DISCOVER THE VAST AND VARIED POLISH BAKING TRADITION, OLD AND NEW, JEWISH AND DIASPORIC, IN THIS EXTENSIVE RECIPE BOOK.

Poland's distinctive baking culture is a product of its rich and complicated history, from the World Wars to the rise of communism to the modern-day cultural exchange that inevitably happens to a country with seven neighbors and endless migration. In this repertoire-expanding baking book, Laurel Kratochvila dives deep into the story of Polish baking to bring you more than 120 recipes to make at home.

PLUM BUTTER CARNIVAL DONUTS:
Pączki z Powidłami

ROSE AND ALMOND JEWEL RUGELACH:
Rogaliki z Różą i Migdałami

SAUERKRAUT AND MUSHROOM ROLLS:
Paszteciki z Kapustą i Grzybami

SUNFLOWER RYE LOAF:
Chleb Żytni Słonecznikowy

CHOCOLATE AND WHIPPED CREAM WARSAW CAKE: Wuzetka

Cheesecakes, wafer cookies, gingerbread, sourdough country loaves: These recipes aren't just for those curious about the new wave of Polish bakeries or nostalgic for the old world treats of childhood—they're for any home baker looking to fill their cookie jars and bread boxes with inspiration.

DOBRE
DOBRE

Baking from Poland and Beyond

DOBRE

BY LAUREL KRATOCHVILA

PHOTOS BY MAŁGOSIA MINTA

CHRONICLE BOOKS
SAN FRANCISCO

DOBRE

Library of Congress Cataloging-in-Publication Data

Names: Kratochvila, Laurel author | Minta, Małgosia photographer
Title: Dobre dobre : baking from Poland and beyond / by Laurel Kratochvila ; photos by Malgosia Minta.
Other titles: Baking from Poland and beyond
Description: San Francisco : Chronicle Books, [2025] | Includes index.
Identifiers: LCCN 2025009304 | ISBN 9781797232096 hardcover
Subjects: LCSH: Cooking, Polish | Cooking--Poland | LCGFT: Cookbooks
Classification: LCC TX723.5.P6 K737 2025 | DDC 641.59438--dc23/eng/20250319
LC record available at https://lccn.loc.gov/2025009304

Manufactured in China.

Prop styling and food styling by Laurel Kratochvila and Małgosia Minta.
Design by Vanessa Dina.
Typesetting by Pamela Geismar.

10 9 8 7 6 5 4 3 2

Chronicle books and gifts are available at special quantity discounts to corporations, professional associations, literacy programs, and other organizations. For details and discount information, please contact our premiums department at corporategifts@chroniclebooks.com or at 1-800-759-0190.

Chronicle Books is represented in the UK and Europe by Abrams & Chronicle Books, 22 Ely Place, London EC1N 6TE, abramsandchronicle.co.uk, and Média-Participations, 57 rue Gaston Tessier, 75166 Paris CEDEX 19, media-participations.com.

Chronicle Books LLC
680 Second Street
San Francisco, California 94107
chroniclebooks.com

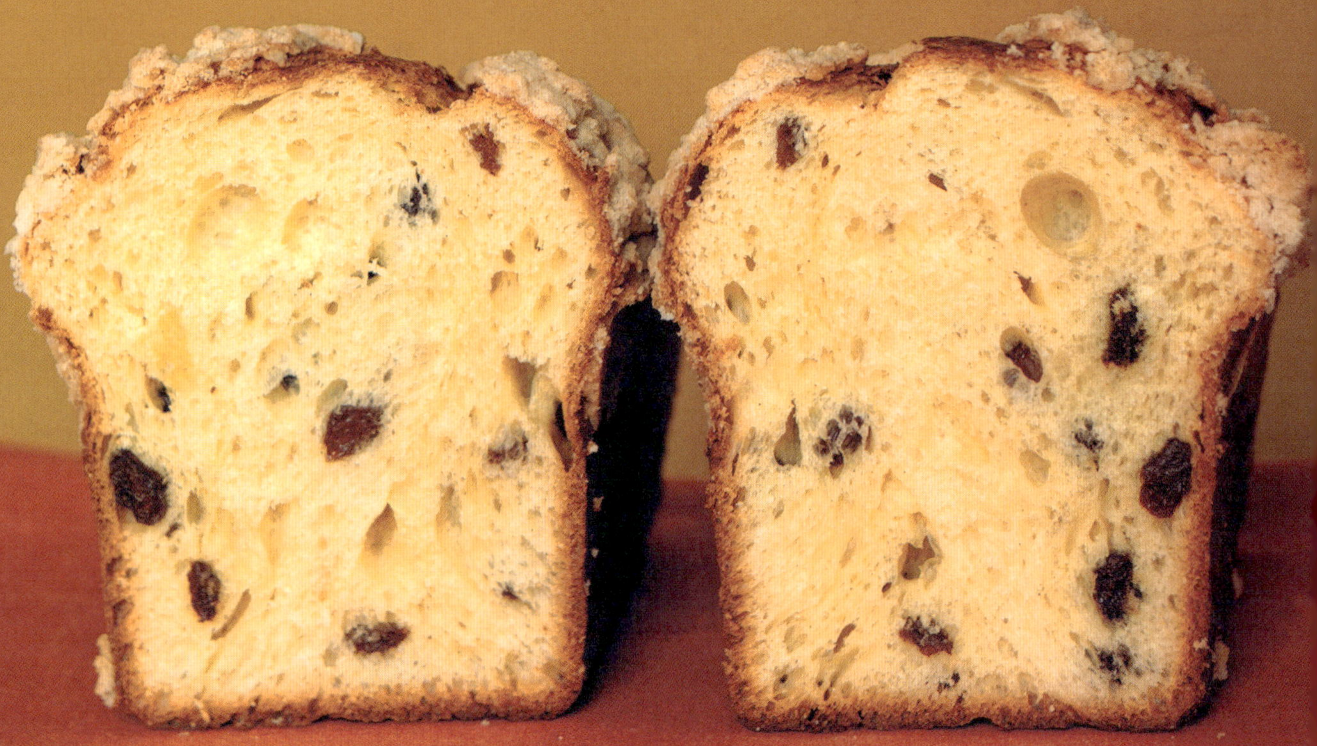

FOR MOLLY. SEVEN YEARS AGO,
YOU DIDN'T FLINCH WHEN I RAN INTO
YOUR BED WHEN A BAT FLEW INTO
OUR ATTIC IN STARE BIELANY.
I LOVE YOU FOREVER.

/1 CHLEB: BREADS, ROLLS & BAGELS

/2 DROŻDŻE: YEASTED BUNS & BREADS

/3 CIASTKA: SLAB CAKES, LAYER CAKES & BUNDTS

/4

CIASTECZKA: COOKIES, SMALL-BITES & WAFERS

/5 PTYSIE, BEZY & SERNIKI CHOUX MERINGUES & CHEESECAKES

/6 EXTRAS: FILLINGS, CREAMS & TOPPINGS

I fell in love with Polish baking because I didn't like the pickles in the Czech Republic. Hear me out.

It was 2009, and I'd moved to Prague from Boston a year earlier, twenty-three years old and aimless. I bartended at night and made mistakes at the grocery store during the day. Baking cookies with rye flour instead of wheat. Putting caraway seeds in a curry instead of cumin. The usual things that happen when you're fumbling around a new language. Eventually I learned, and food shopping became less of a crapshoot. Except for one thing: the pickles.

This was Central Europe—it was supposed to be prime pickle territory, but I couldn't catch so much as a whiff of a good half sour, let alone a kosher dill. Czechs make their pickles sweet. Every jar I took home, whether store-bought or lovingly canned by a coworker's mother, had sugar. This was useless to me—I hate sweet pickles.

I'd almost given up when I went on a date with a nice Moravian guy. He understood the problem, and what was more, he knew where the good pickles were. "So, we put sugar in our pickles," he said. "You don't like it? No problem. The Poles don't." Which was how I wound up on a second date, skidding around snow drifts to cross the border into Poland, the first time anyone in my family had been back in about a hundred years.

We pulled up to a vegetable stand at the first little town on the Polish side and acquired pickles easily (in a bucket, sold by weight, "2 kilos, *proszę*!"). Date #2 seemed to be going well, and I was eager to prolong it. Across the street was the steamed up window of a bakery and pastry shop. It would do. "Should we have a look?" I asked.

Lugging the handle of the enormous plastic pickle bucket together, we sloshed across the street and into the warm, yeasty bakery, and everything hidden behind the foggy window came into view: an almost impossible variety of streusel cakes, Danishes, and jammy yeast buns, many of them uncannily familiar. To one side were trays of tiny tea cookies in every shape and flavor. Against the wall, stacked on racks, were loaves of seeded rye bread, fluffy white rolls, and—what was that? I paused for only a second before I pushed the pickle bucket into my date's arms and stepped up to the counter, squinting. The woman behind it raised an eyebrow.

"Is that challah?" I asked.

"Chałka."

"Yes! Challah!"

"Nie. Chałka."

This lady clearly didn't know what she was talking about. A neat stack of glossy golden braids sat on the shelf right behind her head. Challah. I'd know it anywhere. Despite our obvious misunderstanding, she smiled as though we were on the same page while she wrapped one in paper.

Back on the street, the Czech and I ripped into the still-warm loaf and stuffed long strands of fragrant egg bread into our mouths. That nice man who'd driven me all the way there was looking at me expectantly. This wasn't just challah. This was a very good challah. This was the challah I grew up on. The kind made by the ever-fewer proper Jewish bakeries around Boston. This was the stuff my great-grandparents baked in their one-room flat in a village outside Warsaw to support the family before they emigrated. Was this loaf in my hands the ancestor, offspring, or lost cousin of those baking traditions they brought with them?

I looked from the challah to the pickles and back again. Pieces were falling into place. How was it that we'd traveled little more than an hour and suddenly, in this little bakery in this little Polish town, I felt more at home than I had in a year? I looked at my date. We smiled at each other. I was falling in love with Polish bakeries. And maybe with the guy who drove me here.

More than sixteen years have gone by since that trip to Poland. In that time, I married the guy, moved to Berlin, trained as a baker in Paris, opened my own bakery, wrote a cookbook, and never stopped returning to Poland. As a professional baker whose bakery focuses on heritage Jewish baking, Polish bakeries and cake shops—*piekarnie* and *cukiernie*, respectively—have become my way of connecting to that culinary heritage in the wild.

I recall a school assignment—one of those history ones where you look into your family background. I wrote that my maternal family was Polish, but my grandmother stopped me. "We were never Polish," she said. Then, deciding not to go into it much further, she said, "It was Russia back then anyways." It was one of those it'll-make-more-sense-when-you're-older answers. Distancing oneself from Poland was hardly unusual for American Jews of her generation. The terrible antisemitism in the country's history made for a tricky relationship.

It's a loaded thing, identity. Particularly when you get to a country like Poland. A country so fought-over by Germany and Russia for more than six hundred years that at times it has disappeared from the map, only for another war to be fought and the country to reappear, populations altered and repatriated across new borders. Most recently, this border shuffle occurred in 1945—after the world wars, the occupations, the Holocaust—but the culture would continue to be heavily changed both by communism and then by rapid-onset capitalism. This complicated history has deeply influenced and forever changed Poland's populations, physical borders, character, and culture—including its food culture.

Ask a historian what they think the most influential inflection points have been for Polish food, and you'll get moments scattered across centuries. Some credit the Italian queen Bona Sforza with bringing the country its soup vegetables: onions, carrots, and parsnips. Others attribute the return of exiled Polish kings from France. Still others point to the Second World War and the subsequent thirty-seven years of communism as the most transformational period, as it took the sophisticated prewar cuisine and baking culture and changed its ingredients and style through shortages—all the things that weren't available—into something else. And while all of Polish cuisine, baking included, has given and taken from other European traditions—French, Austro-Hungarian, Italian—I'd posit that there is no greater influence on Poland's bakery culture in the present day than the Jewish bakers of its past.

While an exact number isn't known, some speculate that until the Second World War, up to half of Poland's bakers were Jews. There was almost no city or town without at least one Jewish bakery and it wasn't unusual if half or even all the bakeries—as in the city of Kock—were Jewish. This disproportionate representation of a minority that made up a mere ten percent of the population was a result of the historical ghettoization of Jews into limited professions. But all that changed in the war and through the rest of the twentieth century. Even if Jewish bakers basically don't exist in today's Poland, their influence certainly does. The overlap of what is Jewish and what is Polish is so complete that there's no point in trying to disentangle them. Rugelach, onion breads, apple cakes—everyone makes them, so what belongs to whom? Of course, there is no answer to this question. Food is cultural and cultural borders are porous. As one Polish woman I met while researching the book said about the overlap, "We share the same garden. The same earth. Of course, we share the same baking."

I think of another conversation I had with the Italian pastry chef Alessia Di Donato, a resident of Białystok and enthusiastic advocate for the bialy—the long-gone, regional onion-and-poppy seed bun that was a specialty of Jewish bakeries in Białystok before the war and which now exists only abroad, particularly in New Jersey and New York. Traveling often around Poland to teach Jewish baking history, Alessia tells me, "I've asked myself a thousand times why Białystok (and Poland in general) lacks awareness of Jewish cuisine, and the answer in the end is that there are simply no—rather, too few—Jews left. Unlike other minorities still in the Białystok area—Muslim Tartars and Orthodox Ukrainians—who have the opportunity to use the kitchen as a place of identity and exchange, Jews cannot. The identity path of the Jewish community in Białystok—and elsewhere—was interrupted after the war, because of the Holocaust, because of the diaspora, and then because of the expulsion of Jews from Poland in 1968. So, I say that it's simply a sad reality."

But to reduce Polish baking to what it has lost would be unfair. Better to say that it is a cuisine that has transformed and transformed again. Stroll through Warsaw today and you'll see how much it's gained, even in the last decade: small bakeries specializing in Georgian khachpuri; tandoor stands making decorated Uzbek breads; and patisseries run by new Ukrainian arrivals.

What's more, contemporary Poland has one of the most robust artisan bakery scenes in Europe, on par with that of Copenhagen and Paris. It's growing fast and building on the strong foundations of the preexisting Polish bakery culture. Traditional and nostalgic recipes are being reinvented. Pastries are evolving, sourdough is booming. Butter is replacing cheap margarine, homemade jams are supplanting the mass-produced, supermarket variety. People are expressing their preference for grains and flours that are both local and sustainable. And while industrial bakeries are probably here to stay, seasonal bilberries, plums, sour cherries, onions, and wild mushrooms, as well as local honey, rye, and farmer's cheese, proudly dominate the repertoires of bakeries throughout Poland—even within the most French-style pastry shop.

The legacy of Polish baking is global: from the New York bagel to pletzalej in Argentina to the French baba au rhum. Populations exiled from Poland transmitted the baking culture to their new homelands, where it's been reinvented time and again. Polish and Polish-Jewish traditions exist in bakeries from Chicago to Brooklyn, Tel Aviv to Melbourne, Bangkok to San Luis Potosí in Mexico. Today, in Paris, you can find an old-fashioned onion board in Sacha Finkelsztajn's on Rue de Rosiers as easily as a fashionable chocolate yeast babka at Mamiche on Rue Chateau d'Eau. You can sit in Melbourne's renowned Bar Liberty, sipping natural wine, and be served a piece of their signature, midcentury Warsaw cake, wuzetka, or cure your hangover in London with soft Brick Lane beigels smothered in mustard and salt beef.

Among these bakeries there is massive variation. Some are holders of tradition, nearly frozen in time, like a language spoken by only a few on a desert island. Others, especially the North American Jewish bakeries, are the natural continuation of a baking tradition that has been adapted in diaspora, absorbing new influences, tastes, and ingredients. There is no one way to look at Polish baking and no one way to define it. Though if you had to, I think the affectionate compliment toward good Polish baking (and pickles) from which this book gets its name will do it: *Dobre, dobre, nie za słodkie. Good, good, not too sweet.*

This book is not the be-all and end-all of Polish baking. It's one perspective, influenced by my own travels, friends, family, research, and unapologetic affection for Polish baking. The canon is so broad that a definitive book on the subject is another story altogether, but here is my curation. Some tradition, some modernization. The diasporic and the contemporary. The delicious and the more delicious.

A note on using this book: The recipes in this book were tested using weight measurements, though volume measurements are also provided. The best thing you can do for yourself as a home baker, especially with bread and enriched dough recipes, is to get a kitchen scale and weigh everything. Your results will be more consistent and you'll have much less cleanup.

/1

CHLEB: BREADS, ROLLS & BAGELS

The first loaf of Polish bread I remember eating was in college. I'd enrolled in an art history class with a visiting professor, a formerly exiled Czech performance artist. The class had absolutely no work, and we just listened to his stories of life under communism. The nostalgia for the struggle was palpable. In class, our professor would cut chunks from an enormous loaf of impossibly crusty, round bread—it must have been two feet across, at least—that he'd bought from a Polish bakery across town. He'd pass them around with slices of head cheese, onions, and vinegar, and we'd wash it all down with beers. The giant loaf had a well-floured exterior and the coloring of light rye and a soft crumb that held up when mopping vinegar. The class was hardly rigorous, but I took away one very important lesson: If you wanted a good loaf of bread in Boston—a real loaf of bread—you had to go to the Polish bakery.

Apropos the scale of that bread, which was not unlike that of a traditional chleb Prądnicki (page 75): Back in 1984, Saul Bellow did an interview with journalist Mimi Sheraton that was entirely about his food preferences in his hometown of Chicago. He had this to say: "'And I won't tell you the name of the delicatessen,' he went on, as he unwrapped the lean, fine-grained, fragrant slices. 'But it's in East Rogers Park. As for the rye bread, it is the best in the city, but it's not nearly up to the standards of my cousin Louis. He had a fine old Russian-Jewish bakery in Chicago. It was the Imperial Baking Company, and his rye bread was famous. He also made black Russian pumpernickel in huge ovals, each about the size of a three-month-old infant. Carrying it home was hard work. No one makes that kind of pumpernickel, anymore.'" While Bellow was speaking to a different variety of Eastern European rye bread, his size metaphor stands.

Really, though, the bread my professor brought to class wasn't the first Polish bread I'd ever eaten. Hell, I was raised on Polish bread. So many of us are, without even noticing. Bagels, challahs, and deli ryes were the breads of Jewish bakeries, most of Polish origin, that blossomed in America; first seen as ethnic immigrant food through the midcentury, then as a standard part of the American diet. Recall the tagline of the classic Levy's Real Jewish Rye advertisement from the 1960s: "You don't have to be Jewish to love Levy's." While history has seen to it that many of these particularly Polish-Jewish breads thrive only outside of Poland, to quote a friend, "In the old country, food was food." If one group made a particular bread, it was eaten by another. They all became part of the bakery landscape.

Today, it would be hard to sum up Polish bread culture with one bagel, one roll, or one loaf. Poland is a land of light white rolls, hearty rye sourdoughs, and fragrant onion breads. All of these breads have been shaped by history to some extent—whether they're made using centuries-old regional recipes, or they've been affected by the standardization of communism and industrialization or by the influx of Western additives in the switch to capitalism. As in many countries, tastes over the last century erred toward lighter, white yeast breads, once a rare luxury food. While many fluffy, white rolls have slipped into the Polish bakery, daily bread in Poland is still heavy on whole grains, seeds, and zakwas—sourdoughs—largely resisting the Wonderbreadification of much of the world. The Polish tradition of rye, a grain cultivated in Poland since Roman times, keeps things real.

In the last decade or so, the artisanal bakery movement in Poland has popularized more open-crumbed sourdoughs. While it's easy to reduce this recent craft bakery boom and its breads to a derivative of the trendy Scandinavian bakery school, that would be wrong. Throughout the country, the new wave of bakery artisans draws its influence from traditional Polish breads alongside more globalized flavors. Incorporations like potato, kefir, and sunflower seeds are taken from the classic bakery style. And yet these are expanded on: A smoked sheep's cheese from the Southern mountains might go with a touch of miso in a Danish; pumpkin seeds toasted with a splash of tamari top a bialy; zaatar is heaped on a loaf of chałka.

There are so many varieties of breads in Poland and the bakeries beyond—classic, experimental, Jewish—that it would require a book unto itself to include them all. This chapter draws from some of the best and more distinctive bread traditions.

• WORKING WITH

The different yeasted doughs in the first two chapters of the book—simple and light for fluffy white bulkie rolls, rich and buttery for Danishes and yeast babkas—all follow a pattern. Every yeast dough goes through several steps, each of them important to the final product. The preferment, the mix, the bulk rise, the shaping, the proof (the final rise!), and the bake. Here's a step-by-step guide to working with yeasted breads and enriched yeast doughs.

THE YEAST

The recipes in this book are designed for two types of yeast: fresh yeast and instant yeast. I prefer not to use dry active yeast, as it has to be activated with warm water and a bit of sugar, which can change the composition of the final dough. Fresh yeast and instant yeast have a 2:1 substitution ratio by weight (two parts fresh yeast for one part instant yeast) and while both can go directly into a dough, much of Polish baking uses yeast in preferments (more on this below). If using fresh yeast, be sure that it's truly fresh! It can expire, especially if opened or left out of the fridge. It should have a very light chalky white-gray color and a fresh smell, and flake apart in rubbery pieces. If it is a darker beige or gray color with a strong beer-like smell and a sticky or clay-like texture, it's past its prime and won't be as strong.

THE PREFERMENT

Yeasted preferments—rozczyn (quick sponge) or poolish (overnight yeast culture)—are very typical of Polish yeast doughs. They give the dough a wonderful fluffiness and help keep the final product soft longer than if the yeast was added directly. A preferment is simply a mixture of yeast, flour, liquid, and sugar left to sit until bubbly, domed, and on the point of collapse. Each recipe using a preferment will give you specific instructions.

THE MIX

The mix, or the kneading, is the first step in building the gluten network that will give your dough the structure and elasticity it needs to hold its shape in the final product. For the enriched yeasted doughs of chapter 2, which incorporate fats from butter, milk, egg yolks, and/or oil, it's important to give a very good mix, as these ingredients can work against the development of that gluten network. Each recipe will give you a specific kneading time, but you should also use your eyes and hands to check your dough. The best way to do this is to pinch off a portion of the final dough, about the size of a large marble, and stretch it gently into a thin film. Hold it up to a window and, if you can see the light from behind it without it ripping, it has passed what's called the windowpane test. This means your dough has enough stretch. If it rips, give your dough a few more minutes of kneading.

THE BULK PROOF

The bulk proof, or first rise of your dough, is essential to its final shape and the development of the dough's gluten network. The dough is formed into a smooth ball and placed in a greased bowl, then covered with a tea towel or plastic wrap. The bowl should be at least twice as large as the initial dough to provide room for expansion. Once the dough has bulk proofed, it will have grown by at least 50 percent and be light and jiggly but not collapsed. If you press a finger into the dough, it should slowly spring back about halfway. The timing of the bulk proof is given in each recipe but will vary depending on the temperature of your kitchen. On a warm day, your dough can rise very quickly and be done up to a half hour before the recommended rise; on a cold winter day, you might need to wait an extra half hour for it to rise. Always keep an eye on your dough and look for signs of readiness.

Many recipes in this book give the option for a bulk proof in the fridge. The cold environment of the fridge will slow down the rise of your dough, allowing you to prepare a dough in the evening and then shape and bake it in the morning. This is a great timing technique for breakfast and brunch baking. Chilling the dough also makes it claylike and more moldable for complicated shaping.

DIVIDING AND PRESHAPING YOUR DOUGH

Once your dough has bulk proofed, it's time to divide and shape your dough. Each recipe calls for a different size and shape of dough. The best way to divide the dough is with a bench knife and a kitchen scale, but you can also eyeball the size.

Shaping the dough usually has two steps, the preshape and the final shape. The preshape is the first shaping into balls, followed by a 10- to 15-minute rest. The dough is then degassed (that is, the air is pressed out) and given the final shape. This little extra step of preshaping before shaping gives your final product more structure.

THE FINAL SHAPE

The final shape takes a little technique and therefore practice to master. Most of the shapes in this book are either balls for buns and Danishes or logs for braided breads.

TO FORM A BALL: Press a divided portion of dough to degas, then fold up the sides into the middle to form a rough ball. Flip over so the folded portion is on the underside and the smooth portion is facing up. Form your hand into a cage shape, then roll the ball around until tight and smooth, using the friction of your work surface to help. If the dough is very sticky, you can lightly flour the surface of the ball of dough before rolling—but just barely: If you can avoid using flour altogether, you'll have more success. Let your dough balls rest for 15 minutes, smooth-side up. (See photos on page 22.)

TO FORM A LOG FOR BRAIDING: Flip one ball smooth-side up on your work surface. As with shaping a ball, the less flour on your surface, the better. Using a rolling pin, roll it out to form a long, flat oval. Starting from one of the long sides, use your hands to roll the oval up until you have a tight tube. Use your thumbs to press the seam together where the dough meets. You now have a slightly tapered sausage-shaped log. Using both hands, roll the log to elongate it, starting at the center and moving your hands outward as you go, pressing harder the closer you get to the ends. This stage is where your judiciousness with flour will come in handy! You actually want a bit of friction when you roll the dough. Too much flour and your log will slip around but stay the same size. For braiding, the final log should be about 12 in [30.5 cm] long, tapered on the ends and fat in the middle. Repeat for the remaining portions of dough. (See photos on page 23.)

THE FINAL RISE

Also called a final proof. At this stage, you'll have shaped and set all your items on a baking sheet lined with parchment paper to let them rise one last time. Once they've been arranged on the sheet, they cannot be moved, otherwise you'll risk deflating them and they'll lose the nice pillowy rise you're giving them. Be careful not to let your dough dry out during this stage. Many of the enriched yeasted doughs of chapter 2 call for an egg wash once before the dough has risen, and a second time before it goes into the oven. For recipes that don't call for an egg wash, you can prevent drying by covering your trays or pans lightly with plastic wrap or with a large, airtight box set on top of your tray without touching the rising dough. This will help keep the surface moist.

When your final products are finished, they will be puffed to almost double in size and jiggle a bit when you shake your pan. When pressed gently with a finger, the dough will slowly spring back about halfway. Use these signs to confirm your items have properly risen before you bake to prevent a dense, raw interior. Ensuring you've given your items a sufficient final rise is one of the best ways to ensure full baking.

BAKING

For most of the recipes in this book, I suggest placing your pan on a middle rack and using the convection setting on your oven for a faster, more even bake. If you don't have a convection setting, you may need to increase the baking time by about 25 percent and rotate your items as you bake. Keep in mind that every oven is a little different. A setting of 350°F [180°C] on my oven might be 325°F [165°C] on yours. If you're doing a lot of baking, it's a good idea to verify your oven temperatures with a thermometer. Get to know your oven and check if it has any hot spots—areas where things get dark faster than other areas—and rotate your pans while baking as necessary. Note that some recipes, like bagels, require a hotter temperature than others, like a sweet, enriched yeasted Danish, for example. Each recipe will give you specific baking instructions.

CHECKING FOR DONENESS WITH A THERMOMETER

One of the best ways to tell when your breads are ready is to use an instant-read thermometer. Stick the thermometer into the center of the item and wait for it to register 195°F [90°C]. That's the sweet spot and indicates that your dough is fully baked.

COOLING AND STORING YOUR BAKES

It's important to allow your baked goods to properly cool before you cut into them. They will continue to bake once out of the oven. Especially for loaf-style bakes, cooling helps keep their structure. If not serving the same day, store your fully cooled baked goods according to the instructions in each recipe.

FORMING A BALL

FORMING A LOG

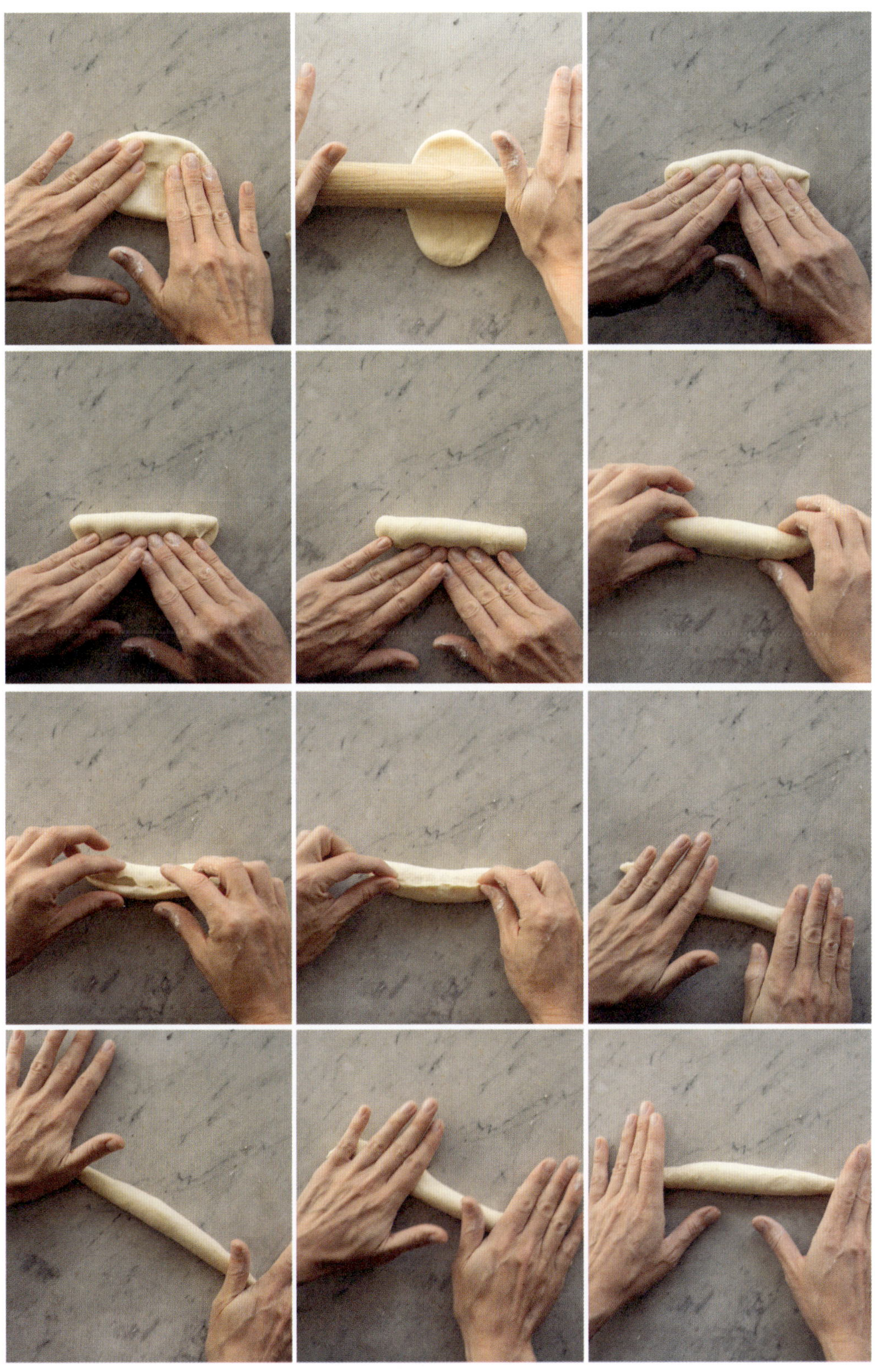

• WORKING WITH

Like yeasted doughs, making sourdough bread requires a series of steps and stages that, with a little variation, are pretty standard, from maintaining a sourdough starter, to building a leaven, to mixing, rising, shaping, proofing, and, finally, baking the dough. Here's a guide to working with sourdoughs.

THE SOURDOUGH

Sourdough is a culture of natural yeasts and bacteria that live off the sugars in flour. They eat these sugars and release gasses, which create the bubbles in your bread that make it rise. The sourdough culture goes through several phases of activity, with its lowest activity right after it has been refreshed (fed) and the peak after it has risen. After it reaches its peak, it will decline in potency and become weaker and unpleasantly acidic. That's why it is best to use and feed your sourdough at its peak. In much Polish sourdough baking and in the recipes in this book, a powerful rye-based sourdough is used. I find rye sourdoughs a bit more forgiving and easier to work with than wheat sourdoughs. If you're new to sourdough and don't have a starter going, you can build this sourdough in about a week, then store it in your fridge, refreshing it once or twice a week so that it's ready to use when you are.

If you already have a starter going, but it isn't with rye, you can simply add a spoonful of whatever starter you have and give it a couple maintenance feedings over a day or two according to the recipe below, and you'll soon have an active rye sourdough. You can also do this with a sourdough starter borrowed from a friend.

SOURDOUGH STARTER (WHOLE-RYE ZAKWAS)

DAY 1

½ cup [50 g] whole-rye flour
¼ cup [60 g] water

Mix flour and water in a jar until it's a stiff paste and cover loosely with a lid or tea towel. Let sit for 24 hours at room temperature.

DAY 2

1 Tbsp [25 g] starter from Day 1
½ cup [50 g] whole-rye flour
3½ Tbsp [50 g] water

Discard all but 25 g of the starter from Day 1 from your jar. Add the new flour and water and mix into a thick paste.

DAYS 3 TO 5

Repeat the process from Day 2. Each day the starter should start to bubble a bit more as it gains activity.

DAYS 6 TO 8

By the time you've reached Day 6, the starter should be bubbling, growing to the point of having a domed top, and releasing an eggy aroma. It's getting ready to be useful! Now that the starter is so active, it will need to be fed twice a day according to the proportions of Day 2, once in the morning and once before bed.

DAY 8 ONWARD

At this point, your starter should be ready to use and you'll have to keep it on a maintenance schedule. You can either continue to feed it twice a day at room temperature, or you can feed it once a week and refrigerate it in between feedings.

STORING YOUR SOURDOUGH

ROOM TEMPERATURE: This is for people who want to bake every day or several times a week. It's an ambitious undertaking and often leads to the lament "I killed my sourdough." If you do want the committed sourdough lifestyle, give your sourdough two feedings a day, once in the morning and once in the evening, according to the proportions from Day 2.

FRIDGE: Once your sourdough is active, it's not necessary to keep it at room temperature and feed it twice a day unless you're planning to bake every day. The cold of the fridge slows down the activity of the starter, meaning you don't have to feed it as much. Simply give your starter a last feeding at peak activity, cover with a loose lid, and refrigerate. Every few days, or even once per week, remove the starter from the fridge and give it a refreshment according to the proportions from Day 2. When you want to bake with your refrigerated starter, give it a couple days of refreshments at room temperature to return it to peak activity.

SOURDOUGHS

TESTING FOR RIPENESS

Your sourdough starter is at peak activity, or ripeness, when it has doubled in size from its maintenance feeding, is bubbly, and smells a bit eggy but not too sour. A small portion placed in a bowl of water will float. This is the stage at which you want to either refresh your starter or turn it into a leaven to be used for bread.

BUILDING YOUR LEAVEN

Your leaven (zaczyn) is the preferment that will rise your bread. It's really just a bigger quantity of your sourdough starter, risen to its peak activity point, then mixed into your dough. Think of it as the natural equivalent to adding yeast. Each sourdough recipe in this book will give you a recipe for the leaven.

THE MIX

The mix is the first step in building the gluten network that will give your dough the structure and elasticity it needs to hold its shape in the final product. Most of these sourdough breads use a hand mix in a large bowl, as opposed to the yeast dough recipes, which use a stand mixer. Sourdough breads rise more slowly than yeast breads, and they build their structure through a series of stretch and folds of the dough during its bulk rise stage, as opposed to strong kneading.

BULK RISE/PROOF AND STRETCH AND FOLDS

After you've mixed your dough, it will go through a long bulk rise phase. This is the first rise of the dough, before it has been shaped. To build up the gluten structure of the dough, you will periodically give it stretch and folds. To stretch and fold your dough, there are two methods. The first is to dip your hands in water (to prevent sticking) and pull up one side of the dough from the bottom of the bowl, stretch it up as far as you can, and fold it back over the top. Turn the bowl and do the same gesture, working your way around the whole bowl until you've built up tension in your dough. The second method is to wet both of your hands, reach all the way under the resting dough, and pull it up from the middle, allowing both overhanging sides to stretch downward with gravity, and fold under the middle of the dough as you place it back into its bowl. Turn the bowl and repeat several times until you've gone around the whole bowl.

Whichever method you choose, these stretch and folds are usually repeated every half hour or so during the bulk rise, building the tension and elasticity in the dough each time.

PRESHAPING YOUR DOUGH

After the dough has finished its bulk proof, some bread doughs will be preshaped for a last short rest before getting their final form. The preshape helps with the final shape and structure of your bread. Generally the dough is preshaped into a loose ball by folding in the sides, then flipping it smooth-side up. After the preshape, your dough will get a bench rest—a short rest on your work surface to relax it enough for you to give it its final shape. See photos on pages 26–27 for preshaping a round loaf.

THE FINAL SHAPE

Before the final proof, you will shape the dough. The bread recipes in this book use a few different forms. On page 28, you can see the shaping of the essential round boule form.

THE FINAL RISE/PROOF

The final proof is the shaped rise of your loaf before baking. For the recipes in this book, this either happens in a proofing basket or a loaf pan. Some breads can be slowed down and risen overnight in the fridge, making your bake easy and convenient for the morning. Each recipe will tell you how and when to give your dough its final proof. At the end of the final proof, you can check for doneness by pressing a finger into your loaf. If it springs back slowly about halfway, this means your bread is ready to bake.

SCORING YOUR BREAD

Scoring your bread is the process of slashing your risen loaf with a sharp knife or baker's lame (razor). The purpose of scoring your bread is to help it expand and rise in a uniform way. If you don't score your bread, it can expand or burst out the sides as it bakes. To score your bread, hold your blade at a 45-degree angle from the surface of the bread, and give it a firm, long slash about ½ in [1 cm] deep. For round breads, it's nice to make several slashes to form a square or triangle. For long loaf breads, a long slash down the middle or several diagonal slashes is ideal.

PRESHAPING

PRESHAPING

SHAPING A ROUND BOULE

BAKING

Bread, unlike cakes and pastries, bakes at a high temperature. It's how you get a beautiful caramelization of the crust. To achieve this nice crust, you'll also need steam and a hot surface. The steam allows the bread to expand before the top crust forms and hardens. The hot surface allows the bottom crust of a loaf of bread to form.

BAKING IN A CAST-IRON POT OR DUTCH OVEN: This is one of the most popular home bread baking techniques, and for good reason. The closed cast-iron pot creates a steamy environment that allows for the expansion of the loaf. To bake in a cast-iron pot, simply heat the oven to the required temperature in the recipe, usually 450°F [240°C], and preheat the pot and its lid for at least a half hour. Once the oven and pot have preheated, remove the pot from the oven, invert your fully proofed final loaf into the pot, score the bread as the recipe suggests, then re-cover and bake for about 20 minutes with the lid on. Those 20 minutes will be enough for your bread to expand. Remove the lid, lower the oven heat to the temperature suggested in the recipe, usually 400°F [200°C], and continue baking. Without the lid on, the bread will brown.

BAKING ON A CAST-IRON BAKING PAN OR PIZZA STONE: This is another method for baking bread in a home oven. In this method, you'll have to add steam to the oven yourself. Preheat your oven, as well as a cast-iron pan or pizza stone on the middle rack in the oven, and an old metal pan on the bottom of the oven for at least 1 hour. When you're ready to bake, invert your loaf onto a pizza peel or a baking sheet with no edges lined with parchment paper. Score the loaf, then slide the loaf, paper and all, onto the preheated pan or pizza stone. Toss several ice cubes in the hot pan at the bottom of the oven, then close the door. The ice cubes will create enough steam to allow the loaf to expand. Once the steam has evaporated, the loaf will brown and get crusty.

CHECKING FOR DONENESS

There are a couple ways to verify if your bread is fully baked. An instant-read thermometer inserted into the middle will read at least 195°F [90°C]. This is the best way to be absolutely sure, especially for stickier breads like rye loaves. You can also turn your loaf upside down (use potholders) and knock on the bottom. If your bread is done, you should hear a slightly hollow sound.

COOLING YOUR BREAD

It's important to cool your bread fully before cutting into it. The reason is that your bread will continue to bake and set once out of the oven. If you cut into it, you will release all of its hot steam and interrupt this process. This is particularly important for rye breads.

STORING YOUR BREAD

Sourdough breads stay fresh for much longer than yeast breads. You can wrap your bread in a tea towel and store it at room temperature for several days and often up to a week. As the days wear on, toast your bread to refresh it.

Matzo

Maca

Some of you dear readers might come from houses that had a box of matzo in the cupboard not just on Passover, but all 365 days of the year. After all, who knew when there'd be a winter storm, a power outage, or an apocalypse that would have us running for the canned goods and crackers? Matzo is magic, not just because it sustained the Jewish people for the long walk out of Egypt, but also because it's somehow impervious to spoilage—not even pantry moths can be bothered to touch the stuff—so in a last-ditch emergency situation, the bread of affliction it is. Oddly, this distinct flatbread is still widely available in Poland, primarily prepackaged for supermarkets or convenience stores and entirely distanced from its Jewish origins. And yet, there it is, serving the exact same function as the unchanging box of matzo in my childhood home: pantry longevity.

None of this preamble is to say that store-bought matzo is any good. It isn't. It's more or less crunchy cardboard that, with every bite, shatters and scatters like chicken feathers all over the floor. That's why you should make your own. Passover requires a set 17-minute start-to-finish mix-and-bake, making homemade matzo impractical if you're observant. Outside of Passover though, this is just a gorgeous crispbread, perfect for dips or crumbled over a salad for a fattoush-style crunch. This recipe uses a bit of rye flour to give it a touch of rustic nuttiness.

MAKES 20 matzos

2 cups [250 g] all-purpose flour
1 cup [100 g] light rye flour
1 heaping tsp [7 g] kosher salt
1 Tbsp [14 g] olive oil
½ cup plus 2 Tbsp [150 g] water, plus more if needed

TOPPINGS (OPTIONAL)

Sesame seeds, rosemary, poppy seeds, flaky sea salt, dried garlic, chili flakes, sumac, caraway seeds, nigella seeds, or your preferred topping

Preheat the oven to 450°F [240°C] with the convection setting turned on. Line two baking sheets with parchment paper.

Begin by mixing the dough. In the bowl of your stand mixer fitted with the dough hook attachment, combine the all-purpose flour, light rye flour, salt, olive oil, and water and mix on medium speed for 5 minutes, until the mixture has come together into a stiff, elastic dough. If you still have dry bits of dough, add an extra tablespoon or two of water, but only enough to bring the dough together. Use your hands to form the dough into a ball and let it rest on your work surface for 5 minutes.

Using a bench knife, divide the dough into twenty portions, each about 1½ oz [40 g]. Roll each into a ball (see page 22). Heavily dust both the work surface and the top of a portion of dough with rye flour, then roll out the dough ball into a paper-thin circle or oval. Take one end of the circle and drape it around your rolling pin so you can transport it to the baking sheet without damaging it. Gently unroll the circle onto one of the baking sheets, leaving space for another matzo, then repeat with a second portion of dough.

Use a fork to perforate all around the surface of the two dough circles, then, if using toppings, brush the surfaces lightly with water and sprinkle on the toppings of your choice. Bake for 3 minutes, or until the surface bubbles and is just starting to get golden brown. While the first batch bakes, prepare your next baking sheet, and so forth, until all the matzos are baked.

Cool completely and store airtight for up to a month or more.

Stovetop Flatbread

Podpłomyk

Podpłomyk is an ancient flatbread, exceedingly simple to make. According to the chef Piotr Wójcik, who serves a yogurt-based and flame-grilled version in his Warsaw restaurant, you can find a thousand recipes for the same thing. The most authentic, he says, is a simple lavash-style with no more ingredients than flour, water, and salt. Michał Pajdosz, a natural winemaker in the Silesian village of Jakubów, who just happens to also be a scholar of the ancient Slavs, pushes it further. "It's from the Mesolithic and Paleolithic times. Before cultivated flour was widely used, ground seeds of wild grasses, acorns, and cattail rhizome were all used for it. Grains came later, sometimes adding beer for puffiness and grilling on a flat stone." Today's versions remain modest with a fast knead, a paper-thin roll, and a quick dry fry on a cast-iron skillet for a soft, warm bread with crunchy little blackened bubbles. Serve as a sandwich wrap or torn and drowned in herby dips.

NOTE: This recipe can easily be halved for smaller servings.

MAKES 20 podpłomyki

4 cups [500 g] all-purpose flour
⅓ cup plus 1 Tbsp [50 g] whole-wheat flour
1¼ tsp [9 g] kosher salt
2 Tbsp [27 g] sunflower oil
2 tsp [14 g] honey
1⅔ cups [400 g] boiling water

Begin by mixing the dough. In the bowl of your stand mixer fitted with the dough hook attachment, combine the all-purpose flour, whole-wheat flour, salt, sunflower oil, honey, and boiling water. Knead on medium-high speed for 5 minutes. The boiling water will slightly gelatinize the dough, which will be thick enough to handle but slightly sticky when finished.

Heat a cast-iron or heavy-bottomed skillet on medium-high heat. Line a plate or basket with a large tea towel and set aside. While the pan heats up, turn out the dough onto a well-floured work surface. Use your bench knife to divide the dough into twenty even portions of about 1¾ oz [50 g] each and form the pieces into balls (see page 22). Flouring the dough and rolling pin as needed to prevent sticking, roll out one portion of dough until it's a paper-thin circle or oval. Lay the rolled dough onto the hot pan and allow to cook for about 1 minute on each side. You'll see small air pockets and bubbles forming. The finished bread will look like a flour tortilla. Set the podpłomyk in the waiting tea towel and wrap up sides to cover. This will keep the podpłomyk soft. Roll, dry fry, and repeat for the rest of the podpłomyki.

These are best made and enjoyed the same day.

Sour Milk and Soda Buns

Proziaki

Proziaki are Carpathian soda buns that taste a lot like American-style drop biscuits (dare I say Bisquik?) but look just like English muffins. The name *proziaki* comes from the regional word for baking soda. These simple-to-make buns have been around since the mid-nineteenth century, when baking soda made its debut in Poland. And since they're Polish, of course a soured milk product gets snuck into the mix. I use kefir, but if you can't find it locally, a thick buttermilk or loose sour cream will give you just as much success. Make proziaki for breakfast instead of pancakes and top with honey, butter, and a bit of flaky salt, or serve for dinner alongside a heavy stew for dipping. They work just as well sweet as they do savory. Just don't confuse the word *proziaki* with *prosiatko*—the latter means piglet.

MAKES 8 to 10 proziaki

1 cup plus 2 Tbsp [300 g] kefir
1½ Tbsp [25 g] unsalted butter, melted
1 egg
4 cups [500 g] all-purpose flour
1½ Tbsp [20 g] sugar
1½ tsp [7 g] baking soda
1 tsp [6 g] kosher salt

Begin by mixing the dough. In a medium mixing bowl, whisk together the kefir, melted butter, and egg. In the bowl of your stand mixer fitted with the paddle attachment or in a large mixing bowl with a wooden spoon, mix together the flour, sugar, baking soda, and salt. Add the liquids, then mix just enough to have a thick lumpy dough with no dry pockets. Cover the bowl loosely with a tea towel and set aside for 15 minutes.

After 15 minutes, the dough will have puffed and gotten lighter. Turn it out onto a well-floured work surface. Flour the top of the dough and roll it out to ¾ in [2 cm] thickness. Using a 3 in [7.5 cm] circular cookie cutter or the rim of a large glass, cut out circles of dough. You can press the scraps back together and reroll to make extras. Allow the cut-out buns to sit and rise for another 15 minutes.

Line a plate or basket with a large tea towel and set aside. Preheat a heavy-bottomed pan, ideally cast iron, over medium heat. Once the pan is hot, working in batches, place buns 1 in [2.5 cm] apart, directly onto the dry surface of the pan. Cover the pan (if you don't have a cover, use a baking sheet or another larger pan), and cook the buns on one side for about 2½ minutes, then remove the cover, flip to the other side, and cook for another 2½ minutes. Each side should be a deep golden brown, not burned. Remove the buns from the heat and wrap in the waiting tea towel to cool. This will keep moisture and steam in. Repeat the dry-frying process for the rest of the buns, then eat.

These are best eaten warm from the pan.

Poznań Split Rolls

Bułki Poznańskie

Bułki Poznańskie, or Poznań rolls, are simple split white yeast buns. An in-country source who wishes to remain anonymous told me, "They have to look like butts." A thin, crispy crust and a very light and soft crumb make this an ideal sandwich or dinner roll.

MAKES 9 rolls

TIMING
Poolish: 6 to 12 hours
Mix: 10 minutes
Bulk proof: 1 hour
Preshape and bench rest: 10 minutes
Final proof: 1½ hours
Bake: 12 to 15 minutes

POOLISH
¾ cup plus 1 Tbsp [100 g] bread flour
Pinch of instant yeast (less than ⅛ tsp)
7 Tbsp [100 g] room-temperature water

DOUGH
All of the Poolish
4 cups [500 g] bread flour
1 Tbsp [20 g] light barley malt syrup
1 egg yolk
2¼ tsp [7 g] instant yeast
1½ tsp [10 g] kosher salt
¾ cup plus 3 Tbsp [225 g] water
1 Tbsp [14 g] sunflower oil

Begin by preparing the poolish. If baking in the morning, start the night before. If baking in the evening, start in the morning. Mix the flour, yeast, and water into a paste, then cover loosely with a tea towel and leave to ferment for 6 to 12 hours. It will bubble and double in size.

When the poolish is ready, mix the dough. In the bowl of your stand mixer fitted with the dough hook attachment, combine the poolish, flour, barley malt syrup, egg yolk, yeast, salt, and water. Mix on medium-low speed for 8 minutes until a supple, slightly tacky dough that pulls away from the sides of the bowl has formed. Continuing to mix, drizzle in the sunflower oil. The dough will come apart and then come back together. Once the dough is smooth again, about 2 minutes, stop mixing and remove it from the bowl. Form the dough into a smooth and tight ball, then set it in a lightly oiled medium mixing bowl. Cover airtight and set aside for 1 hour to rise, until it has grown by almost two thirds in size.

Once the dough has risen, turn it out onto a very lightly floured work surface—the dough shouldn't be very sticky. Using a bench knife, divide the dough into nine even portions of about 3¾ oz [105 g] each. Form each portion of dough into a tight ball (see page 22) and set seam-side down on your work surface, about 2 in [5 cm] apart. Cover loosely with a damp tea towel or plastic wrap and let rest for 10 minutes.

After the dough has rested, take one ball of dough and flip it smooth-side down. Flatten the ball, then reform it into a tight ball. I know, I know—why did we just do that? We're building strength in our dough for the shape. Take the reformed tight ball and give it a few gentle rolls to form it into a fat oval. Use a chopstick or a clean pencil held horizontal to your work surface to press the long way down the roll, almost all the way through. This will create the split look. Note: If you don't press far enough down, the roll won't hold the shape.

Set the roll on a baking sheet lined with parchment paper, then repeat with the remaining balls of dough, arranging the buns 2 in [5 cm] apart. Very

cont'd

lightly cover with plastic wrap and set aside to rise for 45 minutes to 1 hour, until puffed and light.

Shortly before the rolls have finished rising, preheat the oven to 350°F [180°C] with the convection setting turned on and place an old metal baking pan at the bottom of the oven to heat.

When the oven is hot and the rolls are fully risen, use a small sieve to dust the rolls with flour, then put them in to bake. Just before closing the oven door, toss a few ice cubes in the preheated baking pan to create steam. This will help the rolls open nicely. Bake for 12 to 15 minutes, or until golden brown. Transfer to a cooling rack and allow to cool, then eat immediately.

If you aren't eating these the same day, store in an airtight container in the freezer for up to a couple of months. Thaw and toast or warm in the oven when you want to eat them.

Kaiser Rolls

Kajzerki

If you're from Boston like me, you'd call these bulkie rolls. It's a regional quirk. I always figured it was because the buns were, well, bulky. Not quite. Years later I was in Warsaw and walked into a milk bar—the Bar Mleczny Rusałka in the Praga district, to be precise. Milk bars are traditional Polish cafeterias and the menus tend to be tiny-lettered affairs hung on the wall. Without thinking, I ordered a żurek—a soup—and a roll. Except I didn't know the word for roll in Polish. But it was automatic. I didn't even have to think about it: bułka. Of course it's a roll. Turns out the Bostonian word for roll comes from the Yiddish *bulke*, which derives from the Polish *bułka*, which traces back to an old Slavic word meaning *something round*. While there are many kinds of bułki, kaiser rolls are some of the most common, and it's what they handed me with my soup that day. Made from a light white dough and rolled and knotted into a flower shape, they're a perfect bun for a little sandwich or to dip in a soup.

MAKES 9 kaiser rolls

TIMING
Poolish: 6 to 12 hours
Mix: 10 minutes
Bulk proof: 1 hour
Preshape and bench rest: 10 minutes
Final proof: 1½ hours
Bake: 12 to 15 minutes

POOLISH
¾ cup plus 1 Tbsp [100 g] bread flour
Pinch of instant yeast (less than ⅛ tsp)
7 Tbsp [100 g] room-temperature water

DOUGH
All of the Poolish
1 Tbsp [20 g] light barley malt syrup
1 egg yolk
2¼ tsp [7 g] instant yeast
¾ cup plus 3 Tbsp [225 ml] water
4 cups [500 g] bread flour
1½ tsp [10 g] kosher salt
1 Tbsp [14 g] sunflower oil

GLAZE
1 egg white
2 Tbsp [30 g] water

TOPPING
2 Tbsp [20 g] sesame seeds or poppy seeds

Begin by preparing your poolish. If baking in the morning, start the night before. If baking in the evening, start in the morning. Mix the flour, yeast, and water into a paste, then cover loosely with a tea towel and leave to ferment for 6 to 12 hours. It will bubble and double in size.

When the poolish is ready, mix the dough. In the bowl of your stand mixer, whisk together the poolish, barley malt syrup, egg yolk, yeast, and water. Add the flour and salt, then, with the dough hook attachment, mix on low speed until the dough comes together. Increase the speed to medium and mix for 8 minutes until a supple, slightly tacky dough has formed that pulls away from the sides of the bowl. Continuing to mix, drizzle in the sunflower oil. The dough will come apart and then come back together. Once the dough is smooth again, about 2 minutes, stop mixing and remove it from the bowl. Form the dough into a smooth and tight ball, then set it in a lightly oiled medium mixing bowl. Cover airtight and set aside for 1 hour to rise, until it has grown by almost two thirds in size.

cont'd

Once the dough has risen, turn it out onto a very lightly floured work surface—the dough shouldn't be very sticky. Using a bench knife, divide the dough into nine even portions of about 3¾ oz [105 g] each. Form each portion of dough into a tight ball (see page 22) and set seam-side down on your work surface, about 2 in [5 cm] apart. Cover loosely with a damp tea towel or plastic wrap and let rest for 10 minutes.

After the dough has rested, take one ball of dough and flip it smooth-side down. Flatten the ball, then roll it up into a tight log (see page 23). Using both hands, roll the log out into a long snake, about 16 in [40.5 cm] long. Take both ends and tie them in a knot, leaving a 2 to 3 in [5 to 7.5 cm] loop and two 3 in [7.5 cm] ends. Wrap each end around the loop and through the middle, tucking the ends on the underside to create a flower shape. Set the roll on a baking sheet lined with parchment paper, then repeat with the remaining balls of dough, arranging the rolls 2 in [5 cm] apart. Very lightly cover with plastic wrap and set aside to rise for 45 minutes to 1 hour, until puffed and light.

Shortly before the rolls have finished rising, preheat the oven to 350°F [180°C] with the convection setting turned on. Place an old metal baking pan at the bottom of the oven to heat.

When the oven is hot, make the glaze. In a small bowl, whisk the egg white and water, then brush on the rolls, sprinkle with sesame or poppy seeds, and put them in the oven. Just before closing the oven door, toss a few ice cubes in the baking pan to create steam. This will help the rolls open nicely. Bake for 12 to 15 minutes, or until golden brown. Transfer to a cooling rack, allow to cool, then eat immediately.

If you aren't eating these the same day, store in an airtight container in the freezer for a couple of months. Thaw and toast or warm in the oven when you want to eat them.

Adrian Klonowski's Steamed Buns

Pampuchy

If you're ever in Bangkok, you'd be lucky to meet the chef and baker Adrian Klonowski. Originally from Gdańsk, he's one of the true sweethearts in the food world, always with a big smile and something delicious to share. Back in 2020, when he got stuck in Bangkok at the start of the pandemic, he turned lemons into lemonade and opened a bakery and deli, Larder BK, serving Polish sourdough breads and house-made smoked meats alongside Asian additions like shokupan, to a predominantly Thai clientele. When I asked him for a recipe for the book, he immediately suggested pampuchy. Pampuchy are steamed buns, served either sweet—as Adrian remembers from his childhood—with kefir, buttermilk, curd cheeses, honey, or fruit compotes to top—or, in more southern parts of the country like Silesia, salty with meat stews, roulades, and sauces. "It's really a food that makes me think of austerity," Adrian says. "Our grandparents made it when they didn't have a lot. There's just flour, salt, water, yeast, and a tiny bit of oil."

Pampuchy are found all over Poland, as well as in Ukraine, and they bear more than a passing resemblance to the steamed buns of Central Europe, such as Czech ovocné knedlíky and German Dampfnudeln. But what adds another dimension to pampuchy is their near-identical texture and similarity to South Asian bao buns. In his Bangkok catering jobs, Adrian serves versatile pampuchy with both Thai and Polish fillings and sides. Regardless of how you plan to serve them, this recipe yields impossibly soft, cloud-like buns and requires no special equipment but cheesecloth and a large pot.

MAKES 20 pampuchy

TIMING

Mix: 8 minutes
Bulk proof: 1 hour
Final proof: 45 minutes
Steam: 10 minutes per batch

DOUGH

2 cups plus 2 Tbsp [500 g] water
7 Tbsp [100 g] whole milk
2 Tbsp plus ¾ tsp [21 g] instant yeast
8 cups [1 kg] all-purpose flour
1 Tbsp [20 g] kosher salt
1 egg
1 egg yolk
½ cup [110 g] sunflower or olive oil

KEFIR SAUCE

¾ cup plus 1 Tbsp [200 g] kefir
¾ cup plus 1 Tbsp [200 g] plain whole-fat yogurt

FOR SERVING

Jam or stewed fruits

Begin by mixing the dough. In the bowl of your stand mixer, whisk together the water, milk, and yeast. Add the flour, salt, egg, and egg yolk. Using the dough hook attachment, mix for about 8 minutes on medium-low speed until a smooth dough has formed. Remove the dough and form into a tight ball, then place smooth-side up into a lightly oiled medium mixing bowl. Cover the bowl airtight with plastic wrap, and let rise at room temperature for about 1 hour. While the dough rises, cut twenty 3 in [7.5 cm] squares of parchment paper and set aside.

cont'd

Once the dough has risen, it will have grown by about two thirds in size and be soft and domed. Turn it out onto a very lightly floured work surface, and divide it into twenty 2.8 oz [80 g] portions using your bench knife. Preshape each portion into a tight ball (see page 22), and set each on a square of parchment paper smooth-side up. Allow to rise for another 45 minutes to 1 hour, until soft and puffed.

Shortly before the buns are ready, prepare a steamer with a water bath on your stove. You can do this with a proper steamer or make your own steamer as Adrian does. To do this, take a large saucepan, fill it with 2 in [5 cm] of water, and tie a cheesecloth over the entirety of the saucepan's opening, knotting it on the handle. The cheesecloth should form a concave hammock to cradle your pampuchy as the steam rises from below. Place the steamer over medium-high heat.

Pour the oil onto a small plate. Once the water is boiling, gently remove several buns from their papers and dip the bottom of each in the oil to prevent sticking before placing them in the steamer. Cover and steam for 10 minutes, until the surface is glossy. Remove the cooked buns and store under a tea towel to keep their heat. Repeat for the rest of the buns.

To make the sauce, mix the kefir and yogurt in a small bowl until smooth. Plate several buns together and drizzle on the sauce. Top with a few spoonfuls of jam and serve.

While these are nicest served fresh off the steamer, you can refrigerate airtight for a few days and revive using the same steaming method until just warm. Store the sauce and jam separately.

Poppy Seed Sticks

Paluchy z Makiem

Paluch means big toe in Polish—the appendage you're likely to stub if you've been enjoying wódka and beer all evening with your friends. There's a universal need for bar snacks that transcends nations, and while these breadsticks are not limited to drink mitigation, they do pair excellently with an icy cold Żubr or Tyskie. A savory snack with poppy seed and salt and just a touch of sweetness in the dough, these are great any time of day.

MAKES 10 to 12 paluchy

TIMING

Mix: 8 minutes
Bulk proof: 1 hour
Final proof: 2 hours
Bake: 15 minutes

DOUGH

4 cups [500 g] all-purpose flour
2¼ tsp [7 g] instant yeast
1½ tsp [10 g] kosher salt
1 egg
1 egg yolk
1 Tbsp [20 g] light barley malt syrup
¾ cup plus 1 Tbsp [200 g] water
1 Tbsp [14 g] sunflower oil

EGG WASH

1 egg and 1 egg yolk, whisked until smooth

TOPPING

2 Tbsp [20 g] poppy seeds
1 Tbsp flaky sea salt

Begin by mixing the dough. In the bowl of your stand mixer fitted with the dough hook attachment, mix the flour, yeast, salt, egg, egg yolk, barley malt syrup, water, and sunflower oil on medium speed for 8 minutes, or until you have a smooth and stretchy dough. Remove the dough from the mixer and form into a tight ball, then set in a lightly oiled medium mixing bowl and cover loosely with a tea towel or plastic wrap. Let the dough rest for 1 hour, until it has puffed and grown by almost two thirds in size.

Once the dough has risen, turn it out onto a lightly floured work surface. Lightly flour the top of the dough, then roll it out to a bit larger than a 10 in [25 cm] square. Measure out 1 in [2.5 cm] intervals along two opposite sides, then use a pizza cutter or a flat-edged knife to cut ten to twelve even strips. To shape, transfer one strip to a baking sheet lined with parchment paper and then twist each end until you have a twisted log. Do the same with the rest of the strips, setting them about 1 in [2.5 cm] apart. Brush each with egg wash, then set aside to rise for about 2 hours, until puffed and soft. Shortly before the paluchy are risen, preheat the oven to 350°F [180°C] with the convection setting turned on.

When the oven is hot, brush the paluchy a second time with egg wash and sprinkle with poppy seeds and flaky salt. Bake for 15 minutes, or until the egg wash is a rich dark golden color.

Serve these the same day with dips and beers.

New York Bagels

Nowojorskie Bajgle

The bread most emblematic of the Polish Jewish bakery is also one of the least available in modern Poland. A food that thrived in twentieth century New York, it all but disappeared in postwar, post-Shoah Poland. But the bagel in Poland once formed its own economy. The bagel baker was a special, lower class of baker, separate from the general bakeries, both in Poland and New York City. Often renting out the filthy basements of bakeries, bagel bakers in Poland wholesaled to peddlers, who in turn sold the bagels on sticks or ropes on the street for pennies. In New York, these exclusive bagel bakeries were heavily unionized, the Yiddish-speaking bagel union 338 a threat to any non-unionized baker with a death wish and the audacity to make bagels themselves. Today the New York–style bagel—a malted dough with a long, cold rise and a sweet-salty boil then bake—is the most classic of all bagels, crispy on the outside, chewy on the inside. Make and shape the dough at night, then bake these off in the morning for a perfect bagel brunch.

MAKES 12 bagels

TIMING
Sponge: 1 hour
Mix: 15 minutes
Bulk proof: 1 to 1½ hours
Preshape: 10 to 15 minutes
Final proof: 12 to 18 hours
Boil and bake: 12 to 15 minutes

SPONGE (ROZCZYN)
2 cups [250 g] bread flour
2¾ tsp [9 g] instant yeast
2 Tbsp [40 g] light barley malt syrup
2 cups plus 2 Tbsp [500 g] water

DOUGH
All of the Sponge
6 cups [750 g] bread flour
7 to 10½ Tbsp [100 to 150 g] cold water
2¾ tsp [18 g] kosher salt

FOR BOILING
8½ cups [2 L] water
1 Tbsp [20 g] light barley malt syrup
1¼ tsp [9 g] kosher salt

TOPPINGS (OPTIONAL)
Poppy seeds, sesame seeds, dried garlic, salt flakes, nigella seeds, and so on

Begin by making the sponge. In a medium mixing bowl, whisk together the flour, yeast, barley malt syrup, and water until smooth. Let sit for about 1 hour, until light, bubbly, and domed but not collapsing.

When the sponge is ready, mix the dough. In the bowl of your stand mixer fitted with the dough hook attachment, combine the sponge, flour, water, and salt. Mix on medium speed for 10 minutes, until a stiff dough has formed. Because the dough is stiff, you should watch for signs of overheating or struggle with your mixer. (If the mixer is straining, remove the dough and continue the kneading by hand.) When the dough is well-mixed and smooth and no dry bits remain, remove the dough and give an extra 5 minutes of kneading by hand, until the dough is smooth and taut. Form into a ball and place in a large, lightly oiled mixing bowl and cover airtight with plastic wrap with room for expansion. Allow the dough to rise for 1 to 1½ hours, until puffed by about two thirds in size and a finger pressed into the dough springs back slowly.

Once the dough has risen, turn it out onto an unfloured work surface—the dough shouldn't be

cont'd

sticky—and use a bench knife and a kitchen scale to divide the dough into twelve equal portions of 4½ oz [130 g]. Form each into a tight ball, arrange smooth-side up, cover loosely with plastic wrap or a damp tea towel, and set aside to rest for 10 to 15 minutes.

Once the dough has rested, take one ball of dough and flip it smooth-side down. Use a rolling pin to roll into a large, wide oval. Roll up the oval into a tight log, from the top to the bottom, then pinch the seam to seal (see page 23). Roll out the log to about 10 to 12 in [25 to 30.5 cm], then, with one hand on either end, roll the ends in opposite directions to twist the log. This will help your bagel keep its structure. Form a ring by bringing the ends together with an overlap of about 1 in [2.5 cm], maintaining the twist. Push one end into the other, then wrap the underside of the dough around the other, and pinch where it meets, forming a tight seal. Repeat for each bagel and arrange them 2 in [5 cm] apart, seam-side down, on a baking sheet or large brownie pan lined with parchment paper. (I use brownie pans because of the tall edge, which allows you to wrap the tray airtight in plastic wrap without touching the bagels.) Wrap in plastic wrap, allow to sit at room temperature for about 20 minutes, then refrigerate for 12 to 18 hours overnight. Your fridge settings should be low, between 37 and 41°F [3 and 5°C].

In the morning, preheat the oven to 425°F [220°C] with the convection setting turned on. Line two baking sheets with parchment paper and set aside.

Add the water, barley malt syrup, and salt to a medium pot and bring to a boil. The water should be at least 4 in [10 cm] deep (add more if needed). Boil a few bagels at a time, turning with a slotted spatula, allowing at least 1 minute on each side. Place about 1 in [2.5 cm] apart on a prepared baking sheet and sprinkle with toppings while the bagels are still wet. The moisture will act as glue for your toppings. Once all the bagels are boiled and topped, bake for about 12 to 15 minutes, or until golden brown. Serve with cream cheese, lox, onions, and capers.

These bagels are best served the first day. If making in advance, store in an airtight plastic bag with the air sucked out in the freezer for up to 2 months. When ready to eat, thaw at room temperature, then toast.

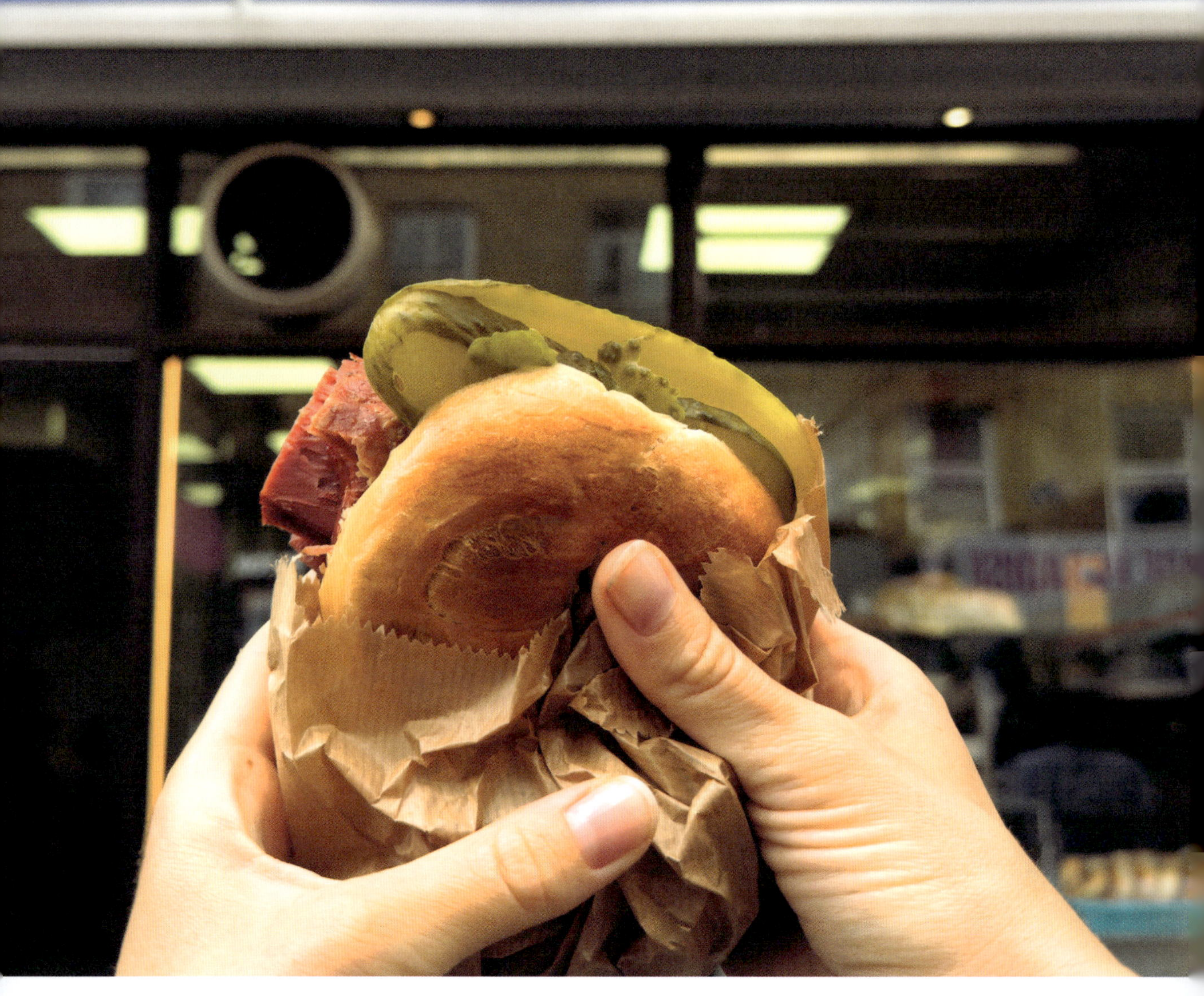
EL BAKE
ANE BAKERY
HOURS 7 DAYS
Tel. 071-729

Beigel Bake's Brick Lane London Beigels

In the great bagel diaspora, New York and Montreal get all the attention, but there's a third bagel, the London beigel, that stands on its own. This bagel, or beigel (pronounced *buy-gel* if you're old school), was popularized in large part by Beigel Bake, the narrow bakery storefront running twenty-four hours a day on East London's Brick Lane, selling dripping hot salt beef and hot mustard sandwiches. This sandwich is as much a part of London hang-over street food as kebabs. While the soft and sweet London beigel was initially a product of the Polish Jewish immigrant bakeries and was sold alongside every other kind of pastry and bread, it was a family of Yemenite Jews, the Cohens, who truly launched the beigel into the cult status it has today.

Daniel Cohen, the current owner of Beigel Bake and son of its founder, tells an origin story that starts when his family moved to London from Israel in the 1950s, following an uncle who'd been baking in those very same Polish bakeries. Noting that these general bakeries didn't enjoy adding the fussy production of beigels to their already busy shops, Daniel's uncle left to open a purely wholesale beigel bakery in the 1970s to supply the other Jewish bakeries around town. Daniel's father followed—working nights at the shop to take advantage of the cheaper nighttime electricity rates—and did his own wholesaling, eventually breaking off from the uncle's shop and opening Beigel Bake. While the shop started as a wholesale business, the residents of the surrounding neighborhood started coming around for beigels as well. Solidifying itself to legendary status, the bakery started making their salt beef beigel sandwiches, taking inspiration from the salt beef at London's famed Bloom's delicatessen.

MAKES 10 beigels

TIMING
Mix: 15 minutes
Bulk proof: 30 to 40 minutes
Preshape and bench rest: 5 minutes
Final proof: 30 to 40 minutes
Boil and bake: 30 minutes

6½ cups [800 g] all-purpose flour
5 Tbsp [60 g] sugar
2½ tsp [10 g] diastatic malt powder (available online)
2½ tsp [14 g] kosher salt
2¼ tsp [7 g] instant yeast
1¾ cups plus 1 Tbsp [440 g] room-temperature water

Begin by mixing the dough. In a medium mixing bowl, whisk together the flour, sugar, malt powder, salt, and yeast. In the bowl of your stand mixer, add the water, then the dry ingredients. Using the dough hook attachment, mix for 15 minutes on low speed until a smooth, medium-firm dough has formed that can be stretched thin without ripping. Form the dough into a tight ball and place in a lightly oiled bowl, then cover loosely with plastic wrap or a damp tea towel. Allow to rest for 30 to 40 minutes, until the dough has puffed and grown by almost two thirds in size and a finger pressed into the dough springs back slowly.

Once the dough has risen, it might be a little tacky but not sticky. Turn it out onto an unfloured work surface and divide the dough into ten even portions of about 4½ oz [130 g] each. Flatten each portion to degas, then roll into a tight ball (see page 22). Let the balls rest, seam-side down, on the work surface, loosely covered with plastic wrap or a damp tea towel, for 5 minutes.

While the balls rest, line a baking sheet with parchment paper and brush lightly with oil. Set aside.

cont'd

To shape the beigels, roll a ball into a fat sausage, about 8 in [20 cm] long (see page 23). With the log horizontal on the work surface, hold your right hand out above the log, perpendicular, with your palm facing up. Keeping your palm facing up, take the right end of the log between your thumb and forefinger, then flip your palm toward the work surface, taking the right end of the log with you. The log is now completely wrapped around your fingers. Overlap the right end of the log with the left end by 2 in [5 cm], then press and roll until it's tightly joined. Repeat for all the beigels.

Place the beigels on the lined baking sheet 2 in [5 cm] apart. Cover very loosely with plastic wrap and let rest for 30 to 40 minutes, until puffed and soft. Shortly before the beigels are risen, preheat the oven to 400°F [200°C] with the convection setting turned on and bring a large pot of water to boil on your stove.

Boil the bagels in batches for 2 to 3 minutes, flipping halfway with a slotted spatula, then return to the baking sheet, touching each other. (Crowding the beigels on the pan will give them the distinct nearly square shape of London beigels.)

Bake for 25 to 30 minutes, until golden brown. Serve immediately with warm salt beef or pastrami, loads of spicy mustard, and generous slices of sour pickles. Leftovers can be stored airtight in the freezer for a couple months.

Twisted Kraków Bagels

Obwarzanki

If you've ever been to the southern city of Kraków, you're sure to have noticed vendors selling obwarzanki, twisted bagels, out of blue-painted pushcarts. These bread rings have a long history and a protected status in modern times. Before the nineteenth century, as per a fifteenth-century law, only certain bakers (read: non-Jews) chosen by the bakery guild, were allowed to sell obwarzanki within the city walls. Once the rules relaxed, the quality and freshness of obwarzanki was still strictly monitored. Vendors set themselves up around the city before dawn to sell breakfast to the town's citizens as they went to work. Unlike the more familiar New York– or Montreal-style bagels, Kraków's obwarzanki are made with a twisted double strand and a much larger middle hole. They are, however, boiled and seeded like their single-stranded counterparts; in fact, the name *obwarzanki* comes from the verb meaning *parboil*. Serve these hot from the oven with cream cheese or butter.

NOTE: All the hard work in this recipe starts the night before. The long fermentation means a more complex and delicious flavor profile. The final boil-and-bake is minimal effort for a hot breakfast.

MAKES 12 obwarzanki

TIMING
Mix: 15 minutes
Bulk proof: 45 minutes to 1 hour
Preshape: 15 minutes
Final proof, refrigerated: 12 to 18 hours
Boil and bake: 12 minutes

DOUGH
5½ cups plus 2 Tbsp [700 g] bread flour
2¼ tsp [7 g] instant yeast
2 tsp [12 g] kosher salt
1½ Tbsp [30 g] honey
1⅔ cups [400 g] lukewarm water

FOR BOILING
4½ cups [1 L] water
2 Tbsp [40 g] kosher salt
2 Tbsp [42 g] honey

TOPPING
Sesame seeds, poppy seeds, or nigella seeds

Begin by mixing the dough. In the bowl of your stand mixer filled with the dough hook attachment, mix the flour, yeast, salt, honey, and water on low speed for 10 minutes, until a medium-stiff and smooth dough forms. Remove from the mixer and give it another few minutes of kneading by hand. Form the dough into a ball, cover with a damp tea towel on your work surface, and allow to rise for 45 minutes, or until the dough has grown by almost two thirds in size.

Once the dough has risen, preshape the dough. Divide the dough with a bench knife into twenty-four even portions of about 1¾ oz [50 g] each. Form each portion into a tight ball (see page 22). Cover the balls with plastic wrap or a damp tea towel and allow to rest for 15 minutes.

Line two baking sheets with parchment paper and set aside.

cont'd

Once the dough has rested, shape the bagels. Form the balls into logs (see page 23) and roll out into 10 in [25 cm] strands.

To form the obwarzanki, lay two strands touching lengthwise side-by-side on the unfloured work surface. Put your hands on each end of the strands and move the left hand down and the right hand up to give the strands the signature twist. Move the right side clockwise and the left side counterclockwise to meet in a ring—the direction is important as to not unwind the twist! Overlap the two ends of the twist by about 1 in [2.5 cm], then tuck and pinch together well. Set on a lined baking sheet and repeat for the remaining dough. The obwarzanki should be spaced at least 1 in [2.5 cm] apart. Cover the sheets loosely with plastic wrap or a plastic bag, then refrigerate for 12 to 18 hours overnight. Your fridge settings should be low, between 37 and 41°F [3 and 5°C].

The next morning, preheat the oven to 425°F [220°C] with the convection setting turned on. Combine the water, salt, and honey in a medium saucepan, adding more water if needed to make sure it is at least 4 in [10 cm] deep. Bring to a boil, and boil each obwarzanek for 1 minute, or until slightly puffed, flipping halfway with a slotted spatula. Remove from the water and allow each obwarzanek to drain over the pot before placing it back onto the baking sheet lined with parchment paper, 1 in [2.5 cm] apart. Top with any seeds immediately after removing from water—that's when they're stickiest! Bake for 12 to 15 minutes, or until golden brown.

Serve immediately or let cool and store in the freezer in an airtight plastic bag with the air sucked out for up to 2 months. When you'd like to eat them, thaw, then toast.

Bialy

Biały

That there are no bialys in Białystok is a *shanda*—a shame. It isn't a fun story. Lost to the Holocaust along with its bakers, the flat onion and poppy seed bread has since predominantly only existed in exile on America's East Coast, in New York and New Jersey. Please bear with me while I pick a bone with the way we've been treating the bialy, disrespecting it from the moment it leaves the oven, soft and crisp. Bialys—short for *Bialystoker kuchen*—are the misclassified stepchild of the Jewish Polish bakery canon. Perennially described as a cousin, close relative, or even sibling of the bagel—often with a qualifier like "neglected" or "forgotten" or "less beloved"—a good bialy truly has nothing to do with a bagel other than that it occasionally runs in the same circles or is sold at the same shops. Sure, they were born in the same country and moved away from home for good almost a century ago, but where the bagel is boiled, the bialy is not. Where the bagel is a ring, the bialy is a disk. And crucially—despite the insistence of many a bagel shop who will make a facsimile of a bialy using a stiff bagel dough—the bialy has a much softer dough, which turns out a far lighter bread. To put it plainly, the bialy is an entirely different animal. Let's let it stand alone.

NOTES: Because the dough can be prepared days in advance and the bake only takes a few minutes, you can serve these hot without throwing off your schedule. This recipe suggests baking on a pizza stone or cast-iron baking pan, but you can also use a regular baking sheet. Just adjust the bake time to about 12 minutes. The resulting bialys will be a little crispier and drier but still delicious.

MAKES 14 bialys

TIMING

Mix: 8 minutes

Bulk proof with stretches and folds, room temperature: 1½ hours

Continued bulk proof, refrigerated: 18 hours to 4 days

Final proof: 3 hours

Bake: 12 minutes

DOUGH

2¾ cups [655 g] water

1 Tbsp [20 g] light barley malt syrup or honey

¾ tsp [2 g] instant yeast

6⅔ cups [900 g] Italian Type 00 Pizza flour

¾ cup [100 g] whole-wheat flour

2¾ tsp [18 g] kosher salt

Cornmeal, for dusting

FILLING

4 medium yellow onions or 6 shallots, finely diced

1 head garlic, finely diced

¼ cup [55 g] olive oil

TOPPINGS

¼ cup [35 g] poppy seeds

Flaky sea salt

Ground black pepper

Fresh thyme (optional)

Begin by mixing the dough. In the bowl of your stand mixer, whisk together the water, barley malt syrup, and yeast, then add the pizza flour, whole-wheat flour, and salt. With the dough hook attachment, mix on low speed until all ingredients are incorporated, then increase the speed to medium for 8 minutes. You should have a smooth, slightly sticky dough that pulls away from the sides of the bowl. Dip your hands in water to prevent sticking, then transfer the dough from the mixer to a lightly oiled medium mixing bowl. Give the dough a series

cont'd

of stretches and folds (see page 25) and form into a tight ball, resting smooth-side up. Cover the bowl loosely with a tea towel.

After resting for a half hour, repeat the process of stretching and folding the dough. Re-cover the bowl and after another half hour, repeat the stretch and folds, for a total of 1½ hours room temperature bulk proof. Cover the bowl airtight with plastic wrap and refrigerate for 18 hours or up to 4 days.

Once the dough has rested, and about 3 hours before you'd like to bake, remove the dough from the fridge. Turn it out onto a lightly floured work surface and divide into fourteen portions, each about 4 oz [115 g]. Flatten each portion and then form into a tight ball (see page 22). Place seam-side down in a plastic storage container or loosely covered in plastic wrap on a baking sheet that has been well-dusted with cornmeal. Each ball should be placed about 2 in [5 cm] apart. If they stick to each other as they grow, they're hell to separate. Let the dough have a final rise of about 3 hours at room temperature.

About an hour before your dough is finished with its final proof, preheat the oven with a pizza stone or cast-iron baking pan inside to 450°F [240°C]. The preheat begins early because these kinds of baking surfaces take longer to absorb the oven's heat than the oven takes to preheat.

To prepare the filling, mix together the onion, garlic, and olive oil in a small bowl and set aside.

When the dough is ready and the oven is heated, line a baking sheet or cutting board with a sheet of parchment paper. Any flat board without an edge will work. Pick up each ball of dough and, using gravity to your advantage, turn and stretch the ball into a disk with a fat lip around the edge. Place each shaped bialy on the tray, about 1 to 2 in [2.5 to 5 cm] apart. You'll fit about six per tray and do three rounds of baking.

Generously spoon the onion mixture in the center of each bialy, then sprinkle with poppy seeds, sea salt, pepper, and thyme (if using).

Use the tray to slide the sheet of bialys onto the pizza stone. Bake for 4 to 5 minutes, until puffed, pillowy, and with attractive brown spots all over. To remove, use the same tray to slide under the parchment paper and scoop the bialys off the stone and transfer to a cooling rack. Repeat the process for the remaining bialys. Serve immediately.

Any leftovers can be frozen in an airtight plastic bag with the air sucked out for up to 2 months. Thaw then toast or warm in the oven when you're ready to eat them.

Horseradish, Beet, and Summer Greens Bialy

Biały z Chrzanem, Burakami, i Nowalijkami

There is one Warsaw baker who has done more for living Polish bialy culture than any other. Monika Walecka, arguably one of the most important contemporary bakers in the country, is the pioneering sourdough queen behind the beloved Cała w Mące Piekarnia and Cukiernia Tonka. Bialys have always been part of her repertoire, even back when she first started her bakery in a miniature upstairs room of an industrial bakery complex and only sold her bread at markets. Her signature full-sourdough potato and nigella seed bialy is a creative offshoot of the traditional onion-and-poppy-seed version and feels like the closest thing in Poland to a natural and playful progression in an interrupted food history. Meanwhile in America, there are more extreme examples of the bialy evolution. These days you can treat yourself at Philadelphia's Reading Terminal Market to an artisan cheesesteak or Buffalo chicken bialy, variations nearly unrecognizable as bialys but there you have it. After all, bialys are perfect vehicles for creative toppings of all kinds.

This is my submission to the modern bialy oeuvre: a light and crispy bialy loaded with the Polish flavors of horseradish, sour cream, poached asparagus, peas, and wild garlic. Serve as a salty breakfast or an aperitif snack with a glass of wine.

While you might not have year-round access to these spring vegetables, substituting frozen or seasonal veggies according to your tastes and regional availability is a great way to keep this recipe going all year. For example, in the heart of winter, oven-roasted beets, parsnips, and squash can replace the springtime greens.

MAKES 14 bialys

TIMING

Mix: 8 minutes

Bulk proof with stretches and folds, room temperature: 1½ hours

Continued bulk proof, refrigerated: 18 hours to 4 days

Final proof: 3 hours

Bake: 12 minutes

DOUGH

2⅔ cups plus 1½ Tbsp [650 g] water

¾ tsp [2 g] instant yeast

1 Tbsp [20 g] light barley malt syrup or honey

6⅔ cups [900 g] Italian Type 00 Pizza flour

¾ cup [100 g] whole-wheat flour

2¾ tsp [18 g] kosher salt

Cornmeal, for dusting

FOR BAKING

Olive oil

Sea salt

TOPPINGS

12 thin asparagus stalks, trimmed and cut into 2 in [5 cm] pieces

1 cup [160 g] fresh green peas

½ cup [30 g] mixed chopped fresh herbs (dill, wild garlic, parsley, chives, etc.)

Olive oil, for drizzling and to garnish

Sea salt

Juice of ½ lemon

¼ cup [70 g] beet horseradish

2 cups [460 g] cream cheese

½ cup [120 g] full-fat sour cream

cont'd

Begin by mixing the dough. In the bowl of your stand mixer, whisk together the water, yeast, and barley malt syrup, then add the pizza flour, whole-wheat flour, and salt. With the dough hook attachment, mix on low speed until all ingredients are incorporated, then increase the speed to medium. Mix for 8 minutes, until you have a smooth, slightly sticky dough that pulls away from the sides of the bowl. Dip your hands in water to prevent sticking, then transfer the dough from the mixer into a lightly oiled medium mixing bowl. Give the dough a series of stretches and folds (see page 25) and form into a tight ball, resting smooth-side up. Cover loosely with a tea towel.

After a half hour rest, repeat the process of stretching and folding the dough. Re-cover the bowl and, after another half hour, repeat the stretch and folds, for a total of 1½ hours room temperature bulk proof. Cover the bowl airtight with plastic wrap and refrigerate for 18 hours or up to 4 days.

After the dough has rested and about 3 hours before you'd like to bake, remove the dough from the fridge, turn out onto a lightly floured work surface and divide into fourteen portions, each about 4 oz [115 g]. Flatten each portion and then form into a tight ball (see page 22). Place seam-side down in a plastic storage container or loosely covered in plastic wrap on a baking sheet that has been well-dusted with cornmeal. Each ball should be placed about 3 in [7.5 cm] apart. If they stick to each other as they grow, they're hell to separate. Let the dough have a final rise of about 3 hours at room temperature.

About an hour before your dough is finished with its final proof, preheat the oven with a pizza stone or cast-iron baking sheet inside to 450°F [240°C]. The preheat begins early because these kinds of baking surfaces take longer to absorb the oven's heat than the oven takes to preheat. (If you don't have a pizza stone, see the Notes on page 59.)

When the dough is ready and the oven is heated, line a baking sheet or cutting board with a sheet of parchment paper. Any flat board without an edge will work. Pick up each ball of dough and, using gravity to your advantage, turn and stretch the ball into a disk with a fat lip around the edge. Place each shaped bialy on the tray about 1 to 2 in [2.5 to 5 cm] apart. You'll fit about six per tray and do three rounds of baking.

Drizzle the center of each bialy with olive oil and a bit of sea salt, then use the tray to slide the sheet of bialys onto the pizza stone. Bake for 4 to 5 minutes, until puffed, pillowy, and with attractive brown spots all over. To remove, use the same tray to slide under the parchment paper to scoop the bialys off the stone. Repeat the process for the remaining bialys.

While the bialys bake and cool, make the toppings. Fill a medium bowl with ice water and set aside. Bring a medium saucepan of salted water to a boil. Add the asparagus and peas and cook for about 4 minutes, until just softened but still vivid green. With a slotted spoon, remove the vegetables from the pot and put directly into the ice bath to halt the cooking process. This will keep the vegetables snappy and bright. As soon as the vegetables are cool, drain and combine with the herbs, a drizzle of olive oil, a dash of sea salt, and the lemon juice in a medium bowl. In a small mixing bowl, whisk together the horseradish, cream cheese, and sour cream until smooth.

To assemble your bialys, schmear a generous portion of the horseradish cream in the center of each, then place a spoonful of the vegetable mix on top. Serve immediately.

Pletzl

Onion Flatbread

Pletzl is many different things to many different people. In the Jewish bakeries of London, it's a puffy onion bun, nearly interchangeable with the East Coast America version of a bialy. In Paris, it's a square-cut bread closer to a focaccia. In Argentina, it's called pletzalej, a sweet bun closer to Cebularz (page 125). And amongst most Americans, pletzl is a crispy risen flatbread. According to Stanley Ginsberg's *Inside the Jewish Bakery*, the Polish—or specifically Varsovian—version is also the flatbread style common in America. And so, that's what we'll do here, embellished with spring onions and seeds for color and flavor.

NOTE: This dough starts the day before you're ready to bake. It comes together easily and, with a little planning ahead, is ready for your lunch, dinner, or snack.

MAKES 3 pletzl

TIMING

Mix: 8 minutes
Bulk proof, room temperature: 1 hour
Continued bulk proof, refrigerated: 18 hours to 4 days
Final proof: 3 to 4 hours
Bake: 5 minutes

DOUGH

1⅓ cups plus 2 tsp [325 g] water
1 Tbsp [21 g] honey
Tiniest pinch [1 g] of instant yeast
3⅓ cups [450 g] Italian Type 00 Pizza flour
½ cup [50 g] whole-rye flour
1¾ tsp [11 g] kosher salt
1½ Tbsp [25 g] olive oil

FOR BAKING

Cornmeal, for dusting

FILLING

2 medium onions, finely chopped, about 2 cups
6 spring onions, finely chopped, about 1 cup
½ cup [110 g] olive oil

TOPPINGS

2 Tbsp [20 g] sesame seeds (optional)
1 Tbsp nigella seeds (optional)
1 Tbsp poppy seeds (optional)
Flaky sea salt

Begin by mixing the dough. In the bowl of your stand mixer, combine the water, honey, and yeast and whisk until smooth. Then add the pizza flour, rye flour, and salt and, with the dough hook attachment, mix on low speed until all the ingredients are incorporated. Increase the speed to medium and continue mixing for 8 minutes, or until the dough is smooth and starts to pull away from the sides of the bowl. Turn the speed to low and drizzle in the olive oil in a thin stream. The dough will come apart and then return to a smooth mass within a couple minutes. Once the olive oil is entirely incorporated, turn off the mixer.

Coat your palms with oil to prevent sticking, and transfer the dough into a lightly oiled medium mixing bowl. Pick up the dough with two hands and allow gravity to stretch the overhanging dough under itself. Turn the bowl and repeat, until you have a smooth ball of dough. Cover the bowl loosely with a tea towel, then allow the dough to rest for 1 hour at room temperature. After 1 hour, give the dough another set of stretch and folds, cover the bowl airtight with plastic wrap with some room for expansion, and let it rest in the fridge for 18 hours or up to 4 days.

After the dough has rested and about 3 hours before you're ready to bake, remove the dough from the fridge and divide into three even portions. With

cont'd

oiled hands, form each portion into a tight ball (see page 22), then place on an oiled surface, loosely covered with plastic wrap or an inverted bowl, and allow to rest for about 3 hours.

While the dough rests and rises, prepare your topping. In a bowl, mix the onions, spring onions, and olive oil, then set aside.

About a half hour before you're ready to bake, preheat the oven to 450°F [240°C] with a rack in the middle and the convection setting turned on. Line a baking sheet with parchment paper and dust with cornmeal.

Stretch one of the balls of dough, using the weight of gravity, as thin as it can go before it becomes too unwieldy, then place it on the baking sheet. Continue stretching until you have a nearly transparently thin oval. Spread one third of the onion mixture evenly over the dough. Sprinkle with sesame, nigella, and poppy seeds (if using), and flaky salt to taste. Bake for 5 minutes, or until the pletzl is golden brown and the onions are sizzling. Remove from the oven and slide onto a cooling rack.

On your work surface, dust a sheet of parchment paper with cornmeal and repeat the shaping process, then transfer the paper and pletzl onto the hot pan and bake. Repeat with the third pletzl. Serve sliced as an appetizer or snack, or as an accompaniment to salads or soups.

The Modern Polish Country Loaf on Leaves

Chleb na Liściu

The contemporary artisan Polish baking movement is heavily influenced by classic Polish breads, local grains, and the transcendent sourdoughs of Scandinavian-style baking. Since communism ended, the Polish food scene has rapidly changed as chefs and bakers moved abroad to work in the gastro scenes of London, Paris, Copenhagen, and New York. These bakers merged newfound techniques and styles with the established Polish culture of local eating, kitchen gardens, and old-style breads. These days there's no need to leave Poland to develop technique, and the European baking community often gravitates toward Polish bakeries, with bakers coming from all over to learn from the new generation of sourdough masters.

This recipe is representative of the new Polish sourdough: open-crumbed but with a portion of whole rye and baked on spicy horseradish leaves, a traditional touch meant to add moisture and flavor. If you can't find horseradish leaves, grape leaves, beet leaves, or savoy cabbage leaves will also work.

MAKES one 1½ lb [680 g] loaf

TIMING
Leaven: 8 hours
Mix and bulk proof: 3½ hours
Bench rest and preshape: 20 minutes
Proof and final rise, refrigerated: 8 to 10 hours
Bake: 45 minutes
Cool: 4 hours

LEAVEN (ZACZYN)
1 tsp [5 g] sourdough starter
½ cup [50 g] whole-rye flour
¼ cup [60 g] room-temperature water

DOUGH
All of the Leaven
2 cups [475 g] water
3 cups plus 3 Tbsp [400 g] bread flour
¾ cup [90 g] whole-rye flour
⅓ cup plus 1 Tbsp [50 g] whole-wheat flour
1¾ tsp [11 g] kosher salt

FOR BAKING
2 or 3 horseradish, beet, grape, or savoy cabbage leaves, washed and dried

The morning of the day before you wish to bake, prepare the leaven. Mix the sourdough starter, flour, and water into a uniform paste with no dry lumps of flour, then cover loosely with a tea towel and leave to rise at room temperature for 8 hours, until domed and bubbly.

The afternoon or evening after you've prepared your leaven and it is at peak activity, mix the dough. In a large mixing bowl, whisk together the leaven and water. Add the bread flour, whole-rye flour, whole-wheat flour, and salt, and hand mix until a medium-thick, uniform dough has formed. At this point, the dough will be sticky with a batter-like texture but will develop stretch as it rises. Scrape down the sides of the bowl with a dough scraper (and do the same to clean your hands!). Cover the bowl loosely with a tea towel and set aside for 1 hour.

After the dough has rested for an hour, give the dough a set of stretch and folds (see page 25) every 30 to 45 minutes for the next 2½ hours, for a total of 3½ hours bulk proof. With each stretch and fold, the dough will develop more elasticity.

At the end of the series of stretch and folds, turn the dough out onto a floured surface. Fold in the sides to preshape the loaf (see page 26), then allow to rest smooth-side up for about 20 minutes.

cont'd

Meanwhile, flour your proofing basket and set aside. For an extra flourish, add a leaf to the base of the proofing basket before flouring to decorate what will be the top of your loaf.

After the dough has rested, use your bench knife to flip it smooth-side down, and fold in the sides to shape it into a boule (see page 28). Flip the boule smooth-side down into the proofing basket. Lay your leaves on top of the loaf. Let the dough rest for another 20 minutes at room temperature, then refrigerate overnight for 8 to 10 hours.

Then next morning, preheat the oven to 450°F [240°C] with the convection setting turned on and a large, covered cast-iron pot inside. Once the oven has preheated for at least 30 minutes, remove the pot and set on a heatproof surface. Uncover the pot and invert the dough into the middle, leaves and all. Using a sharp knife or razor, make several ½ in [1 cm] slashes in the pattern of your choice across the top. Re-cover immediately with the lid, and return the pot to the oven. Bake covered for 20 minutes, then remove the lid, lower the heat to 400°F [200°C], and continue to bake for about 25 more minutes, until a thermometer inserted in the bread reads at least 195°F [90°C]. Remove from the oven and set the loaf on a cooling rack. Allow to cool completely before cutting, about 4 hours.

Store for up to a week at room temperature wrapped in a tea towel. As the week goes on, toast to reinvigorate your bread.

Kefir Loaf

Chleb z Kefirem

The Polish love of fermented dairy is no secret—buttermilks, yogurts, fresh cheeses, and kefirs exist in more permutations than is wise to count. Fermented dairy also makes its way into breads. While not incredibly common, it's always a treat to find a loaf spiked with yogurt or kefir. It gives the texture a bit of extra chew and moisture as well as a discernible tang. This loaf is modeled after an artisan loaf I had in a Kraków market. Made in the style of modern sourdough, its open crumb and chewy crust was unforgettable, a meal unto itself. Start your leaven 24 hours before you wish to bake—starting it in the morning means an evening mix and a morning bake.

MAKES **one 1½ lb [680 g] loaf**

TIMING
Leaven: 8 hours
Mix and bulk proof: 3½ hours
Bench rest/preshape: 20 minutes
Proof and final rise, refrigerated: 8 to 10 hours
Bake: 45 minutes
Cool: 4 hours

LEAVEN (ZACZYN)
1 tsp [5 g] sourdough starter
⅓ cup plus 3 tsp [50 g] whole-rye flour
¼ cup [60 g] room temperature water

DOUGH
All of the Leaven
1⅓ cups [330 g] kefir
⅓ to ⅔ cup [100 to 150 g] water
3 cups plus 3 Tbsp [400 g] bread flour
1 cup plus 2½ tsp [135 g] whole-rye flour
1¾ tsp [11 g] kosher salt

The morning of the day before you wish to bake, prepare the leaven. Mix the sourdough starter, whole-rye flour, and water into a uniform paste with no dry lumps of flour. Cover loosely with a tea towel and leave to rise at room temperature for 8 hours until domed and bubbly.

The afternoon or evening after you've prepared the leaven and it is at peak activity, mix the dough. In a large mixing bowl, whisk together the leaven, kefir, and water. Add the bread flour, whole-rye flour, and salt, and hand mix until a medium thick, uniform dough has formed with no dry lumps of flour. At this point, the dough will be sticky, with a batter-like texture, but will develop stretch as it rises.

Scrape down the sides of the bowl with a dough scraper (and do the same to clean your hands!). Cover the bowl loosely with a tea towel and set aside for 1 hour.

After the dough has rested for 1 hour, give the dough a set of stretch and folds (see page 25) every 30 to 45 minutes for the next 2½ hours, for a total of 3½ hours bulk proof. With each stretch and fold, the dough will build more elasticity. After the bulk proof, turn the dough out onto a floured surface. Fold in the sides to preshape the loaf (see page 26), then turn smooth-side up and allow to rest for about 20 minutes. While it rests, flour a proofing basket.

After the dough has rested, use your bench knife to flip the dough smooth-side down, and fold in the sides to shape it as a boule (see page 28). Flip the boule smooth-side down into the floured proofing basket. Let rest for another 20 minutes, then refrigerate overnight for 8 to 10 hours.

The next morning, preheat the oven to 450°F [240°C] with the convection setting turned on and a large, covered cast-iron pot inside. Once the oven

cont'd

has preheated for at least 30 minutes, remove the pot and set it on a heatproof surface. Uncover the pot and invert the loaf into the middle. Using a sharp knife or razor, make several ½ in [1 cm] slashes in the pattern of your choice across the top. Re-cover immediately with the lid and return to the oven. Bake covered for 20 minutes, then remove the lid and reduce the heat to 400°F [200°C] and continue to bake for about 25 more minutes, until a thermometer inserted in the bread reads at least 195°F [90°C].

Remove the pan from the oven and set the loaf on a cooling rack. Allow to cool completely before cutting, about 4 hours.

Store for up to a week wrapped in a tea towel. As the week goes on, toast to reinvigorate your bread.

Kraków Potato and Bran Flake Loaf

Chleb Prądnicki

A true chleb Prądnicki is a giant round bread, its weight starting at a minimum of 10 pounds [4.5 kg], with large loaves reaching almost 33 pounds [15 kg]. The scale is incredible, often stretching well beyond 3 feet [1 m] across. Its soft, light crumb made succulent with a bit of potato contrasts with a thick, brown crust coated in bran flakes. This bread's impressive size is matched only by its impressively long history. Chleb Prądnicki was first made in Kraków six hundred years ago and named for the river Prądnik, where a cluster of villages built flour mills that took advantage of the river's hydropower. In the late fifteenth century, King Jan I Olbracht (John I Albert) allowed the bakers of these villages to sell their breads in Kraków one day a week, a commercial activity normally restricted to residents of the city. The tradition has endured, and you can still buy a chunk of these huge breads at market stands in Kraków.

NOTE: Your oven can't fit a real chleb Prądnicki. There's no way. This recipe makes a home-friendly size loaf.

MAKES one 1½ lb [680 g] loaf

TIMING

Leaven: 8 hours
Mix and bulk proof: 3½ hours
Bench rest and preshape: 20 minutes
Proof and final rise, refrigerated: 8 to 10 hours
Bake: 45 minutes
Cool: 4 hours

LEAVEN (ZACZYN)

1 tsp [5 g] sourdough starter
½ cup [50 g] whole-rye flour
¼ cup [60 g] room-temperature water

DOUGH

All of the Leaven
¾ cup [100 g] riced or finely blended mashed potatoes
1½ to 1⅔ cups [350 to 400 g] water
2½ cups plus 1 Tbsp [320 g] bread flour
1¾ cups [180 g] whole-rye flour
1¾ tsp [11 g] kosher salt

FOR SHAPING

1 cup [80 g] bran flakes

The morning of the day before you wish to bake, prepare the leaven. In a small mixing bowl, mix the sourdough starter, flour, and water by hand into a uniform paste with no dry lumps of flour. Cover loosely with a tea towel and leave to rise at room temperature for about 8 hours, until domed and bubbly.

The afternoon or evening after you've prepared your leaven and it is at peak activity, mix the dough. In a large mixing bowl, whisk together the leaven, mashed potatoes, and water. Add the bread flour, whole-rye flour, and salt, and mix by hand until a medium-thick, uniform dough has formed. At this point, the dough will be sticky with a batter-like texture but will develop stretch as it rises. Scrape down the sides of the bowl with a dough scraper (and do the same to clean your hands!). Cover the bowl loosely with a tea towel and set aside for 1 hour.

cont'd

After the dough has rested for an hour, give it a set of stretch and folds (see page 25) every 30 to 45 minutes for the next 2½ hours, for a total of 3½ hours bulk proof. With each stretch and fold, the dough will develop more elasticity.

After the bulk proof, turn the dough out onto a surface well-coated in bran flakes. Fold in the sides to preshape the loaf (see page 26), then turn smooth-side up and allow to rest for about 20 minutes. While it rests, generously sprinkle a proofing basket with more bran flakes and set aside.

After the dough has rested, use your bench knife to flip it smooth-side down, and fold in the sides to shape it into a boule (see page 28). Flip it smooth-side down into the proofing basket. Let rest for another 20 minutes, then refrigerate overnight for 8 to 10 hours.

The next morning, preheat the oven to 450°F [240°C] with the convection setting turned on and a large, covered cast-iron pot inside. Once the oven has preheated for at least 30 minutes, remove the pot and set it on a heatproof surface. Uncover the pot and invert the loaf into the middle. Using a sharp knife or razor, make several ½ in [1 cm] slashes in the pattern of your choice across the top. Re-cover immediately with the lid, and return the pot to the oven. Bake covered for 20 minutes, then remove the lid, lower the heat to 400°F [200°C], and continue to bake for about 25 more minutes, until a thermometer inserted in the bread reads at least 195°F [90°C]. Remove from the oven and set the loaf on a cooling rack. Allow to cool completely before cutting, about 4 hours.

Store for up to a week wrapped in a tea towel. As the week goes on, toast to reinvigorate your bread.

Everyday Light Rye Bread

Chleb Baltonowski

There was a funny phenomenon during communism in Eastern Bloc countries: hard currency stores. These were places where, for foreign currency, you could buy Western goods: clothes, radios, tobacco, you name it. They started off serving the elite, but by the 1970s, they also catered to the general public. In the People's Republic of Poland, there were a couple of these shops, namely Pewex and Baltona. Baltona didn't start off as a hard currency retail shop though—it was originally a supplier to ships, government buildings, diplomatic posts, and airlines. And one of the items they supplied to these ships and planes and halls of power, and later sold in their stores, was chleb Baltonowski. According to some, this simple rye-wheat bread with a soft but tight crumb was, improbable as it sounds, synonymous with luxury. It spread in popularity and is today one of the most eaten breads in Poland, sold at almost every bakery. No need to buy it in foreign currency, złoty will do just fine.

NOTE: This bread uses a large portion of leaven as a preferment, making the bulk rise after the dough mix faster than the other sourdough recipes in this book. You've basically already done half the rising with the preferment!

MAKES one 1½ lb [680 g] loaf

TIMING

Leaven: 8 hours to overnight
Mix: 7 minutes
Bulk proof: 45 minutes to 1 hour
Proof and final rise: 1½ to 2 hours
Bake: 1 hour
Cool: 4 hours

LEAVEN (ZACZYN)

1½ tsp [8 g] whole-rye sourdough starter
2⅓ cups [240 g] light rye flour
1½ cups plus 1 Tbsp [375 g] water

DOUGH

2 tsp [12 g] kosher salt
½ cup [125 g] water
All of the Leaven
2¾ cups plus 2 Tbsp [360 g] bread flour

FOR BAKING

Bran flakes, cornmeal, or whole-grain flour

The night before you're ready to bake, prepare the leaven. In a large mixing bowl, mix the starter with the flour and water by hand into a uniform paste with no dry lumps of flour. Cover loosely with a tea towel and leave to rise overnight, about 8 hours, until domed and bubbly.

The next morning, when your leaven is ready and at peak activity, mix the dough. In a small bowl, whisk together the salt and water to dissolve. In the bowl of your stand mixer fitted with the dough hook attachment, mix together the leaven, bread flour, and salt water on medium speed for 7 minutes, until the dough starts to pull away from the sides of the bowl.

Dip your hands in water to prevent sticking, then, keeping the dough in the mixing bowl, give the dough some extra tension by folding it into as tight a ball as you can manage. Cover loosely with a tea towel and let the dough rest and bulk proof for 45 minutes to 1 hour, until visibly puffed.

Once the dough has risen, turn it out onto a well-floured work surface. Press the dough into a thick oval, then fold up and narrow the shorter sides to create a tapered shape. Roll up the long side of the

cont'd

oval, creating an oval loaf shape. Place the loaf into a floured oval-shaped proofing basket, smooth-side down. (If you don't have an oval proofing basket, you can form it into a boule and place in a round proofing basket.) Let rise for 1½ to 2 hours. When the loaf has fully risen, it will have grown by almost two thirds in size and a finger pressed into the dough will spring back slowly about halfway.

About an hour before you're ready to bake, preheat the oven to 450°F [240°C] with the convection setting turned on and a pizza stone or cast-iron baking pan on the middle rack. Put an old metal baking pan at the bottom of the oven to preheat.

Generously dust a flat baking sheet or pizza peel with bran flakes, cornmeal, or whole-grain flour. Invert your loaf onto the baking sheet and use a sharp knife or razor to score the length of the top of the bread, about ½ in [1 cm] deep. Open the oven and slide the loaf onto the preheated pizza stone. Toss several ice cubes into the preheated pan at the bottom of the oven to release steam, then quickly close the door. Bake for 20 minutes, then lower the heat to 400°F [200°C] and continue baking for about 40 minutes, until a thermometer inserted in the loaf reads 195°F [90°C]. If the surface of the loaf starts to get too dark, cover loosely with aluminum foil for the remainder of the bake. Remove from the oven and slide onto a cooling rack. Allow the bread to cool completely before you cut into it, about 4 hours.

Store for up to 4 days wrapped in a tea towel. As the days go on, toast to reinvigorate your bread.

słonecznik
5 szt.

Wholemeal Rye Loaf

Chleb Żytni Razowy

One of the great historians of twentieth century and communist Eastern Europe is Anne Applebaum. American by birth, she's a Polish dual citizen, married to the politician Radosław Sikorski, and spends half of her time in Poland. While she's won the Pulitzer and is celebrated for her journalism and history books, in 2012 she also wrote one of the best English-language cookbooks on Polish cuisine: *From a Polish Country House Kitchen*. With her extensive knowledge of Polish food culture, I asked her what Polish baking speaks to her the most. Her answer was simple: a slice of rye bread, spread with butter.

Polish rye breads are a wonderful and hearty thing. Made with zakwas—sourdough—they are full of the flavor of whole grains, with a touch of acid and natural sweetness. Chleb żytni razowy is a dense and crusty bread best served with, as Ms. Applebaum suggests, a thick schmear of butter.

NOTE: I prefer to prepare this loaf directly from start to finish, with no rest in the fridge. It's a great bread to make on a day off, prepping your starter the night before you wish to bake, mixing the dough in the morning, and baking it mid-afternoon.

MAKES one 9 x 5 in [23 x 13 cm] loaf

TIMING

Leaven: 8 hours to overnight
Mix and bulk proof: 3½ hours
Proof and final rise: 2½ hours
Bake: 45 minutes
Cool: 4 hours

LEAVEN (ZACZYN)

1 tsp [5 g] sourdough starter
½ cup [50 g] whole-rye flour
¼ cup [60 g] room-temperature water

DOUGH

All of the Leaven
2 cups plus 3¾ Tbsp [530 g] water
1 Tbsp [21 g] honey or light barley malt syrup
1⅔ cups [165 g] light rye flour
1⅔ cups [165 g] whole-rye flour
1⅓ cups [165 g] bread flour
1¾ tsp [11 g] kosher salt

FOR BAKING

Sunflower oil
Whole-rye flour

The evening before the day you wish to bake, prepare the leaven. In a medium mixing bowl, mix the sourdough starter, flour, and water by hand into a uniform paste with no dry lumps of flour. Cover loosely with a tea towel and leave to rise at room temperature overnight, about 8 hours, until domed and bubbly.

The next morning, when the leaven is ready, mix the dough. In a large mixing bowl, whisk together the leaven, water, and honey. Next add the light rye flour, whole-rye flour, bread flour, and salt. Mix by hand until it's a uniform, sticky dough. Scrape down the sides of the bowl with a dough scraper (and do the same to clean your hands!). Cover the bowl loosely with a tea towel and set aside for 1 hour to start the bulk proof.

Dip your hands in water to prevent sticking, then give the dough a series of stretch and folds (see page 25). The dough will be loose and highly

cont'd

hydrated without a lot of stretch due to the high percentage of rye.

After the dough has rested for an hour, give it a set of stretch and folds every 30 to 45 minutes for the next 2½ hours, for a total of 3½ hours bulk proof. With each stretch and fold, the dough will build more elasticity. While the dough bulk proofs, brush your loaf pan very lightly with sunflower oil and set aside.

Once the dough has risen, shape the loaf. Give the dough one last set of stretch and folds in the bowl, turning it into a tight oval or ball (see page 22), then use the dough scraper to slide the folded dough into the greased pan. Don't worry if the dough doesn't spread immediately to fill the entire pan; it will as it rises. Sift a dusting of whole-rye flour over the top, then let the loaf rise at room temperature for 2½ hours, until puffed and domed and risen just past the top of the pan and the flour on top has cracked. A finger pressed into the dough will spring back slowly about halfway.

Shortly before the dough is finished rising, preheat the oven to 450°F [240°C] with a rack in the middle and the convection setting turned on. Put an old metal baking pan at the bottom of the oven to heat.

Put the loaf in the oven and toss a few ice cubes into the pan to make steam, then quickly close the door. Bake for 20 minutes at 450°F [240°C], then lower the temperature to 400°F [200°C] and continue baking for another 25 to 30 minutes, until a thermometer inserted in the bread reads at least 195°F [90°C]. If the top of the loaf starts getting too dark, cover with aluminum foil for the remainder of the bake. Allow the bread to cool for 1 hour, then turn the loaf out of the pan onto a cooling rack. Cool completely before cutting, about 3 hours.

Store for up to a week wrapped in a tea towel. As the week goes on, toast to reinvigorate your bread.

Sunflower Rye Loaf

Chleb Żytni Słonecznikowy

The Polish farming countryside at the peak of summer is a technicolor wonder. Hot fields of sunflowers and bright red poppies await harvest. Whole giant sunflower heads appear in vegetable stands, the fresh seeds ready for snacking. Meanwhile, the shelled seeds are used heavily in baking, adding a rich, nutty signature to many buns, cookies, and loaves. Here, rye and a touch of sweet malt complement a hearty sourdough bread that's as easily paired with vinegary herrings and wódka as it is meaty tomatoes and fresh twaróg—farmer's cheese.

NOTE: I prefer to prepare this loaf directly from start to finish, with no rest in the fridge. It's a great bread to make on a day off, prepping your starter the night before you wish to bake, mixing the dough in the morning, and baking it mid-afternoon.

MAKES one 9 x 5 in [23 x 13 cm] loaf

TIMING
Leaven: 8 hours to overnight
Mix and bulk proof: 3½ hours
Proof and final rise: 2½ hours
Bake: 45 minutes
Cool: 4 hours

LEAVEN (ZACZYN)
1 tsp [5 g] sourdough starter
½ cup [50 g] whole-rye flour
¼ cup [60 g] room-temperature water

DOUGH
1¾ cups [250 g] sunflower seeds, plus more for topping
All of the Leaven
2 cups plus 3¾ Tbsp [530 g] water
1 Tbsp [21 g] honey or barley malt syrup
1⅔ cups [165 g] light rye flour
1⅔ cups [165 g] whole-rye flour
1⅓ cups [165 g] bread flour
1¾ tsp [11 g] kosher salt

FOR BAKING
Sunflower oil

The night before you wish to bake, prepare the leaven. In a medium mixing bowl, mix the sourdough starter, flour, and water by hand into a uniform paste with no dry lumps of flour. Cover loosely with a tea towel and leave to rise at room temperature overnight, about 8 hours, until domed and bubbly.

Preheat the oven to 350°F [180°C] with the convection setting turned on. Lay out two thirds of the sunflower seeds on a shallow pan. Toast the seeds for about 10 minutes, until golden brown and fragrant. Place the seeds in a bowl and mix with about a half cup of water. Set aside to absorb the water until the next day.

The next morning when the leaven is ready, mix the dough. In a large mixing bowl, whisk together the leaven, the 2 cups plus 3¾ Tbsp [530 g] water, and honey. Add the light rye flour, whole-rye flour, bread flour, and salt. Mix together by hand until it's a uniform, medium-thick, sticky dough with no dry pockets of flour. Scrape down the sides of the bowl with a dough scraper (and do the same to clean your hands!). Cover the bowl loosely with a tea towel and set aside for 1 hour.

Drain the sunflower seeds of any excess water and add them to the dough. Dip your hands in water to prevent sticking and give the dough a series of stretch and folds (see page 25) to incorporate the seeds and build tension. The dough will be loose and highly hydrated without a lot of stretch due to the high percentage of rye.

cont'd

After the dough has rested for an hour, give it a set of stretch and folds every 30 to 45 minutes for the next 2½ hours, for a total of 3½ hours bulk proof. With each stretch and fold, the dough will build more elasticity. While the dough proofs, brush your loaf pan very lightly with sunflower oil and set aside.

Once the dough has risen, shape the loaf. Do this by giving the dough one last set of stretch and folds in the bowl, turning it into a tight oval or ball (see page 22), then use the dough scraper to slide the folded dough into the greased pan. Don't worry if the dough doesn't spread immediately to fill the entire pan; it will as it rises. Sprinkle the top with sunflower seeds, then let the loaf rise at room temperature for 2½ hours, until it is puffed and risen just past the top of the pan. A finger pressed into the dough will spring back slowly about halfway.

Shortly before the dough is finished rising, preheat the oven to 450°F [240°C] with a rack in the middle and the convection setting turned on. Put an old metal baking pan at the bottom of the oven to preheat.

Use a sharp knife or razor to score a long line about ½ in [1 cm] deep across the top of the loaf. Put the loaf in the oven, toss several ice cubes into the bottom pan to make steam, then quickly close the door. Bake for 20 minutes at 450°F [240°C], then lower the temperature to 400°F [200°C] and continue baking for another 25 to 30 minutes, until a thermometer inserted in the bread reads at least 195°F [90°C]. If the top of the loaf starts getting too dark, cover with aluminum foil for the remainder of the bake. Allow the bread to cool for 1 hour, then turn the loaf out of the pan onto a cooling rack. Cool completely before cutting, about 3 hours.

Store for up to a week wrapped in a tea towel. As the week goes on, toast to reinvigorate your bread.

Lithuanian Black Bread

Chleb Litewski

The blackest rye breads of Eastern Europe come from farther afield than Poland, the most famous coming from the Baltic states. But with practically every other bakery in Eastern Poland selling a chleb Litewski, Lithuanian black bread, it is arguably a part of the Polish bakery canon. This unique rye loaf's presence in the Polish bakery world makes sense: The exchange between the two countries is hardly negligible. There have been long periods of history when the ever-flexible borders meant Poland and Lithuania were one. For more than two centuries, between 1569 and 1795, they were the powerful Polish-Lithuanian Commonwealth. After the partition, as food stories tend to go, no demarcation on a map could create an arbitrary separation of national breads. Chleb Litewski is a sweet, dark rye bread, its mysterious color attributed to a variety of sweeteners and colorants—from molasses to coffee and cocoa powder. But for the truest, most complex flavor and color, here we use roasted malt powder, a touch of molasses, and a bit of caraway.

NOTE: Dark roasted rye or barley malt powder can be sourced through beer brewing stores, or you can make your own by toasting baker's malt on a pan in a 350°F [180°C] oven with the convection setting off for 20 to 30 minutes, stirring occasionally, until the color of ground coffee.

MAKES one 9 x 5 in [23 x 13 cm] loaf

TIMING
Leaven: 8 hours to overnight
Mix and bulk proof: 3½ hours
Proof and final rise: 2½ hours
Bake: 45 minutes
Cool: 4 hours

LEAVEN (ZACZYN)
1 tsp [5 g] sourdough starter
½ cup [50 g] whole-rye flour
¼ cup [60 g] room-temperature water

DOUGH
All of the Leaven
2 cups plus 2 Tbsp [500 g] water
1 Tbsp [21 g] molasses
2 tsp [10 g] sunflower oil
¼ cup [35 g] dark roasted rye or barley malt powder
1⅔ cups [165 g] light rye flour
1⅔ cups [165 g] whole-rye flour
1⅓ cups [165 g] bread flour
1¾ tsp [11 g] kosher salt
1 tsp [5 g] ground caraway

The night before you wish to bake, prepare the leaven. In a medium mixing bowl, mix the sourdough starter, flour, and water by hand into a uniform paste with no dry lumps of flour. Cover loosely with a tea towel and leave to rise at room temperature overnight, about 8 hours, until domed and bubbly.

The next morning when the leaven is ready, mix the dough. In a large mixing bowl, whisk together the leaven, water, molasses, sunflower oil, and malt powder. Next add the light rye flour, whole-rye flour, bread flour, salt, and caraway. Mix together by hand until it's a uniform, sticky dough with no dry pockets of flour. Scrape down the sides of the bowl with a dough scraper (and do the same to clean your hands!). Cover the bowl loosely with a tea towel and set aside for 1 hour to start the bulk proof.

Dip your hands in water to prevent sticking, then give the dough a series of stretch and folds. The dough will be loose and highly hydrated without a lot of stretch due to the high percentage of rye. Give the dough a set of stretch and folds every 30 to 45 minutes for the next 2½ hours, for a total

cont'd

of 3½ hours bulk proof. With each stretch and fold, the dough will build more elasticity. While the dough bulk proofs, brush a metal loaf pan very lightly with sunflower oil and set aside.

Once the dough has risen, shape the loaf. Give the dough one last set of stretch and folds in the bowl, turning it into a tight oval or ball (see page 22), then use the dough scraper to slide the folded dough into the greased pan. Don't worry if the dough doesn't spread immediately to fill the entire pan; it will as it rises. Let the loaf rise at room temperature for 2½ hours, until puffed and domed and risen just past the top of the pan. A finger pressed into the dough will spring back slowly about halfway.

Shortly before the dough is finished rising, preheat the oven to 450°F [240°C] with a rack in the middle and the convection setting turned on. Put an old metal baking pan at the bottom of the oven to heat.

Put the loaf in the oven and toss several ice cubes into the pan to make steam, then quickly close the door. Bake for 20 minutes at 450°F [240°C], then lower the temperature to 400°F [200°C] and continue baking for another 25 to 30 minutes, until a thermometer inserted in the bread reads at least 195°F [90°C]. If the top of the loaf starts getting too dark, cover with aluminum foil for the remainder of the bake. Allow the bread to cool for about 1 hour, then turn the loaf out of the pan onto a cooling rack. Cool completely before cutting, about 3 hours.

Store for up to a week wrapped in a tea towel. As the week goes on, toast to reinvigorate your bread.

BAWOLE
8 00
KG
BAWOLE
ŹOŁtE
12 00
KG

Mateusz's Łódź Bread with Coffee and Raisins

Łódzki Żulik

Żulik is a soft and gently sweet bread from the city of Łódz, the former garment industry capital of Poland now known best for its film school. It's a dark brown bread heavy on caramel notes made with coffee and molasses, studded with raisins, and enriched with butter and milk. Perhaps not the most politically correct name, *żulik* can mean *little thief* or sometimes *a street alcoholic*, depending on whom you ask. The bread was invented by a Turkish baker, Mehmet Erol, who began his baking career in Lublin in the 1930s, before moving to work in a Turkish bakery in Kraków. After a complicated war story—arrests by Nazi German occupiers and constant moving—he finally settled in Łódź in the post-war 1940s, opening a Turkish confectionary and then, in the 1960s, the Erol bakery where he began baking the city's beloved żulik.

Mehmet Erol is now long gone, but his żulik isn't. And if you ask anyone today where the best żulik in Łódź is, the answer will always be Ania Słonka's Okruchy Mikropiekarnia. Entering the bakery, you're greeted by Ania and the cake-and-spice aroma of racks of cooling żulik. It's there that Ania keeps the legacy of not only żulik and Mehmet Erol active, but also that of her late husband, Mateusz.

Ania and Mateusz started Okruchy (Crumbs), in 2019, first baking at home and selling at farmer's markets before opening their own brick-and-mortar bakery. The ethos of Okruchy has always been to work fully with sourdough and to use healthy grains and local products. Mateusz's take on the traditional Łódzki żulik melds regional culture with a contemporary style of baking. His recipe is fully sourdough and takes 24 hours to complete, but the results are worth it. Today Ania continues with Okruchy, the żulik warm and inviting, preserving the memory of Mateusz, Mehmet, and the city of Łódź.

MAKES two 1 lb [455 g] loaves

TIMING

Leaven: 8 hours to overnight
Mix: 15 to 20 minutes
Bulk proof: 3½ hours
Bench rest and preshape: 1½ hours
First proof and rise, room temperature: 3 hours
Continued proof and final rise: 8 to 10 hours, refrigerated, plus 1½ to 2 hours, room temperature
Bake: 30 to 45 minutes
Cool: 4 hours

LEAVEN (ZACZYN)

¼ tsp [1 to 2 g] sourdough starter
¼ cup [30 g] whole-rye flour
2 Tbsp [32 g] room-temperature water

DOUGH

¾ cup [180 g] whole milk, at room temperature
¾ cup plus ½ tsp [180 g] room-temperature water
3½ Tbsp [75 g] molasses
All of the Leaven
3⅔ cups [460 g] bread flour
¼ cup plus 1 Tbsp [25 g] very finely ground coffee
1 heaping tsp [7 g] kosher salt
3 Tbsp [40 g] unsalted butter, at room temperature
¾ cup plus 1½ Tbsp [120 g] raisins

EGG WASH

1 egg, beaten

cont'd

The morning of the day before you wish to bake, prepare the leaven. Mix the sourdough starter, whole-rye flour, and water by hand into a paste with no dry lumps of flour. Cover loosely with a tea towel and leave to rise at room temperature for about 8 hours, until domed and bubbly.

When your leaven is ready and at peak activity, mix the dough. In the bowl of your stand mixer, whisk together the milk, water, molasses, and leaven. Add the bread flour, coffee, and salt, then mix on medium speed with the bread hook attachment for 15 to 20 minutes, until the dough is glossy and smooth and starts to pull away from the sides of the bowl. Continuing to mix, add the butter and allow to incorporate for 3 to 5 minutes. The butter will make the dough come apart at first, but then it will re-form into a smooth dough. Turn the mixer speed to low, then add the raisins and mix for 1 to 2 minutes until fully incorporated. Form the finished dough into a ball and set in a lightly greased bowl, covered loosely with a tea towel, and allow to proof at warm room temperature (about 82°F [28°C]) for 3½ hours. Halfway through the proof, give the dough a set of stretch and folds to add elasticity and strength.

Once the dough has risen, divide it into two even portions. Form into balls and allow to rest on a lightly floured work surface, smooth-side up, loosely covered with plastic wrap, for 1½ hours.

After the bench rest, form the breads into tight balls (see page 22), then set smooth-side down in a lightly floured proofing basket. Allow to sit at room temperature for 3 more hours, then refrigerate overnight, 8 to 10 hours. The next morning, remove the dough from the fridge and let it warm up at room temperature for 1½ to 2 hours. At this stage the loaves will have almost doubled in volume since the initial shaping.

Shortly before the dough has finished rising, preheat the oven to 400°F [200°C] with the convection setting turned on. Place an old metal baking pan at the bottom of the oven to heat. Line a baking sheet with parchment paper, then invert the loaves onto the parchment. Gently brush off any excess flour, then brush with egg wash and bake for 30 to 45 minutes, until a thermometer inserted into the center reads 195°F [90°C]. Allow to cool completely before cutting, about 4 hours. Serve with butter and powidła—Plum Filling (page 333)—or jam and, of course, a coffee.

Store for up to a week wrapped in a tea towel. As the week goes on, toast to reinvigorate your bread.

BAGIETKI
PSZENNE Z DODATKAMI
ORKISZOWE

/2

DROŻDŻE: YEASTED BUNS & BREADS

It's hard not to play favorites. But if there's one area where Polish baking shines above all else, it's yeast baking. In terms of cultural significance and importance, drożdżówki (yeast buns) are to Poland what viennoiseries are to France. Pillowy and eggy, slightly sweet yeast doughs form the bases of endless Danishes, slab cakes, challahs, and donuts. This style of baking blurs the boundaries between breads and cakes. There is hardly a special occasion that isn't marked with a yeast bake: brioche-y babka on Easter; spiraling poppy seed makowiec for Christmas; and fat, plum-filled pączki for Carnival.

Polish yeast baking influences bakery shelves well beyond the country's borders. It mingles with German and Austro-Hungarian baking. It shows up in American donut shops and trendy French bakeries. In Israel, it's one of the few old-world food cultures that truly stuck despite the rejection of Yiddishkeit during pre- and post-Holocaust migration. As the *Haaretz* food journalist Ronit Vered puts it, "Yeast cakes entered the canon in a way that most of the Eastern European food didn't." The sticky, yeasted rugelach, babkas, sufganiyot, and challahs that originated in the Eastern European tradition took root in Israeli culture and thrived.

The origins of Polish yeast baking date back to the nineteenth century, when commercial yeast was first brought to Poland and embraced wholeheartedly. In these early days of commercial yeast, bakers in Poland invented an economical method of transforming a small quantity of then-pricey yeast into a preferment, or sponge, capable of rising much more bread than the yeast could on its own. This preferment became known around the world as a poolish, from the word *Polish*. Though yeast has now become cheap, the technique remains, as it not only maximizes the yeast but also adds a more complex flavor, extensibility, and better fermentation to doughs. The most widely known application of poolish globally is in France's famed *baguette tradition*, with the poolish adding to its characteristic open crumb and crisp crust.

Nowadays, rozczyn, a faster, modified poolish, is commonly used in Polish yeast baking, resulting in an extra soft and delicate enriched dough when compared with many European counterparts. Rozczyn is generally a very quick preferment; it kick-starts yeast activity and adds to the suppleness and longevity of the final product. It's from these incredible yeast doughs that some of the most beloved Polish baking is born.

While the vast majority of Polish yeast baking is sweet and filled or topped with fruits, streusels, puddings, or sweet cheeses, newer bakeries and market stalls have been adding more savory drożdżówki to their repertoires, incorporating salty and smoky Polish cheeses like bryndzą and oscypek, roasted vegetables, forest mushrooms, and spring greens. One of my favorite new-style drożdżówki I've come across was at the Zbożna Piekarnia in the Powiśle neighborhood of Warsaw. Proprietors Aneta Pawlińska and Michał Krul have turned the classic pudding drożdżówki on its head by using a filling inspired by pierogi leniwe—a gnudi-style Polish dumpling made with curd cheese and topped with dripping brown butter, sugar, and grated nutmeg. It's one of the many playful takes on yeast pastry you can find in the new Polish baking world. In this chapter, you'll find both the classic yeast pastries as well as sweet and savory twists.

For practical basic information about working with yeasted doughs, refer to pages 20 to 21 in chapter 1.

SOFT MILK DOUGH

Chałka Dough

Soft milk doughs form the base of ciasta drożdżowe, the everyday yeasted pastries in Poland. The prevalence of chałka in the Polish bakery is a relic of the days when Jewish bakers made up a vast part of the profession; even today, the lost Jewish bakery has left an indelible mark on the way contemporary Poles bake. Infinitely versatile, these milk doughs can be braided into a loaf, folded into fruit pockets, balled into simple buns, and more. As with the other base doughs in this chapter, this recipe uses a rozczyn, or sponge: a preferment that improves flavor and rise. Enriched with butter, milk, and eggs, Polish milk doughs are, in terms of texture and flavor, what would happen if a brioche and a challah had a baby. When baked, this dough has a similar texture to a Japanese shokupan—the industry standard for fluffiness.

NOTE: This recipe can be bulk-proofed at room temperature or in the fridge, but there are a few advantages to a refrigerated bulk proof. The first is that the resulting dough will be stiff and easier to shape. The second is that you can make your dough the night before, making for a much easier morning bake for serving at breakfast or brunch. The third is that a longer, slower ferment will make your bread more flavorful and easier to digest.

MAKES about 34 oz [960 g] of dough (about 12 medium buns or 2 large loaves)

TIMING

Sponge: 1 hour
Mix: 10 minutes
Bulk proof: 1 hour 15 minutes, room temperature, or 8 to 36 hours, refrigerated
Final proof: 2 to 2½ hours

SPONGE (ROZCZYN)

1¼ cups [150 g] all-purpose flour
¾ cup plus 3 Tbsp [225 g] whole milk, at room temperature
2¼ tsp [7 g] instant yeast
2¼ tsp [10 g] sugar

DOUGH

All of the Sponge
5 egg yolks
1 tsp vanilla extract
2¾ cups [350 g] all-purpose flour
1 Tbsp [15 g] sugar
1¼ tsp [9 g] kosher salt
7 Tbsp [100 g] unsalted butter, cubed and at room temperature

Begin by preparing the sponge. In a medium mixing bowl, whisk together the flour, milk, yeast, and sugar, then cover with a damp tea towel and allow to rise for 1 hour. When the sponge has bubbled and doubled in size with a domed top on the verge of collapse, it's ready to use.

To make the dough, in the bowl of your stand mixer, combine the sponge, egg yolks, and vanilla and whisk together until smooth. Add the flour, sugar, salt, and butter, then, using the dough hook attachment, mix on low speed. Once the butter has fully incorporated into the dough and there are no dry pockets of flour, increase the speed to medium-low and continue mixing for 10 minutes, until the dough is smooth and supple and pulls away from the sides of the bowl. Pull off a small piece of dough. The dough should be able to stretch until it's thin and transparent without tearing and passes the windowpane test (see page 20).

With lightly greased or oiled hands, remove the dough and place it in a lightly oiled or greased bowl. Pick up the dough with two hands and allow gravity to stretch the overhanging dough under itself. Turn the bowl and repeat, until you have a smooth ball of dough. Cover the bowl airtight with room for expansion and bulk proof. You can do this in one of two ways:

OPTION 1: Allow to rise at room temperature for about 1 hour 15 minutes, or until almost doubled in size and a finger pressed into the dough springs back slowly about halfway.

OPTION 2: Let the dough rest at room temperature for about 30 minutes, then chill in the fridge (set between 37 and 46°F [3 and 8°C]) for at least 8 hours or up to 36 hours. (See Note.)

However you choose to bulk proof the dough, now it's ready to shape according to the recipes or your creativity. After shaping, factor in a final proof of 2 to 2½ hours before baking.

SOFT EGG DOUGH

Challah Dough

Challah and chałka are closely related doughs with a fundamental difference: dairy. While chałka has butter and milk, challah stays parve, or neutral in a kosher sense, so it can be eaten at any meal, be it milchik or fleischik (dairy or meat). Challah takes its richness from egg yolks and oil. The resulting dough is wonderfully fluffy and flavorful and works not just for challah loaves but also as an alternative base for any recipes that call for a milk dough.

NOTE: Because this recipe uses oil rather than butter, it has a faster rise than the chałka dough.

MAKES about 32 oz [910 g] of dough (about 12 medium buns or 2 large loaves)

TIMING
Sponge: 1 hour
Mix: 10 minutes
Bulk proof: 1 hour and 15 minutes, room temperature, or 8 to 10 hours, refrigerated
Final proof: 2 to 2½ hours

SPONGE (ROZCZYN)
1 cup [125 g] all-purpose flour
¾ cup plus 1½ Tbsp [200 g] room-temperature water
2¼ tsp [7 g] instant yeast
2¼ tsp [10 g] sugar

DOUGH
5 egg yolks
3½ Tbsp [50 g] sunflower oil
1 tsp vanilla extract (optional)
2 Tbsp [25 g] sugar
1¼ tsp [9 g] kosher salt
All of the Sponge
3 cups [375 g] all-purpose flour

Begin by preparing the sponge. In a medium mixing bowl, whisk together the flour, water, yeast, and sugar, then cover with a damp tea towel and allow to rise for about an hour. When the sponge has bubbled and doubled in size with a domed top on the verge of collapse, it's ready to use.

In the bowl of your stand mixer, whisk by hand the egg yolks and sunflower oil until smooth, then whisk in the vanilla (if using), sugar, and salt. Add the sponge and the flour to the egg mixture, then, using the dough hook attachment, begin mixing the dough on low speed. Once a dough has formed with no dry pockets of flour remaining, increase the speed to medium-low and continue mixing for 10 minutes, until the dough is smooth and supple and pulls away from the sides of the bowl. It should not be so wet that it's too sticky to form a ball, but not so dry that the dough hook struggles to mix it.

With lightly oiled hands, remove the dough and place it in a lightly oiled large mixing bowl. Pick up the dough with two hands and allow gravity to stretch the overhanging dough under. Turn the bowl and repeat, until you have a smooth ball of dough. Cover the bowl airtight with room for expansion and allow it to bulk proof. You can do this in one of two ways:

OPTION 1: Allow to rise at room temperature for about 1 hour 15 minutes, or until grown by almost two thirds in size and a finger pressed into the dough springs back slowly about halfway.

OPTION 2: If allowing your dough to rise overnight, put the covered bowl directly in the fridge (set between 37 and 46°F [3 to 8°C]) for 8 to 10 hours.

However you choose to bulk proof the dough, now it's ready to shape according to the recipes or your creativity. After shaping, factor in a final proof of 2 to 2½ hours before baking.

RICH AND LIGHT YEAST DOUGH FOR CAKES AND LOAVES

Placek Dough

Between you and me, this is the best yeast dough in the book. A meltaway dough that will keep its softness all week so long as it's stored airtight, it's the base of the uniquely luscious Polish babka loaves and yeasted fruit and streusel sheet cakes. The particular texture owes in part to the high volume of eggs. There are stories of bakeries whose large batches of placek doughs use as many as 100 egg yolks—but maybe that's just legend. As with plenty of good things, this dough takes a bit more skill than the others, due to its very high hydration, but it's well worth it.

NOTE: Because this dough has such a high hydration and soft texture, working with it takes skill. If you're not feeling confident or are just starting to work with yeast doughs, feel free to replace any recipes in the book that call for Placek Dough with Chałka Dough (page 98), for a slightly different texture.

MAKES two 9 x 5 in [23 x 13 cm] loaves or 1 large sheet pan cake

TIMING

Sponge: 45 minutes
Mix: 25 minutes
Bulk proof: 1 hour 15 minutes
Final proof: 2 to 2½ hours

SPONGE (ROZCZYN)

½ cup [125 g] whole milk
½ cup plus 2 Tbsp [75 g] all-purpose flour
2¼ tsp [7 g] instant yeast
2¼ tsp [10 g] sugar

DOUGH

All of the Sponge
2½ cups plus 2 Tbsp [325 g] all-purpose flour
⅓ cup plus 2 Tbsp [90 g] sugar
2 eggs
6 egg yolks
2 tsp vanilla extract
1 tsp [6 g] kosher salt
5½ Tbsp [80 g] unsalted butter, melted and cooled

Begin by preparing the sponge. In a small saucepan or the microwave, warm the milk to bath temperature—don't allow it to steam or boil. In a medium mixing bowl, whisk together the flour, yeast, and sugar. Continue to whisk as you pour the warmed milk into the bowl in a thin stream. Mix until just combined and no dry pockets of flour remain; it will be thin and liquidy like pancake batter. Set aside for about 45 minutes. When the sponge has bubbled and doubled in size with a domed top on the verge of collapse, it's ready to use.

In the bowl of your stand mixer fitted with the dough hook attachment, pour in the sponge, flour, sugar, eggs, egg yolks, vanilla, and salt. Begin mixing on low speed until a rough dough has formed and no dry pockets of flour remain, then increase to medium-high speed. Continue mixing for 20 minutes, until the dough is silky and shiny and pulls away from the sides of the bowl. Pull off a piece of dough. The dough should be able to stretch until it's thin and transparent without tearing and passes the windowpane test (see page 20). If it hasn't reached this point, continue mixing for up to another 5 minutes. At this point, slowly pour in the melted butter in a thin stream.

cont'd

Do not, under any circumstances, add the butter at the beginning of your mix. As you continue mixing, the dough will come apart a bit and not want to incorporate the butter, but keep mixing for about 5 minutes, and it will.

Grease your hands with a bit of softened butter and remove the dough from the mixer. Set the dough in a large greased bowl, then pick up the dough with two hands and allow gravity to stretch the overhanging dough under. Turn the bowl and repeat until you have a smooth, domed dough. Cover the bowl airtight with room for expansion and allow it to bulk proof. You can do this in one of two ways:

OPTION 1: Allow to rise at room temperature for about 1 hour 15 minutes, or until doubled in size and a finger pressed into the dough springs back slowly about halfway.

OPTION 2: If allowing your dough to rise overnight, begin the rise for about 30 to 45 minutes at room temperature, then let it rest in a cold refrigerator (set between 37 and 46°F [3 and 8°C]) overnight for 8 to 10 hours to slow the rest of the rise. Your cold dough will be easier to shape and the timing works perfect for brunch bakes.

However you choose to bulk rise the dough, now it's ready to shape according to the recipes or your creativity. After shaping, factor in a final proof of 2 to 2½ hours before baking.

DONUT DOUGH FOR FRYING

Pączki Dough

The Polish word for donuts is *pączki*. The Yiddish word for donuts is *pontshkes*. They both sound a lot like *patchke*, the Yiddish word, colloquially, for things that are a pain in the butt. As in, making pączki and pontshkes is a patchke, albeit a rewarding and delicious one. Pontshkes and pączki are closely related—traditionally jelly donuts with no hole, they've now expanded to include every sort of cream, glaze, crunch, and sprinkle imaginable. Back in the day, pączki were fried in pork lard—szmaltz—and pontshkes were fried in oil or goose schmaltz. Poles made and still make pączki for Tłusty Czwartek—Fat Thursday. For Jews, donuts were and remain a Hanukkah treat, though goose schmaltz has fallen by the wayside. While the pączki culture remains strong in Poland, Chicago, and other Polish enclaves globally, Jewish bakers brought pontshkes to Israel, where they were renamed *sufganiyot*. While it was largely German Jews who brought global fame to donuts—leading to descendants like Portugal's Bolas de Berlim and America's Dunkin' Donuts—Poles deserve a large share of the credit as well.

This dough varies from the chałka dough only in that a small quantity of aquavit or other strong, clear alcohol is added during the final part of the mix. The alcohol stops the dough from soaking up too much oil during frying, resulting in a dry, not greasy texture. There's some debate about whether this is an old wives' tale, but I'll swear by it.

NOTE: This recipe has a larger yield than the other enriched doughs in the book, because once you start frying donuts in oil, you'll want to make it count. Cut the recipe in half for a smaller quantity of donuts. If you're concerned about wasting egg whites, store them frozen and thaw to use in the meringue recipes in chapter 5.

MAKES about 4 lb [1.8 kg] of dough (20 to 24 donuts)

TIMING

Sponge: 1 hour
Mix: 15 minutes
Bulk proof: 1 to 1½ hours, room temperature, or 8 to 36 hours, refrigerated
Final proof: 2 to 2½ hours

SPONGE (ROZCZYN)

2⅓ cups plus 1 Tbsp [300 g] all-purpose flour
1⅔ cups [400 g] whole milk, at room temperature
1½ Tbsp [14 g] instant yeast
1½ Tbsp [20 g] sugar

DOUGH

All of the Sponge
10 egg yolks
2 tsp vanilla extract
5½ cups plus 2 Tbsp [700 g] all-purpose flour
2½ Tbsp [30 g] sugar
2¾ tsp [18 g] kosher salt
14 Tbsp [200 g] unsalted butter, cubed and at room temperature
2 Tbsp [30 g] aquavit, vodka, or schnapps

Begin by preparing the sponge. In a medium mixing bowl, whisk together the flour, milk, yeast, and sugar, then cover with a damp tea towel and allow to rise for about an hour. When the sponge has bubbled and doubled in size with a domed top on the verge of collapse, it's ready to use.

In the bowl of your stand mixer, whisk together the sponge, egg yolks, and vanilla until smooth. Add the flour, sugar, salt, and butter, then, using the dough hook attachment, begin mixing on low speed. Once the butter has fully incorporated into the dough, increase the speed to medium-low and continue

cont'd

mixing for 10 minutes, until the dough is smooth and supple and pulls away from the sides of the bowl. Pull off a small piece of dough. The dough should be able to stretch until it's thin and transparent without tearing and passes the windowpane test (see page 20). At this point, turn the speed to low, and add the aquavit. The dough will come apart and come together again in a few minutes.

Once the dough has come back together, use lightly greased hands to remove the dough and place it in a greased bowl. Pick up the dough with two hands and allow gravity to stretch the overhanging dough under itself. Turn the bowl and repeat, until you have a smooth ball of dough. Cover the bowl airtight with room for expansion and bulk proof. You can do this in one of two ways:

OPTION 1: Allow to rise at room temperature for about 1½ hours, or until doubled in size and a finger pressed into the dough springs back slowly about halfway.

OPTION 2: Let the dough rest at room temperature for about 30 minutes, then chill in the fridge (set cold, between 37 and 46°F [3 to 8°C]) for at least 8 hours or up to 36 hours.

However you choose to bulk rise the dough, now it's ready to shape according to the recipes or your creativity. After shaping, factor in a final proof of 2 to 2½ hours before frying.

HALF-FRENCH DANISH DOUGH

Półfrancuskie Dough

Półfrancuskie, or half-French dough, is more or less a classic Danish dough. It's rich and yeasty, pull-apart yet flaky. Here, the Polish name makes infinitely more sense than the English. Why? Półfrancuskie is a lot like a French croissant dough—but it's easier to make and has rougher layers and a brioche-like texture. Hence half-French. But while croissant dough is a project for the ages, this French, Danish, Polish—whatever you want to call it—alternative has a clever trick that makes it infinitely more user-friendly. All you need is a cheese grater.

NOTE: This is the most complicated dough in the book! That said, if you take it step by step, it's a manageable recipe. I like to start this dough in the evening the day before I want to bake it.

MAKES about 2.2 lb [1 kg] of dough (10 to 12 buns or Danishes)

TIMING

Mix: 15 minutes
Bulk proof: 1 hour 15 minutes, room temperature, or 8 to 36 hours, refrigerated
Preshape, refrigerated: 3 to 24 hours
Lamination: 30 minutes
Post-lamination chill: 1 hour to 24 hours
Final proof: 2½ hours

FOR LAMINATION

10½ Tbsp [150 g] unsalted European-style butter

DOUGH

2 eggs
1 egg yolk
⅔ cup [160 g] whole milk
1 tsp vanilla extract
4 cups [500 g] all-purpose flour
5 Tbsp [60 g] sugar
1½ tsp [10 g] kosher salt
2¼ tsp [7 g] instant yeast
3½ Tbsp [50 g] unsalted butter, cubed and at room temperature

Before you begin, pop the European-style butter in the freezer so it's nice and hard for later when you laminate the dough.

Begin by mixing the dough. In the bowl of your stand mixer, whisk together the eggs, egg yolk, milk, and vanilla. Add the flour, sugar, salt, yeast, and cubed butter, then, using the dough hook attachment, mix on low speed until the dough comes together into a rough and stiff dough. As the butter incorporates into the dough, the dough will loosen and become smoother. Continue mixing until all the butter is incorporated. Once there are no more visible bits of butter in the dough, increase the speed to medium-high and continue mixing for 7 minutes, until the dough is smooth and starts to pull away from the sides of the bowl. Increase the speed to high for 1 minute, then pull off a small piece of dough. The dough should be able to stretch until it's thin and transparent without tearing and passes the windowpane test (see page 20).

Lightly grease your hands, then remove the dough from the mixer—it will be very soft and supple, medium-smooth, and just a little bit sticky. Place the dough in a greased bowl, then pick up the dough with two hands and allow gravity to stretch the overhanging dough under itself. Turn the bowl and repeat, until you have a smooth ball of dough. Cover

cont'd

the bowl airtight with room for expansion and allow to bulk proof. You can do this in one of two ways:

OPTION 1: Allow to rise at room temperature for about 1 hour 15 minutes, until almost doubled in size and a finger pressed into the dough springs back slowly about halfway.

OPTION 2: Let the dough rest at room temperature for about 30 minutes, then chill in the fridge (set cold, between 37 and 46°F [3 to 8°C]) for at least 8 hours or up to 36 hours.

However you choose to bulk rise the dough, now it's ready to laminate and shape.

Remove the dough from the bowl and place it on a large piece of plastic wrap. Press the dough into a rough rectangle, about 8 x 10 in [20 x 25 cm], pressing the air out to degas as you do, then wrap airtight but loosely with the plastic wrap, allowing a little room for expansion. Let chill in the fridge for 3 to 24 hours. After the dough has chilled, it will be much stiffer and easier to work with.

Lightly flour a work surface, and begin to roll out your dough into a longer but narrower rectangle, about 20 x 6 in [51 x 15 cm]. Lightly flour the dough and rolling pin as needed. Remove the butter from the freezer and use the medium holes on a cheese grater to grate the butter evenly over the rectangle.

With the long side of the dough rectangle oriented vertically on your work surface, fold the top down by one third, then fold the bottom up and over by one third. This kind of fold is called a single turn.

After the first single turn, if this was a book, the spine would now be the side of the dough closest to you. You're going to repeat this process another two times, for a total of three single turns.

To continue with your turns, rotate the folded dough by 90 degrees so the spine of the book is vertical and to the left. Press your rolling pin horizontally down the length of the book—this will help the dough roll out evenly. Then roll out the dough a second time, vertically, to about 20 x 6 in [51 x 15 cm]. Fold the top down by one third, then fold the bottom up and over by one third. Repeat the same process for the third turn.

Once your final turn is finished, your dough book will be a nice folded rectangle. Wrap in plastic wrap and chill for 1 hour or up to 24 hours. When you're ready to use, roll out to a thickness of ⅛ in [3 mm] with the desired dimensions as instructed in the recipes. After shaping, factor in a final proof of about 2½ hours before baking.

Chałka

Braided Egg Bread with Streusel

Chałka might be the most common baked good in Poland—I've never seen a bakery without it. What makes this enriched braided egg bread distinct is the generous streusel topping, which gives it a sweet crunch and texture.

Ten years ago, I went to Brok, the small village on the Bug River halfway between Warsaw and Białystok where my great-grandparents were born. I got lost looking for the cemetery, the only trace of Jewish history left in the town, and, as an excuse to ask directions from the unimpressed shopkeeper of the one-room village store, I bought a loaf of chałka. The shopkeeper shook her head at my broken Polish, and I left with no directions and a load of mortification. When I did finally find the Jewish cemetery, I promptly stepped in dog poo, which led to the greater discovery that in fact the whole place was a receptacle for trash of the unmentionable sort, which led to an urgent need to get the hell out of Brok. The chałka, however, was delicious, and kinda made me feel better.

Rather than eating this with a side of angst and disappointment as I did, Małgosia Minta, the photographer of this book, suggests serving chałka with a thick spread of fresh curd cheese and jam.

NOTE: For extra perfect braids, follow the directions for chilling the dough overnight so that you're working with a stiffer, more malleable dough.

MAKES 2 large loaves

DOUGH

1 batch Chałka Dough (page 98)

EGG WASH

1 egg and 3 Tbsp [45 g] whole milk, whisked until smooth

TOPPING

1 batch Streusel (Kruszonka, page 346)

Prepare your chałka dough according to the recipe on page 98 through the bulk proof. When the dough is ready to use, turn it out onto a very lightly floured work surface. If your dough doesn't seem sticky at all, skip the flour altogether. Use a bench knife to divide the dough into eight even portions of 4 oz [115 g] each. Press each portion of dough flat to degas it, then fold in the sides and roll to form a tight ball (see page 22). Set the balls on your work surface smooth-side up and cover lightly with a damp tea towel or plastic wrap. Allow to rest for 15 minutes. Don't skip this rest—it will relax the dough enough so that it doesn't tear while forming into logs for braiding.

After the dough has rested, form each ball of dough into a 12 in [30.5 cm] tapered strand (see page 23).

To braid the chałka, take four strands and press the ends together tightly on one side. Assign each braid position a number 1 to 4, from left to right. As you move each strand, the numbered position doesn't change. If this is confusing, put masking tape labels on your work surface with the numbers 1, 2, 3, 4 at the bottom of each strand.

cont'd

Braid according to the pattern 4 over 3, 2 over 4, 1 over 2, 3 over 1. I've heard this pattern called outside-inside-outside-inside because you cross the right outside over the right inside, the left inside over the right outside, the left outside over the right inside, and the right inside over the left outside.

When you get to the end of the braid, press the ends together and fold slightly underneath the braid. Place your loaf on one side of a baking sheet lined with parchment paper, at least 2 in [5 cm] from the edges, then repeat for the second loaf, placing it at least 4 in [10 cm] from the other loaf and 2 in [5 cm] from the sides of the pan.

Using a pastry brush, give each loaf an egg wash, then set aside to rise for 2 to 2½ hours, or until the loaves have almost doubled in size and indent easily but still spring back when poked with a finger. To help retain moisture and prevent the surface from drying, I like to put the pan in a large plastic bag, held aloft from the rising loaves by an empty bottle.

While the loaves rise, prepare the streusel. Shortly before the loaves have finished rising, preheat the oven to 350°F [180°C] with the convection setting turned on.

Once the loaves are fully risen, brush a second time with egg wash and sprinkle generously with streusel. Bake for about 30 minutes, or until golden brown and a thermometer inserted in the bread reads 195°F [90°C] and comes out clean. Let cool before slicing and eating.

Store airtight for several days or freeze airtight for up to 2 months. From frozen, thaw at room temperature, then warm in the oven to revive.

Challah

There are two stories I remember my great-grandmother telling about her early childhood in Brok. The first story is about cigarettes, the second is about challah. Since we're here to bake, let's just say that as far as the smokes were concerned, they rewarded a good report card for grade schoolers a little differently in the old country. As for the challah, my great-grandmother fondly remembered the big one-room home her family lived in. On one side was a bed, and on the other, a great big oven. There, her mother and aunt used to bake challahs that they then "sold to the peasants." It was how they supported the family. My great-grandmother immigrated to America as a child, stopping in New York before settling in Boston, but she continued to bake challah, very much like these, for the rest of her life.

MAKES 2 large loaves

DOUGH

1 batch Challah Dough (page 100)

EGG WASH

1 egg and 1 egg yolk, whisked until smooth

TOPPING

Poppy seeds or sesame seeds

Prepare your challah dough according to the recipe on page 100, through the bulk proof. When your dough is ready to use, turn it out onto a very lightly floured work surface. If your dough doesn't seem sticky at all, skip the flour altogether. Use a bench knife to divide the dough into eight portions of just under 4 oz [115 g] each. Press each portion of dough flat to degas it, then fold in the sides and roll to form a tight ball. Set the balls on your work surface seam-side down and cover lightly with a damp tea towel or piece of plastic wrap. Allow to rest for 15 minutes. Don't skip this rest—it will relax the dough enough so that it doesn't tear while forming into strands for braiding.

After the dough has rested, form each ball of dough into a 12 in [30.5 cm] tapered strand (see page 23).

Once you've made your strands, it's time to braid the challah. Take four strands and press the ends together tightly on one side. Assign each braid position a number 1 to 4, from left to right. While the strands move as they are braided, the numbered positions don't change. If this is confusing, use masking tape to label positions 1 to 4 on your work surface at the end of each strand.

Braid according to the pattern 4 over 3, 2 over 4, 1 over 2, 3 over 1. As mentioned in the previous chałka recipe, I've heard this pattern called outside-inside-outside-inside because you cross the right outside over the right inside, the left inside over the right outside, the left outside over the right inside, and the right inside over the left outside.

When you get to the end of the braid, press the ends together and fold slightly underneath the braid. Place your loaf on one side of a baking sheet lined with parchment paper, at least 2 in [5 cm] from the side. Repeat for the second loaf, placing it at least 4 in [10 cm] from the other loaf and 2 in [5 cm] from the sides of the pan.

Using a pastry brush, give each loaf an egg wash, then set aside to rise for 2 to 2½ hours, or until the loaves have almost doubled in size and indent easily but still spring back when poked with a finger. To help retain moisture and prevent the surface from drying, I like to put the pan in a large plastic bag, held aloft from the rising loaves by an empty bottle.

cont'd

Shortly before the loaves have finished rising, preheat the oven to 350°F [180°C] with the convection setting turned on.

Once the loaves are fully risen, brush a second time with egg wash and sprinkle with sesame or poppy seeds. Bake for about 30 minutes, or until golden brown and a thermometer inserted in the bread reads 195°F [90°C] and comes out clean.

To soften the crust, cover the loaves with a tea towel immediately upon removing from the oven. Let cool before pulling apart and eating.

Store airtight for several days or freeze airtight for up to 2 months. From frozen, thaw at room temperature, then warm in the oven to revive.

Zosia Barto's Vegan Chałka

There's nothing in Zosia Barto's Kraków bakery, Zaczyn Piekarnia, that tells you her unbelievably soft drożdżowe—chałka and yeast pastries—are vegan. Though most of what she does is naturally plant-based, she never advertises it. Zosia says modestly, "If it's good, it's good." Some customers know her bakes are vegan, some don't, and that speaks to the quality of her dairy-free and eggless dough. Poland, a country known for smoked meats and infinite incarnations of dairy, is also one of the sleeper best countries in Europe for plant-based food and baking, and Zosia is a pioneer in that movement. But to relegate her to pioneer status in vegan baking would be pigeonholing, as she is an important figure in the Polish artisan sourdough bakery movement in general.

In 2014, Zosia was an out-of-work chemist baking at home when she began thinking about getting a permanent place to bake. She opened a kitchen in a neighbor's backyard and began supplying local restaurants and festivals, building her name and reputation as she went. She stayed in that small backyard kitchen until 2018, when she moved into her first real bakeshop. Now she's in a thriving corner spot on Tadeusza Kościuszki Street, with a sunny café and an expansive bread bakery and pastry shop filled with enthusiastic young bakers, eager to bring her vision to life. Even now with the busy shop, Zosia is careful to source only Polish flour, as local and ecological as possible, and heavy on whole grains. Her shelves are full of wheat, rye, and einkorn loaves, as well as innovative flavor combinations like her sweet-salty fennel and millet crisp breads and sesame and miso loaf. Zosia takes inspiration from books, traveling, and other cultures, especially Nordic bakery traditions, but of huge importance to her is her own childhood flavors, and that's where this chałka comes in.

NOTES: Zosia is from Silesia, and there chałka is primarily braided in three fat tresses. Feel free to use the braiding instructions from the recipe for Challah (page 100) for a variation.

If you want a plain vegan chałka without streusel and a shinier glaze, mix 2 Tbsp maple syrup with 1 Tbsp water and brush on before baking.

MAKES 2 loaves

TIMING

Mix: 8 minutes
Bulk proof: 1 to 1½ hours
Final proof: 1 hour

DOUGH

1¼ cups [300 g] plant-based milk (preferably soy or oat, because of their creaminess)
¼ cup [50 g] granulated sugar
¼ cup [50 g] cane sugar or demerara sugar
3½ Tbsp [50 g] odorless (refined) coconut oil
Seeds from 1 vanilla pod (optional)
4 cups [500 g] all-purpose flour
¼ tsp kosher salt
2¼ tsp [7 g] instant yeast

ZOSIA'S STREUSEL (KRUSZONKA)

⅔ cup [80 g] all-purpose flour
¼ cup [30 g] confectioners' sugar
2 Tbsp [30 g] demerara sugar
3½ Tbsp [50 g] odorless (refined) coconut oil, at room temperature (soft but not liquid)
¼ tsp kosher salt

cont'd

Begin by mixing the dough. In a medium saucepan, combine the plant-based milk, granulated sugar, cane sugar, and coconut oil and warm it gently over low heat until the sugars and coconut oil dissolve. Note: Do not let the milk boil. After everything is melted, leave it off heat for about 20 minutes to cool down to about bath temperature so as not to kill the yeast. Mix in the vanilla seeds (if using).

In the bowl of your stand mixer, combine the flour and salt, then add the yeast and the milk mixture. With the dough hook attachment, mix on low speed until it comes together into a rough dough with no dry pockets of flour remaining. Increase the speed to medium and mix for about 8 minutes, until you have a smooth, elastic dough. If it's a little bit tacky, don't worry—you can coat your hands in a bit of coconut oil or flour to help you handle it.

Remove the dough from the mixer, form it into a ball, and place it in a large, lightly oiled mixing bowl. Cover the bowl with a damp tea towel or plastic wrap, then let it rise for 1 to 1½ hours, until nearly doubled in size. The rising time will depend on your kitchen's temperature—a warmer day means your dough will rise faster.

Once the dough has fully risen, turn it out onto a lightly floured work surface and divide it into six equal pieces of 5½ oz [155 g] each. Preshape these into loose balls, smooth-side up, then cover with a damp tea towel or plastic wrap and allow to rest for about 10 minutes.

After the dough has rested, form each ball of dough into a 12 in [30.5 cm] tapered strand (see page 23). To make the braids, take three strands and cross them over themselves at their fat middles. Braid from the center to one end, turn around your loaf, and then braid the other end. Repeat for the second loaf. Place your breads on a baking sheet lined with parchment paper. Cover with a damp tea towel and let them rise for 1 hour, until puffed and soft and almost doubled in size. A finger pressed into the dough springs back slowly.

While the chałka rises, prepare the streusel. In a small mixing bowl, combine the flour, confectioners' sugar, demerara sugar, coconut oil, and salt with your fingers, crumbling it a bit but not overdoing it, working as quickly as possible so as not to melt the coconut oil. Once you have a nice crumbly texture, refrigerate for 15 minutes.

Shortly before the chałka is fully risen, preheat the oven to 350°F [180°C] with the convection setting turned on. Brush the loaves with plant-based milk for a matte glaze or the maple mixture for a shiny glaze, then sprinkle with the streusel. Bake for 25 to 30 minutes, until golden brown. Let cool, then enjoy!

Store in an airtight container for up to 3 days or freeze in a plastic bag with the air sucked out for up to 2 months. If freezing, thaw at room temperature and then warm in the oven to revive.

TheTea
Tanyang Gong Fu Hong Cha
2023
ROASTAINS
ZACZYN
CHAŁKA 16,-
CHAŁECZKA 10,-
BRIOSZKA 12,-
BUŁKA WYTRAWNA
+ passata pomidorowa
+ karczoch
+ czosnek
15,-
BUŁKA WYTRAWNA
+ ziemniaki
+ czarnuszka
17,-
BUŁKA WYTRAWNA
+ passata pomidorowa
+ oliwki
+ czosnek
14,-
PUDDING
+ marcepan
+ wiśnia
14,-

Butter Crescents

Rogale Maślane

If you moved from America to Europe at any point in the last twenty years or so, there was a secret to get your things over the Atlantic on the cheap: the Polish boat. You'd simply bring your boxes to any of the drop-off points at small travel agencies and bodegas in Polish neighborhoods along the East Coast, and they would arrive about 28 days later at a large courtyard parking lot in the city of Częstochowa. Then you'd get a call and drive to Central Poland from wherever you lived only to sit and wait in a small mint green office. The man responsible for releasing your worldly possessions would take anywhere from 6 to 10 hours to fill out the customs forms, a process for which you must be present. It gives one plenty of time to reflect on the irony that somewhere in your boxes are the silver bread knife and the crystal water pitcher your great-grandparents carried with them on a boat from Poland to America. This inevitably leads to wondering whether your ancestors are rolling over in their graves—they left only for you to come back? Oof. Fortunately, those voices quiet at a point, because you realize this isn't going to be a short visit and you've got nothing to eat. One day I spent in that Częstochowa office, the clerks took pity on me and gave me hot tea and a few rogale maślane they'd had left over from breakfast. Rogale maślane are soft crescent rolls, easily thrown together with an overnight batch of chałka dough, then shaped, risen, and baked in the morning. They're usually served at breakfast, spread with jam and butter, or dipped into a soft egg. Most importantly, they make excessively long waits in Częstochowa go faster.

MAKES 12 rolls

DOUGH

1 batch Chałka Dough (page 98)

EGG WASH

1 egg and 3 Tbsp [45 g] whole milk, whisked until smooth

TOPPING

2 to 3 Tbsp [20 to 35 g] poppy seeds

Prepare your chałka dough according to the recipe on page 98 through the bulk proof. Once the dough has risen, turn it out onto a lightly floured surface and divide it into three even portions of about 10½ oz [300 g] each. Form the dough into loose balls and let rest, smooth-side up and loosely covered with a damp tea towel or plastic wrap, for 10 minutes.

Meanwhile, line two baking sheets with parchment paper and set aside.

After the dough has rested, take one ball and use a rolling pin to roll it out to a circle about 12 in [30.5 cm] across. Lightly flour as needed while rolling to prevent sticking. To shape, use a flat knife or pizza cutter to divide the circle into four even triangles. Starting from the wide base of each triangle, roll up the triangle into a rolled crescent that's fat in the middle and thin on the ends. Use both hands to roll and elongate the crescents into tapered logs, still keeping the middle fat. Place the rogale on a lined baking sheet, 2 in [5 cm] apart, with the rolled point of the triangle on the underside of each roll. Curve the ends to make a crescent moon shape. Repeat with the remaining balls of dough to create a total of twelve rogale. Brush each with egg wash and set aside to rise for 2½ hours, until light and puffed.

Shortly before the rogale have fully risen, preheat the oven to 350°F [180°C] with the convection setting turned on. Brush the rogale a second time with egg wash and sprinkle with poppy seeds. Bake for 12 to 15 minutes, until the rogale are golden brown. Enjoy warm, with butter, the same day or freeze airtight for up to 2 months. From frozen, thaw at room temperature, then warm in the oven to revive.

Plum and Walnut Yeast Crescents

Rogale z Powidłami i Orzechami

These rogale are one of the many in the family of Polish rolled yeast pastries. You can find rogale filled with nut paste, and you can find them filled with plum butter. One village bakery I visited outside of Poznań, however, did both, and it was, as you might expect, the best of both worlds, so of course that's what we're doing here. Substitute the ground walnuts for ground almonds or hazelnuts for a different flavor profile if you like.

NOTE: This recipe calls for the dough to be chilled overnight. It is possible to make the dough directly, but the chilled dough will be more malleable and easier to work with for shaping the rogale.

MAKES 20 rogale

DOUGH

1 batch Chałka Dough (page 98), chilled overnight

FILLING

½ batch Walnut Paste (page 340)

1 cup [260 g] Plum Filling (page 333) or thick jam

EGG WASH

1 egg and 3 Tbsp [45 g] whole milk, whisked until smooth

TOPPING

½ cup [60 g] slivered almonds or chopped walnuts

1 batch Glaze (Lukier, page 348)

Prepare your chałka dough according to the recipe on page 98 and allow it to bulk proof overnight.

The day you're ready to bake, prepare the walnut paste according to the recipe on page 340.

Once the dough is ready, turn it out onto a lightly floured work surface and divide it into five even portions of about 6½ oz [180 g] each, then flatten and shape into tight balls (see page 22). Let rest, loosely covered, for about 10 minutes, then roll out into circles 12 in [30.5 cm] across. Divide each circle into four triangles. About ¾ in [2 cm] from the base of each triangle, place a teaspoon of jam and a teaspoon of walnut paste. Fold the wide base of the triangle just over the filling and press in a half-moon shape to contain it. A couple inches of the tail will remain unfilled. Give the tail of the triangle a small stretch, then roll it all up, from the half-moon to the tip of the tail, into a croissant shape. Twist the ends of the croissant in the opposite direction you just rolled, and turn them inward in a crescent moon shape. Repeat for all of the rogale. Space about 2 in [5 cm] apart on two baking sheets lined with parchment paper.

Brush each rogal with egg wash, then allow to rise for 2½ hours, until puffed and very soft. Shortly before they're fully risen, preheat the oven to 350°F [180°C] with the convection setting turned on. Before baking, give each rogal a second egg wash and sprinkle with slivered almonds. Bake for about 15 minutes, or until golden brown.

Remove from the oven and mix up your glaze according to the recipe on page 348. Drizzle the glaze over the cooling rogale, then eat immediately or allow to cool.

Store in an airtight container at room temperature for up to a couple days. If you'd like to freeze the baked rolls, skip the glaze and store in an airtight bag with the air sucked out for up to 2 months frozen. Thaw at room temperature, warm up in the oven, then glaze when ready to serve.

Sweet Cheese Twists

Drożdżówki z Serem

There's a cluster of bakeries in the Greenpoint neighborhood of Brooklyn that produce perfect classic Polish baked goods. Uncannily perfect, that is, except for one thing: size. These bakeries sell just about every traditional cake, bread, and pastry, but the proportions are inflated to a decidedly American scale. In fact, these pastries look as though they went through the space-time continuum, landed in New York, were dipped into the same radioactive puddle as the Ninja Turtles, and quadrupled in size. The first time I had drożdżówki z serem was not in Poland, but rather at one of these Brooklyn bakeries. So I assumed these yeasted sweet cheese twists were always about a foot long. They're not. That's just Polish baking in America. That said, these are soft, creamy, and just sweet-enough pastries, no matter the size. Here, we make them in the more reasonable length you'd find in Poland.

MAKES 16 drożdżówki

DOUGH

1 batch Chałka Dough (page 98)

FILLING

1 batch Sweet Cheese Filling (page 343)

EGG WASH

1 egg and 3 Tbsp [45 g] whole milk, whisked until smooth

GLAZE

1 batch Glaze (Lukier, page 348)

Prepare your chałka dough according to the recipe on page 98 through the bulk proof. For this recipe in particular, I suggest proofing overnight in the fridge to have an easier-to-shape dough.

To make your twists, turn the dough out onto a lightly floured work surface, then roll it out to an about 28 x 12 in [71 x 30.5 cm] rectangle, keeping the long side vertical to you.

Use a spoon or offset spatula to spread the cheese filling evenly on the entire middle two thirds of the rectangle, from short end to short end.

Next, fold both long sides in to meet each other in the middle so the edges touch but don't overlap. This will form a long and narrower rectangle with a seam down the middle. Tightly pinch the dough where it meets along the entire length of the seam to seal. Flip the entire filled rectangle over, so the seam is now on the underside.

Measure 1½ to 2 in [4 to 5 cm] intervals along the long side of the rectangle and use this as a guide to cut sixteen strips. Cut with a flat-edge knife by pressing directly down rather than sawing the dough.

Arrange the strips on two baking sheets lined with parchment paper, keeping the seam on the underside and evenly spaced in lines of four, eight to each sheet.

To shape, twist the ends of each strip over in opposite directions without lifting the strips from the pan. This will create two twists down the center of each. Don't worry if a bit of filling gushes out during this step.

Egg wash the dough and set the twists aside to rise for 2½ hours, until light and puffed. Shortly before the twists are finished rising, preheat the oven to 350°F [170°C] with the convection setting turned on.

Give the twists a second egg wash, and bake for 15 to 20 minutes, until golden brown.

Allow to cool, then finish with a drizzle of glaze and serve. These are best served the same day, but can be stored airtight at room temperature and served for another couple days.

Onion Brioche

Cebularz

If you buy a cebularz, a savory onion brioche, eat it immediately. The good ones will soak oil and butter right through a paper bakery bag, rendering the paper translucent and your hands onion-scented butter bombs. Rich chałka dough is topped with melty onions and poppy seeds and sold as individual rounds or, more rarely and, some might say, sacrilegiously, cut as squares off a sheet pan like focaccia. Likely a relative of the bialy and pletzl, cebularze have a gorgeous sweet-savory softness and make a perfect afternoon snack. They can be made with onions—finely diced, sliced thinly into strings, or large chunks—all lightly sautéed before baking to bring out their sweetness.

MAKES 12 individual cebularze or one 10 x 12 in [25 x 30.5 cm] pan

DOUGH

1 batch Chałka Dough (page 98)

EGG WASH

1 egg and 3 Tbsp [45 g] whole milk, whisked until smooth

FILLING

2 Tbsp [30 g] unsalted butter

4 to 5 medium yellow onions, about 4 cups [400 g], finely diced or cut into strings or large smiles

2 Tbsp [30 g] olive oil

3 Tbsp [35 g] poppy seeds

1 Tbsp thyme, fresh or dried (optional)

Flaky sea salt

Ground black pepper

1 tsp honey (optional)

Prepare your chałka dough according to the recipe on page 98, through the bulk proof. When the dough is ready to use, turn it out onto a very lightly floured work surface, then shape.

To shape individual round cebularze: Divide the dough with a bench knife into twelve even portions of 2¾ oz [80 g] each. Press each portion of dough flat to degas it, then fold in the sides and roll to form a tight ball (see page 22). Set the balls on your work surface seam-side down and cover lightly with a damp tea towel or piece of plastic wrap. Allow to rest for 15 minutes. After the rest, roll out each ball into a large circle about 6 in [15 cm] across and ½ in [1 cm] thick. Place the circles 2 in [5 cm] apart on two baking sheets lined with parchment paper. Brush with egg wash and let rise for 2½ hours, until light and puffed and a finger pressed into the dough springs back slowly.

To shape pan cebularz: Grease a 10 x 12 in [25 x 30.5 cm] pan well with butter, then roll the dough out to the dimensions of the pan. Press the dough into the pan, then give it a coat of egg wash. Set aside to rise for about 2 hours, until light and puffed and a finger pressed into the dough springs back slowly.

While the dough rises, prepare the filling. Melt the butter in a skillet over medium-low heat and sauté the onions until just starting to get translucent. Remove from the heat and transfer to a medium mixing bowl. Mix the onions with the olive oil, poppy seeds, thyme (if using), salt, pepper, and honey (if using).

cont'd

Shortly before your dough is fully risen, regardless of its shape, preheat the oven to 350°F [180°C] with the convection setting turned on.

If making individual round cebularze, give each round a second egg wash just before baking, then prick all over with a fork. Spread an even portion of the onion-poppy mixture almost to the edges of each round. Bake for about 20 minutes, until golden brown.

If making a pan cebularz, give it a second egg wash right before baking, then use your fingers to dimple the dough at about 1 in [2.5 cm] intervals. This will help the dough rise evenly. Cover the dough with the onion-poppy mixture all the way to the edges, then bake until golden brown, about 30 minutes.

Individual cebularze can cool on a cooling rack; the pan bake should be sliced after cooling.

Cebularz can be stored in an airtight box at room temperature for a couple days, or frozen airtight for up to 2 months. From frozen, thaw at room temperature, then warm in the oven to revive.

Danishes with Pudding and Raspberries

Danisze z Budyniem i Malinami

A round Danish, spread with budyń (pudding), fruit, and streusel, is by far the most classic and simple of all the Polish drożdżowe pastries. These sit in any pastry stand, any bakery case. Office workers, teachers, tram drivers, and everyone in between line up at train station coffee kiosks and streetside snack vendors to grab these on the run. While these can be made with any of the yeasted doughs in this chapter, to make this recipe special, I like to use the Placek Dough (page 101). While the delicate dough takes a bit more skill to shape than the other yeasted doughs, the reward is an extra-soft Danish. If you're not up for the challenge, the simpler chałka or challah dough will also yield excellent results. Here I use raspberries, but these can just as easily be made with any ripe berry or soft fruit tossed in sugar.

NOTE: For a morning bake, prepare your dough the night before and allow to proof in the fridge according to the recipe on page 101. When planning for a morning bake, I suggest preparing the budyń and kruszonka at the same time so everything is ready to go in the morning.

MAKES 12 danisze

DOUGH

1 batch Placek Dough (page 101)

FILLING

Double batch Pudding (Budyń, page 342)
6 cups (2.2 lb [1 kg]) raspberries
Granulated sugar, for sprinkling
1 batch Streusel (Kruszonka, page 346)

EGG WASH

1 egg and 3 Tbsp [45 g] whole milk, whisked until smooth

TOPPING

Confectioners' sugar, for sprinkling, or 1 batch Glaze (Lukier, page 348) (optional)

Prepare your placek dough according to the recipe on page 101 through the bulk proof. While it rises, prepare your pudding according to the recipe on page 342 and your streusel according to the recipe on page 346.

Once your dough is ready, turn it out onto a floured work surface and divide it into twelve portions of 2¾ oz [80 g]. Form the divided dough into tight balls (see page 22) and place seam-side down onto two baking sheets lined with parchment paper, evenly spaced at least 4 in [10 cm] apart. Brush each ball with egg wash and set aside to rise.

Allow the dough balls to rise for 2½ hours, until the dough is light and puffed. Shortly before the balls have fully risen, preheat the oven to 350°F [180°C] with the convection setting turned on. Brush the balls a second time with egg wash, then dip a large spoon in the remaining egg wash and press down on the middle of each ball to form a pizza shape about 5 in [13 cm] across, with a flattened middle and a 1 in [2.5 cm] thick rim. If the spoon sticks while you're doing this, dip it again in the egg wash. Whisk the budyń until smooth, then fill the center of each bun with an equal portion of the budyń, spread to the inner edge of the rim. Divide the raspberries evenly among the buns, press them into the budyń, and sprinkle with a little granulated sugar. Cover each pastry with streusel.

Bake for 15 to 20 minutes, or until the buns are golden brown and the raspberries have begun to leak juice. After cooling, for optional sweetness, dust with confectioners' sugar or drizzle with glaze (if using). Store for up to a couple days in an airtight container at room temperature.

Sour Cherry and Salty Sheep's Cheese Danishes

Drożdżówki z Bryndzą i Wiśniami

Though typically a sweet pastry, drożdżówki are now a format for any savory fantasy, often incorporating seasonal vegetables and traditional Polish ingredients. Here, we use bryndzą, the salty and crumbly sheep's cheese found across Poland, Slovakia, and Ukraine. This cheese is very similar to feta, which makes for a perfect substitution when bryndzą is not to be found. The salt of the cheese, the sour of the cherries, the sweetness of the honey, and the earthiness of the thyme nod to some of the very, very good things from the Polish kitchen.

NOTE: For a morning bake, prepare your dough the night before and allow to proof in the fridge according to the recipe on page 98.

MAKES 12 drożdżówki

DOUGH

1 batch Chałka Dough (page 98)

FILLING

6 cups [1 kg] sour cherries, pitted fresh or thawed if frozen
½ cup [110 g] demerara sugar
9 oz [255 g] bryndzą or feta, drained
7 oz [200 g] thick full-fat sour cream
1 Tbsp all-purpose flour
1 egg
2 tsp dried thyme
1 tsp ground black pepper

EGG WASH

1 egg and 3 Tbsp [45 g] whole milk, whisked until smooth

GARNISH

⅓ cup [115 g] pourable honey
Fresh thyme sprigs

Prepare your chałka dough according to the recipe on page 98, through the bulk proof.

Once your dough is ready, turn it out onto a floured work surface and divide it into twelve portions of 2¾ oz [80 g]. Form the divided dough into tight balls (see page 22) and arrange smooth-side up onto two baking sheets lined with parchment paper, evenly spaced at least 4 in [10 cm] apart. These have to be far apart because you'll press them out to shape after they rise. Brush each ball with egg wash and set aside to rise for 2½ hours, until light and puffed.

While the dough balls are rising, prepare the filling. Mix the cherries with the demerara sugar in a small bowl and set aside to soften. To prepare your cheese filling, in a medium bowl, mix the bryndzą, sour cream, flour, egg, thyme, and pepper until all the ingredients are fully incorporated. Set aside.

Shortly before the balls have fully risen, preheat the oven to 350°F [180°C] with the convection setting turned on. Brush the balls a second time with egg wash, then dip a large spoon in the remaining egg wash and press down on the middle of each ball to form a pizza shape about 5 in [13 cm] across, each with a flattened middle and a 1 in [2.5 cm] thick rim. If the spoon sticks while you're doing this, dip it again in the egg wash.

Spoon a generous portion of the cheese filling into the center of each bun, spread to the inner edge of the rim, then press a handful of sour cherries into the middle of the filling. Bake for about 15 minutes, or until the pastry is golden brown, then drizzle all over with honey and garnish with fresh thyme.

These are best served the same day, but can be extended 1 or 2 days when stored airtight at room temperature. Reheat in the oven to warm the cheese before serving, if you like.

Inox

Poppy Seed Swirls

Drożdżowe Bułki z Makiem

There's a *Seinfeld* episode where Elaine can't go on a work trip because she keeps eating lemon–poppy seed muffins and failing a drug test. What is a mere comedic television plotline in America is a real-life problem in Poland. Polish baking is such a hub for poppy seeds that according to journalist Marek Kępa, the country's legal periodical *Problemy Kryminalistyki* published an article titled "Testing the Level of Morphine in Bodily Fluids of Persons That Have Consumed Food Products Containing Poppy Seeds and Its Marking on Such Products." In short, what to do if someone ate a poppy seed pastry before having a drug test? Which leads us to this—one of the most delightful ways to legally compromise yourself: drożdżowe bułki z makiem, sweet butterfly-shaped poppy seed yeast buns.

NOTE: To time this for a morning treat, make the poppy seed paste and chałka dough the night before you want to bake.

MAKES 18 to 20 drożdżówki

DOUGH

1 batch Chałka Dough (page 98)

FILLING

1 batch Poppy Seed Paste (page 337)

1 egg white

EGG WASH

1 egg and 3 Tbsp [45 g] whole milk, whisked until smooth

TOPPING

1 batch Glaze (Lukier, page 348)

2 to 3 Tbsp [20 to 35 g] poppy seeds (optional)

Prepare your chałka dough according to the recipe on page 98, through the bulk proof. Once the dough is ready, turn it out onto a lightly floured work surface and divide it into two even portions. Roll out one portion of your dough to a thin 20 x 8 in [51 x 20 cm] rectangle, keeping the long side horizontal to you.

Using a spoon or offset spatula, spread half of the poppy seed paste evenly over the dough, leaving 1 in [2.5 cm] along the long bottom side unfilled. Brush this unfilled side with egg wash or water. This will act as glue to seal and hold the roll together.

Starting from the long side opposite the side you just brushed with water, roll down the dough, stretching vertically gently to make a fairly tight roll. Once the dough is rolled into a log with the glued seam on the underside, use a large, flat knife to trim the ends of the roll. Measure 2 in [5 cm] marks along the length of the roll, then cut at each interval by pressing directly down with the knife rather than sawing. You'll have nine or ten rolls.

Arrange the rolls on a baking sheet lined with parchment paper, about 2 in [5 cm] apart in two lines of five. They should be upright like fat wagon wheels with the seam on the underside. Repeat for the second portion of dough, arranging the rolls on a second baking sheet lined with parchment paper. To create the distinct butterfly shape of these buns, use a chopstick or clean pencil to press the center of each roll firmly nearly all the way to the pan. Brush each bun with egg wash and set aside to proof for 2½ hours, until light and puffed.

Shortly before the rolls are fully risen, preheat the oven to 350°F [180°C] with the convection setting turned on. Give the buns one last egg wash, then bake for about 20 minutes, or until golden brown. Allow to cool, then use a pastry brush to spread a swoosh of glaze, then sprinkle with poppy seeds (if using), and serve.

These are best eaten the day they're baked, but can be stretched another couple days by storing airtight at room temperature.

Stuffed Fruit Buns

Drożdżówki z Owocami

If you ever want to know what time of year it is in Poland, you've got two options: Check a calendar or go to a bakery and buy drożdżówki z owocami, fruit-stuffed yeast buns. Take a bite, and whatever fruit spills out will make the season abundantly clear. Springtime is strawberries, summer is blueberries and raspberries, early autumn is stone fruit, and winter is, well, whatever got set aside and preserved during the rest of the year. Maybe that's why the strawberry buns feel extra delicious and optimistic—they mean the cold Polish winter is over.

NOTE: What's wonderful about these buns is how the fruit is never made too sweet—just a hint of sugar is enough to let the fruit go jammy but still shine with freshness. However, if you like your fillings sweeter, or if your fruit isn't completely ripe, feel free to add an extra couple tablespoons of sugar.

MAKES 12 drożdżówki

DOUGH

1 batch Chałka Dough (page 98)

FILLING

1 lb 5 oz [600 g] whole ripe small berries like strawberries or raspberries, or larger strawberries, plums, or apricots, cut into 1 in [2.5 cm] pieces

¾ cup [150 g] granulated sugar

1 Tbsp lemon juice

¼ tsp ground cinnamon

¼ cup [55 g] demerara sugar

½ cup [70 g] dry bread crumbs

2 Tbsp [16 g] cornstarch

EGG WASH

1 egg and 3 Tbsp [45 g] whole milk, whisked until smooth

STREUSEL

1 batch Streusel (Kruszonka, page 346)

Prepare your chałka dough according to the recipe on page 98, through the bulk proof. While the dough rises, make the filling. Toss the fruit, granulated sugar, lemon juice, and cinnamon in a medium mixing bowl. Set aside to rest for at least an hour. In another bowl, mix the demerara sugar and bread crumbs. If making your dough in advance and allowing it to bulk proof in the fridge overnight, prepare the fruit about an hour before you'd like to shape your buns.

Once the dough has risen, turn it out onto your work surface and divide it into twelve even portions of about 3 oz [85 g] each. Flatten each piece of dough to degas, then fold in the sides, flip over so the seal is table-side down, and roll into a tight ball (see page 22). Cover the dough balls loosely with plastic wrap or a damp tea towel and allow to rest for 20 minutes.

After the dough has rested and you're ready to shape, drain the fruit through a sieve to get rid of the liquid released while resting, then toss it with the cornstarch. Turn your dough out onto a lightly floured work surface smooth-side down, and roll it out into a large circle, about ¼ in [6 mm] thick. Place the dough circle in a small bowl or the cupped palm of your less dominant hand, so you have a little valley in the middle. Spoon a few tablespoons of the fruit mixture in the dough circle, then sprinkle a spoonful of the bread crumb mixture

cont'd

on top. Fold up the sides of the dough to enclose the fruit, then pinch and fold along the edge like a dumpling or pierogi to seal the bun very tightly. If there are any loose seams, the juice will leak out during baking. Remove the sealed bun from the bowl and set seam-side down on a baking sheet lined with parchment paper. Repeat with each ball of dough, arranging the filled buns 1½ in [4 cm] apart on the baking sheet.

Brush the buns with egg wash and set aside to rise for 2½ hours at room temperature, until light and puffed. Shortly before they are fully risen, preheat the oven to 350°F [180°C] with the convection setting turned on.

Brush the buns a second time with egg wash, and pile high with a handful of streusel on each bun. Bake for 25 minutes, or until golden brown. If a little juice leaks from some of the buns, no problem!

Serve the same day, or store airtight at room temperature for a couple days. These can be reheated in the oven to serve warm.

Z WŁASNEGO GOSPODARSTWA

Rano Piekarnia's Summer Bilberry Buns

Jagodzianki

If you get up early in the morning and walk down the sunny side of the tree-lined Stalowa Street in Warsaw's Praga district—the low and flat residential area on the other side of the Vistula River's sandy banks that can feel like a separate city unto itself—you'll probably see Weronika Nogańska in the window of her bakery, Rano. She might be rushing breads and yeast buns from the oven, piping hazelnut frangipane onto thick brioche slices for bostock, or slicing ogórki małosolne (half-sour pickles) for sandwiches. On the rare occasion that Weronika takes a break and sits on the sunny bench in front of her kitchen, you might also see a small black cat, Ciupek, the bakery ambassador, warming in the sun with her. If they're there, they're most certainly greeting the endless passing by of neighbors and pet dogs. And if it happens to be a hot summer morning when you're there, there might be an impatient line twenty people deep. Because jagodzianki season has begun.

Every summer in Poland, the minute the jagody—wild bilberries—ripen, bakeries rush to make these jammy, stuffed berry and streusel buns. And in turn, customers rush to buy them. People have always loved jagodzianki, but the artisan bakery movement has caused an upswell in their popularity. Weronika notes: "The season is so short—we wait for it all year. The jagody are this gift from the forest." The best jagodzianki are a thin, yeasted pocket of chałka dough filled with barely sweetened fresh berries and topped with loads of crunchy kruszonka, and Weronika, who staged in bakeries in Marseille and Katowice before opening Rano, makes some of the best, in part because she keeps hers so simple and honest, letting the fruit star.

At Rano, on those summer mornings, customers leave with boxes full of jagodzianki, often with one already in hand, waving the pastry to greet their neighbor Weronika, saying *cześć!* (*hello!*) with full mouths, their teeth inky from the berries. If you ask her about the idea behind her bakery, you might expect her to say something about the quality of her bread—which is impeccable—but she won't. "I think I realized a couple years into this that it's about bringing people joy. Making them happy for a minute. This is my community—we all really like each other." And during that brief hot summer when the jagody are plentiful, her jagodzianki might be the surest way she and Ciupek bring joy to her neighbors.

NOTE: Bilberries aren't available everywhere, but they're very similar to wild blueberries, which work perfectly. If necessary, larger domestic berries can be used, but they'll have a different texture and flavor profile. Whatever you do, don't use frozen berries—they'll leak juice everywhere.

MAKES 12 jagodzianki

cont'd

DOUGH

1 batch Chałka Dough (page 98)

FILLING

⅓ cup plus 1 tsp [70 g] sugar

¼ cup [45 g] cornstarch

21 oz [600 g] bilberries or wild blueberries, fresh and dry

EGG WASH

1 egg and 3 Tbsp [45 g] whole milk, whisked until smooth

STREUSEL (KRUSZONKA)

1 cup plus 1 Tbsp [125 g] almond meal

1 cup [125 g] all-purpose flour

½ cup plus 2 Tbsp [125 g] sugar

½ tsp kosher salt

9 Tbsp [125 g] unsalted butter, cold and cut into small cubes

The night before you're ready to bake, prepare your chałka dough according to the recipe on page 98, following the instructions to bulk proof overnight in the fridge.

The next day, line two baking sheets with parchment paper and set aside. In a medium mixing bowl, gently fold the sugar and cornstarch into the berries, trying not to crush them.

Turn your chilled dough out onto a lightly floured work surface and divide into twelve portions of 2½ oz [70 g]. Form the dough into balls (see page 22) and let rest, smooth-side up, for about 15 minutes. Once the dough has rested, it's time to form your jagodzianki. Take one dough ball and flip it over, smooth-side down. Roll it out to a large, thin circle. Place the circle in your less dominant hand, holding it with your fingers cupped to create a well (some people use a small bowl to hold the dough at this stage). Scoop about 1¾ oz [50 g] of berries, or one twelfth of your berries, into the middle of the dough, then fold up the sides and crimp or pleat the dough like a dumpling or pierogi where it meets. The important thing is to create a tight seal. Turn the sealed jagodzianka seam-side down onto one of your baking sheets. Continue for the rest of your jagodzianki, setting them 2 in [5 cm] apart on the pans. Brush each with egg wash, then set aside to rise for 2½ hours, until light and puffed and a finger pressed into the dough springs back slowly.

Shortly before the jagodzianki are fully risen, preheat the oven to 350°F [180°C] with the convection setting turned on.

Prepare the streusel. In a medium mixing bowl, whisk together the almond meal, flour, sugar, and salt. Use your hands to rub the butter into the dry ingredients until you have a crumbly texture and no visible pockets of butter remain. Chill for at least 20 minutes in the fridge before using.

Brush the buns a second time with egg wash, then top with a large pile of streusel and bake for about 25 minutes, until golden brown. Don't worry if one or two leak juice, that's part of the charm.

Serve immediately or store airtight at room temperature for up to 2 days.

Walnut-Paste Babka with Nut Crumble

Strucla z Orzechami Włoskimi

There's a babka problem with Polish baking. The Jewish-style babkas that have surged in popularity around the world have nothing to do with what Poles call babka, or baba. In Poland, babka is a Bundt cake, while the globally better-known, twisted, filled yeast babkas are called strucle. In the last decade's flood of babka recipes, maybe the world doesn't need another one, but if we call it a strucla, maybe that's the loophole to get away with just one more. Here, an impossibly light yeast dough is filled with thick cinnamon-walnut paste and covered in chopped nuts and streusel.

MAKES two 9 x 5 in [23 x 13 cm] loaves

DOUGH

1 batch Placek Dough (page 101)

FILLING

1 batch Walnut Paste (page 340)

WALNUT STREUSEL

¾ cup [100 g] chopped walnuts

1 tsp ground cinnamon

1 batch Streusel (Kruszonka, page 346)

EGG WASH

1 egg and 3 Tbsp [45 g] whole milk, whisked until smooth

CINNAMON SUGAR

¼ cup [50 g] sugar

½ tsp ground cinnamon

Prepare your placek dough according to the recipe on page 101, through the bulk proof. While it rises, prepare your walnut paste according to the recipe on page 340 and your kruszonka according to the recipe on page 346.

To prepare the walnut streusel, toss the walnuts, cinnamon, and kruszonka, then set aside until ready to use.

Once the dough is ready, line two 9 x 5 in [23 x 13 cm] loaf pans with parchment paper. Turn out the dough onto a lightly floured work surface and use your hands to gently stretch it into a thick rectangle, 24 x 8 in [61 x 20 cm]. This dough is very supple and fluffy, so you won't need to use a rolling pin unless you prefer it. Spread the dough evenly with a thick layer of the walnut paste, then roll it all up into a long log, starting with a long edge. Slice the log in half to create two smaller logs. Give one log a small stretch to lengthen it to about twice the length of the loaf pan, then fold it in half and give it one twist. Place it in one of the loaf pans, then repeat for the second loaf. Brush each with egg wash, then set aside to rise for 2 to 2½ hours, or until risen by about half and the loaves are light and soft and a finger pressed into the dough springs back slowly.

In a small bowl, combine the sugar and cinnamon and set aside.

Shortly before the loaves finish rising, preheat the oven to 350°F [180°C] with the convection setting turned on. Brush the loaves a second time with egg wash, then generously cover each babka with the walnut streusel and a bit of cinnamon sugar. Bake for 45 minutes, or until the loaves are golden brown and a thermometer inserted into the middle reads at least 195°F [90°C].

Allow to cool before serving. Store airtight at room temperature for up to several days.

Raisin Streusel Brioche

Placek Drożdżowy z Rodzynkami

This is Polish panettone. It puffs up like a cloud yet holds more butter and richness than its weight belies. It's enjoyed as a teatime snack slathered in cold butter and as a centerpiece bake on a Christmas or Easter table. Make it extra festive and throw in a spoonful of orange zest and a handful of mini dark chocolate chips or cranberries along with the raisins—or stick to the recipe and keep it simple.

MAKES two 9 x 5 in [23 x 13 cm] loaves

MACERATED RAISINS

¾ cup [105 g] raisins
¾ cup plus 1½ Tbsp [200 g] water
3½ Tbsp [50 g] rum, kirsch, or hazelnut liquor (optional)

DOUGH

1 batch Placek Dough (page 101)

EGG WASH

1 egg and 3 Tbsp [45 g] whole milk, whisked until smooth

TOPPING

1 batch Streusel (Kruszonka, page 346)

Begin by preparing the raisins. If using other dried fruits, prepare in the same manner. Boil the water, then pour over the raisins in a small bowl. Add the rum (if using), stir, and set aside to soak for 30 minutes to 1 hour. Once the raisins are plump, drain the liquid and dry the raisins gently on a folded tea towel. Set aside to cool.

While the raisins are cooling, prepare your placek dough according to the recipe on page 101. During the last stage of the mix of the dough, after the butter has been incorporated, turn down the speed of the mixer to low and add the raisins, mixing for 1 to 2 minutes until just incorporated.

Grease your hands with a bit of softened butter, and remove the dough from the mixer. Set the dough in a large greased bowl, then pick up the dough a few times, letting the sides fold under themselves each time, until you have a smooth, domed dough. Cover the bowl airtight with room for expansion, then set aside to rise for 1 hour 15 minutes, until the dough has grown by about two thirds in size.

Meanwhile, line two 9 x 5 in [23 x 13 cm] loaf pans with parchment paper and set aside.

Once the dough has risen, shape the loaves. Turn the dough out onto a lightly floured work surface, and divide it into two equal portions. Press one portion of the dough out into a large rectangle or oval just a bit longer than your loaf pan, sprinkling with flour as needed to prevent sticking. Fold the two shorter sides into the middle. Then fold the two longer sides into the middle. Turn this over so the fold is on the underside and the smooth side is face up. You now have a plump, tube-shaped loaf. Place this in a lined loaf pan, smooth-side up. It's no problem if the loaf is shorter than the pan, as it will spread out as it rises. Repeat for the second loaf. Brush with egg wash, then cover both loaves with streusel. Set aside to rise for 30 to 40 minutes, until they have risen by about two thirds and they are light and soft and a finger pressed into the dough springs back slowly.

Preheat the oven to 350°F [180°C] with the convection setting turned on. Bake the loaves for 35 minutes, or until a thermometer reads 195°F [90°C] or a cake tester comes out clean.

Cool before slicing and store airtight at room temperature for up to several days.

Plummy Yeasted Tray Cake

Placek Drożdżowy ze Śliwkami

At the end of summer, when all the stone fruits in Poland are coming to their peak, drive along tree-lined roads in the countryside and you'll see just-too-ripe plums and apricots dropping on cars and hot pavement like little schnapps bombs. Unfortunately, this timing coincides with the late-season yellow jackets that swarm the sugar-sticky plums on bakery placek cakes like this one, and it's common to see people swatting away bees between bites. An absolute classic of Central European coffee cakes, this plum cake can be made with many different dough bases; my favorite is the ultra-soft placek.

NOTE: This recipe calls for a shorter final proof than other recipes that use placek dough. This gives this cake its distinct slightly dense, cakey texture.

MAKES one 10 x 12 in [25 x 30.5 cm] cake (12 to 16 slices)

DOUGH

1 batch Placek Dough (page 101)

FILLING

3 lb 5 oz [1.5 kg] blue Italian plums
½ cup [100 g] sugar
1 tsp ground cinnamon
1 tsp ground ginger

TOPPING

¼ cup [50 g] sugar
1 batch Streusel (Kruszonka, page 346)

Prepare your placek dough according to the recipe on page 101 through the bulk proof.

Meanwhile, prepare the filling. Halve and pit the plums. In a medium mixing bowl, toss the plums with the sugar, cinnamon, and ginger. Cover the bowl and refrigerate until ready to use. This maceration process will help make your plums jammy when they bake.

While you wait for your dough to rise and your plums to soften, prepare your streusel according to the recipe on page 346 and butter a 10 x 12 in [25 x 30.5 cm] baking pan, line with parchment paper, and set aside.

Once the dough has grown by about two thirds in size, shape the cake. Turn it out directly into the pan and, with greased hands, stretch and press it to fit the pan, pressing out the air in it as you do. The dough will be fluffy and stretchy. Press the plums into the dough in tight lines on an angle or face up, then sprinkle with the sugar. Finally, sprinkle with the streusel—as much or as little as you like. Set this aside to rise for 1½ hours until light and soft.

Shortly before the cake has fully risen, preheat the oven to 350°F [180°C] with the convection setting turned on. Bake the cake for 35 minutes, or until the streusel is very toasted, the plums are jammy and leaking juice, and a knife inserted in the center of the loaf comes out clean. If you're uncertain, give it a few more minutes—it's better to overbake this than underbake!

Allow to cool, then slice into squares and serve. Store airtight at room temperature for up to 3 days.

Yeasted Saffron and Orange-Glazed Easter Bundt

Wielkanocna Baba Drożdżowa

Yeasted baba, or babka, is the brioche Bundt central to every Easter table in Poland. While it's sometimes molded into the arguably cuter form of a little lamb, the Bundt shape is the most popular. These babas decorate bakery windows, glazed in pastel pinks, blues, and yellows, or dusted with confectioners' sugar. Here, the cake's color is deepened to gold with saffron—which also adds a brightening and aromatic touch—and glazed with an orange-flavored icing.

MAKES 1 large Bundt cake

DOUGH

1 batch Placek Dough (page 101)
¼ tsp saffron threads (optional)

FOR THE PAN

½ Tbsp unsalted butter, at room temperature
½ cup [70 g] dry bread crumbs

EGG WASH

1 egg and 3 Tbsp [45 g] whole milk, whisked until smooth

GLAZE

¾ cup plus 1½ Tbsp [100 g] confectioners' sugar
1 to 2 Tbsp [15 to 30 g] whole milk
1 Tbsp grated orange zest

Prepare your placek dough according to the recipe on page 101, adding the ¼ tsp of saffron to the sponge. This will allow the saffron to release its color and flavor before being mixed into the dough along with the sponge. Butter a Bundt pan, coat it with bread crumbs, and set aside.

Once the dough has bulk proofed, shape the baba. Invert the dough onto a well-floured work surface and, with well-floured hands, press it out into a large rectangle, degassing it as you go. Roll up the rectangle of dough into a long log, then twist it to give it some tension and structure. Gently pick up the log and wind it around the center of the Bundt pan in a spiral, overlapping as you need. Brush the top of the spiral with egg wash, then set aside to rise for another 1½ hours, until light and puffed about 1 to 2 in [2.5 to 5 cm] from the top of the Bundt pan. A finger pressed into the dough will spring back slowly.

Shortly before the baba has fully risen, preheat the oven to 350°F [180°C] with the convection setting turned on. Give the top one more brush with cream or egg wash, then bake for about 30 minutes, or until a cake tester comes out clean or a thermometer inserted reads at least 195°F [90°C]. Remove from the oven and cool for about 30 minutes, then invert the baba onto a cooling rack.

To make the glaze, mix the confectioners' sugar and enough milk to make a very thick but pourable glaze, then mix in the orange zest. Drizzle the glaze over the top of the baba and let it spill down the edges.

The baba can be made several days in advance and stored airtight at room temperature. In this case, wait until you're ready to serve it to glaze.

Fritter-Style Apple Pancakes

Racuchy z Jabłkami

Racuchy are light, fluffy yeasted apple or pear fritters doused in confectioners' sugar served as a sweet afternoon snack or dessert rather than breakfast, as is the Central and Eastern European habit. Even if it isn't tradition, don't be afraid to serve these for breakfast. No matter when they're enjoyed, the best way to make these is to go very heavy on the apples-to-batter ratio. While typically the apples are added to the batter raw (which is how I've done it here), my friend Jessica Nadziejko likes to lightly sauté her apples in a spoonful of butter with a sprinkling of cinnamon and sugar for extra flavor.

NOTE: This recipe calls for clarified butter, which allows for easier frying without burning. If you don't have clarified butter, you can use regular butter, but watch your racuchy carefully as you fry them.

MAKES 12 to 15 pancakes

BATTER

¾ cup plus 3 Tbsp [225 g] whole milk
1 egg
1¾ Tbsp [25 g] unsalted butter, melted
2 cups [250 g] all-purpose flour
1 Tbsp [15 g] sugar
1 tsp [3 g] instant yeast
¼ tsp kosher salt
2 or 3 large apples, peeled, cored, and diced

FOR FRYING

½ cup [110 g] clarified unsalted butter or ghee

TOPPING

Confectioners' sugar, for sprinkling

Begin by making the batter. In a large mixing bowl, whisk together the milk, egg, and melted butter. In a smaller mixing bowl, mix together the flour, sugar, yeast, and salt. Pour the dry ingredients into the wet and mix just until no dry pockets of flour remain. It should be a moderately lumpy batter—do not overmix. Add the apples and mix until even. Set aside to rise for 45 minutes to 1 hour.

Once the batter is risen and bubbly, line a cooling rack with paper towels. In a large skillet over medium-low heat, melt about 3 Tbsp [45 g] of clarified butter until a speck of batter sizzles when added. Racuchy are cooked with more fat than American-style pancakes, so the effect is more like a fritter, nearly deep-fried. Spoon out the racuchy batter into the hot clarified butter in large, heaping spoonfuls, keeping each about 1 in [2.5 cm] apart. As the racuchy fry, bubbles will rise to the surface of the dough, signaling it's time to flip. You can also use a spatula to check when the bottom has gotten golden brown—after about 3 minutes—then flip and cook until golden brown on the other side. Remove the browned racuchy from the pan and allow to cool on the rack.

Replenish the clarified butter as needed, allow it to heat, then fry the next batch. Continue until all the racuchy have been fried. Sprinkle generously with confectioners' sugar and serve hot.

Plum Butter Carnival Donuts

Pączki z Powidłami

The family-run Peter Pan Donuts in Greenpoint—the deeply Polish part of Brooklyn—is midcentury Americana coffee shop perfection: low café counter, bottomless coffees, bakery display featuring every possible kind of donut. Funny enough, a lot of people think it's a Polish donut shop. After all, you'll hear Polish greetings between staff and clients. But the owner, Christos Siafakas, came over from Greece, not Poland, in the 1970s. Once in New York, he worked the Polish donut shop circuit until he had enough money to buy his own place. The way his son Demetri tells it, "The family owes a lot to the neighborhood Polish community. [My father] would cross any cultural boundary as long as there was a nice treat to be made."

Each year around Tłusty Cztwartek (Fat Thursday), Peter Pan sells every flavor of the beloved Carnival donut, from the very traditional plum or rose jam, to custard and raspberry. So, for a couple days in February, all the people who think Peter Pan is a Polish donut shop aren't really wrong.

This is a recipe for the most classic flavor of pączki. They're stuffed with powidła—plum butter—then glazed and topped with a bit of orange peel and poppy seed.

MAKES 20 to 24 pączki

DOUGH

1 batch Pączki Dough (page 103)

FOR FRYING

8½ cups [2 L] sunflower oil

FILLING

28 oz [800 g] Plum Filling (page 333)

TOPPING

1 batch Thin Glaze (Lukier, page 348)

½ cup diced Candied Orange Peel (page 332)

DECORATIVE TOPPINGS (OPTIONAL)

2 Tbsp [20 g] poppy seeds

¼ cup [30 g] slivered almonds

Prepare the pączki dough according to the recipe on page 103 through the bulk proof. I like to make the dough the night before and allow it to rise overnight in the fridge so I can have morning donuts.

When the dough is risen and you're ready to shape your donuts, cut out twenty-four 4 in [10 cm] squares of parchment paper and set aside.

Turn your dough out onto a lightly floured work surface and roll to about ¾ in [2 cm] thickness. Use a wide water glass or round cookie cutter to cut out as many circles as possible from the dough. Press the remaining dough back together, allow it to relax for about 10 minutes, then roll it out again and cut the remaining circles. Put each dough circle on a piece of parchment paper and cover loosely with plastic wrap. Allow to rise for 2½ hours, or until light and puffed and a finger pressed into the dough springs back slowly. It's very important to wait until the donuts are well-risen—an underproofed donut won't cook all the way through while frying.

Shortly before your donuts are finished rising, fill a medium pot or home deep fryer with sunflower oil, at least 3 in [7.5 cm] deep. Heat it on medium heat until it reaches 350°F [180°C], checking the temperature with a thermometer throughout the frying process. Any lower and your donuts will be greasy. Any higher and they'll burn without cooking the interior. Meanwhile, line a cooling rack with paper towels.

cont'd

Once your oil is at temperature, use a slotted spatula to place several donuts in the oil, paper and all. (If you're not sure about your oil temperature, it's a good idea to do one test donut first!) The papers will slide off as soon as the donuts hit the oil and can be removed with tongs. Fry the donuts on each side for about 2 minutes, until a rich brown color, then remove and allow to cool and drain on the prepared rack. Repeat with the rest of the donuts.

Fit a pastry bag with a 5 to 8 mm filling piping tip, often called a Bismark tip, and fill the bag with the plum filling, or powidła. When the donuts are cool, insert the tip into the side of each donut and fill generously. Next, mix up the glaze. These donuts usually use a very thin, liquidy glaze, but if you prefer a thicker glaze, use the recipe for Lukier (page 348). Either dip the top of each donut in the glaze or arrange on a cooling rack with a tray underneath and pour glaze over the top of each. Sprinkle with chopped candied orange peel or the decorative toppings of your choice (if using), then serve.

Rose Petal Donuts

Pączki z Różą

I met Rose Ta My at an all-night party at the Château du Feÿ, a castle about an hour south of Paris. I assumed she was French, but at one point in the night she said, "I heard you were writing a book about Polish baking. I'm from Warsaw!" Our insobriety prevented us from having the conversation I needed to have with her at that moment. "What's your favorite Polish pastry?" I shouted at her over the music. "The rose jam pączki! I think because of my name!" she yelled back. While Rose moved from Poland to Paris as a teenager, she still makes sure to go back to Warsaw from time to time to see family and eat her favorite donuts.

Rose petal donuts are a uniquely Polish donut flavor. The edible beach rose petals, *Rosa rugosa*, are collected in the summer and churned with sugar to preserve, then turned into a jam or left as intensely flavored Rose Paste (page 344). While some people prefer the strong rose flavor of pure rose jam, it's popular to mellow the flavor with raspberry or quince jam, as this recipe does. The recipe can easily be doubled for larger batches.

MAKES 20 to 24 pączki

DOUGH

1 batch Pączki Dough (page 103)

FOR FRYING

About 8½ cups [2 L] sunflower oil

FILLING

2 cups [600 g] raspberry jam

½ cup plus 2 Tbsp [200 g] Rose Paste (page 344)

GLAZE (LUKIER)

2 cups plus 1 Tbsp [250 g] confectioners' sugar

2 Tbsp [35 g] Rose Paste (page 344)

3 to 4 Tbsp [45 to 60 g] whole milk

DECORATIVE TOPPINGS (OPTIONAL)

Decorative rose petals, pink glitter, mint leaves, freeze-dried raspberries

Prepare the pączki dough according to the recipe on page 103 through the bulk proof. I like to make the dough the night before and allow it to rise overnight in the fridge so I can have morning donuts.

Cut out twenty-four 4 in [10 cm] squares of parchment paper and set aside.

Turn your dough out onto a lightly floured work surface and roll to about ¾ in [2 cm] thickness. Use a wide water glass or round cookie cutter to cut out as many circles as possible from the dough. Press the remaining dough back together, allow it to relax for about 10 minutes, then roll it out again and cut the remaining circles. Put each dough circle on a piece of parchment paper and cover loosely with plastic wrap. Allow to rise for 2½ hours, or until light and puffed and a finger pressed into the dough springs back slowly. It's very important to wait until the donuts are well-risen—an underproofed donut won't cook all the way through in the oil.

Shortly before your donuts are finished rising, fill a medium pot or home deep fryer with sunflower oil, at least 3 in [7.5 cm] deep. Heat it on medium heat to 350°F [180°C], checking the temperature with a thermometer throughout the frying process. Any lower and your donuts will be greasy. Any higher and they'll burn without cooking the interior. Meanwhile, line a cooling rack with a layer of paper towels.

cont'd

Once your oil is at temperature, use a slotted spatula to place several donuts in the oil, paper and all. (If you're not sure about your oil temperature, it's a good idea to do one test donut first!) The papers will slide off as soon as the donuts hit the oil and can be removed with tongs. Fry the donuts on each side for about 2 minutes, until a rich brown color, then remove and allow to cool on the prepared rack. Repeat with the rest of the donuts.

To make the filling, stir together the raspberry jam and rose paste in a small bowl. Fit a pastry bag with a 5 to 8 mm filling piping tip, often called a Bismark tip, and fill the bag with the raspberry-rose filling. When the donuts are cool, insert the tip into the side of each donut and fill generously. Next, mix up the glaze. In a medium mixing bowl, mix the confectioners' sugar, rose paste, and milk until smooth. Either dip the top of each donut in the glaze or arrange on a cooling rack with a tray underneath and pour glaze over the top of each. Sprinkle decorative toppings of your choice on top (if using), then serve.

Poppy Seed Roll

Makowiec

Makowiec is a poppy seed roll cake that's an essential part of Polish Christmas but is easily found all year long across Central and Eastern Europe and in many old-fashioned Jewish bakeries around the world. The one unifying principle is the more poppy seed, the better. The most extreme makowiec is the makowiec Lubartowski from the Lubartów region near Lublin, in the far east of Poland. There, makowiec is like a reverse babka, with thick rolls of poppy seed ribboned with a thin dough. Here we make a more classic version with a spongy centimeter of yeast dough swirled around about twice that amount of filling, served in slices.

NOTE: Makowiec goes against most traditional bread-making principles in that it uses a yeast dough but doesn't give it a final rise. The end result is a rich, crumbly, and cakey roll. If poppy seed is not your thing, fear not. Walnut Paste (Masa Orzechowa, page 340) is also a traditional filling.

MAKES 2 makowce (serves 20)

DOUGH

1 batch Chałka Dough (page 98)

FILLING

Double batch Poppy Seed Paste (page 337)
¼ to ½ cup [35 to 70 g] golden raisins
¼ to ½ cup [35 to 70 g] chopped dried apricots
2 Tbsp [30 g] rum, walnut liqueur, kirsch, apple juice, or water
3 egg whites
¼ to ½ cup [35 to 70 g] chopped Candied Orange Peel (page 332)

TOPPING

1 batch Royal Icing (page 349)
Whole candied cherries (optional)
Candied Orange Peel (page 332), chopped or julienned (optional)

Prepare your chałka dough according to the recipe on page 98 and bulk proof. I like to make the dough the night before, along with the filling.

Prepare your poppy seed paste according to the recipe on page 337, then set aside to cool before refrigerating overnight, covered airtight. Mix the raisins and apricots in a bowl with the rum and set aside. Cover and let sit overnight.

The next day, preheat your oven to 350°F [180°C] with the convection setting turned on, then finish preparing your filling. In the bowl of your stand mixer fitted with the whisk attachment, whisk the egg whites on medium-high speed until stiff peaks form. Use a spatula to fold the egg whites into the poppy seed paste until the whites are no longer visible and the paste is a spreadable consistency. Drain the fruit you soaked overnight, then fold it into the poppy seed paste along with the chopped candied orange peel.

To shape the makowiec, turn your dough out onto a lightly floured work surface, then divide it in half. Roll one portion out to a rectangle about 20 x 12 in [51 x 30.5 cm] and ½ in [1 cm] thickness, keeping the long side horizontal to you. Using a spoon or an offset spatula, spread half of the poppy seed paste on all but the bottom 1 in [2.5 cm] of dough. Brush that unfilled strip of dough with water. This will act as the glue that seals and holds your roll together. Roll up the dough from the top to the bottom, slightly stretching it vertically to make a tight roll. Roll it all the way up so the seam is on the underside. Repeat to make a second roll with the remaining half of dough and filling.

Cut two pieces of parchment paper to be slightly longer than each of your rolls. Place one roll seam-side down on the top side of the paper, then roll it up in the paper to make a tube. It's important to keep track of where the bottom seam of the dough

cont'd

roll is—it won't necessarily be visible through the parchment paper, and it must stay on the underside of the roll when it bakes, otherwise the spiral won't be perfect.

Place the roll on a baking sheet with the seam on the underside. Don't twist or seal the open ends of the parchment paper the makowiec is wrapped in—you'll want it to be able to expand outward as it bakes.

Repeat the wrapping process for the second makowiec and place it on the pan with the other makowiec, spaced about 2 in [5 cm] apart. Bake for 40 to 50 minutes, or until the exterior of the dough, when unwrapped, is a deep tan.

While the makowiec cools, prepare the icing according to the recipe on page 349. Glaze the cooled cake by either pouring or brushing on the glaze with a pastry brush and decorate with candied cherries or candied orange peel.

Serve immediately or store airtight at room temperature for up to a week.

Sour Cherry and Sweet Cheese Figure Eights

Drożdżówki z Wiśniami i Serem

If you struggle with decision making, these Danishes are for you. Two perfectly formed but distinctly different Danishes in one, shaped like an infinity sign or a figure eight, a different flavor on each side. You'll find these two-flavor Danishes mostly in Western Poland, closer to the German border. Here I use sour cherry filling, but Apple Filling (page 336) is also popular; really, just about any kind of thick seasonal fruit preserves works. Some people prefer to use Budyń (page 342)—vanilla pudding—instead of sweet cheese.

MAKES 10 Danishes

DOUGH

1 batch Półfrancuskie Dough (page 105)

FILLING

1 batch Sweet Cheese Filling (page 343)

1 batch Cherry Filling (page 334)

EGG WASH

1 egg and 3 Tbsp [45 g] whole milk, whisked until smooth

TOPPING (OPTIONAL)

Simple syrup or thinned apricot jam, for brushing

1 batch Glaze (Lukier, page 348)

Prepare your półfrancuskie dough according to the recipe on page 105 and allow to chill overnight in the fridge. The next morning, laminate the dough (see page 106) and chill for at least an hour before shaping your Danishes. When your dough is ready, turn it out onto a lightly floured surface and roll it into a square about 17 x 17 in [43 x 43 cm]. As you roll, run your hands under the dough from time to time to allow the dough to contract and relax. Once the rectangle is the correct size, use a pizza wheel or a flat knife to trim a little less than ½ in [1 cm] from each side of the rectangle to make tidy edges. Use a ruler to measure out 1½ in [4 cm] intervals along opposite sides of the dough, then use the ruler as a guide to cut out ten long strips.

To shape the strips, place one hand on each end of a strip and roll the ends in opposite directions to twist. Loosely roll up one side like a snail, connecting to the center point. Then take the other side of the rope and do the same but in the opposite direction. The coils of the figure eights should be touching but loose enough to allow for a bit of expansion, and the connecting coil should be draped diagonally across the pastry. Place the shaped Danish on a baking sheet lined with parchment paper and repeat for the other strips. Place them about 2 in [5 cm] apart on two baking sheets.

Use a pastry brush to lightly egg wash each Danish, then set them aside to rise for 2½ hours, until puffed and soft. Shortly before the Danishes are risen, preheat the oven to 350°F [180°C] with the convection setting turned on.

Brush the Danishes again with egg wash, then use a spoon to gently press down the middle of each spiral on the figure eights to make a little well. On each Danish, spoon cheese filling into the well on one half of each figure eight, then fruit filling into the well on the other half of each figure eight.

Bake for 15 to 20 minutes, until golden brown. Remove from the oven, and, for a little extra shine, brush the pastry with the remaining juices from the filling, simple syrup, or a bit of thinned apricot jam. If you wish to glaze, let the pastry cool on a cooling rack, then drizzle glaze across the pastry in thin diagonal stripes.

Serve the same day or store airtight at room temperature for up to 3 days.

St. Martin's Croissants

Rogale Świętomarcińskie

The 11th of November is St. Martin's Day. In Poznań, that means rogale świętomarcińskie, St. Martin's croissants. St. Martin was a Roman soldier who, one winter night, encountering a beggar, cut his cloak in half and gave it to the poor man. When St. Martin went to sleep, he dreamed he saw Jesus wearing the cloak. While European countries all celebrate St. Martin's Day differently, Poznań celebrates a second dream, this one from the nineteenth century, in which a local baker imagined he saw a knight riding a horse into town. The horse lost a golden shoe and the knight was . . . St. Martin? Upon waking, the baker went straight to work making a white poppy seed–laden croissant, packed with dried fruit and nuts, to memorialize the horseshoe in the vision. Neither of these stories sounds particularly plausible, but their veracity is unimportant—everyone knows legends make pastry taste better.

St. Martin's croissants can now be found across the country during their short season—the weeks leading up to St. Martin's Day—but Poznań is still the best place to find them.

MAKES 12 croissants

FILLING

1 batch Poppy Seed Paste (page 337) made with white poppy seeds

½ cup [65 g] chopped walnuts or almonds

⅓ cup plus 1 Tbsp [55 g] golden raisins

¼ cup [40 g] finely chopped Candied Orange Peel (page 332)

DOUGH

1 batch Półfrancuskie Dough (page 105)

EGG WASH

1 egg and 3 Tbsp [45 g] whole milk, whisked until smooth

TOPPING

1 batch Glaze (Lukier, page 348)

A few Tbsp chopped walnuts

Chopped Candied Orange Peel (page 332)

The night before you want to bake, prepare the poppy seed paste according to the recipe on page 337 and mix in the nuts, raisins, and candied orange peel. Prepare the base for the półfrancuskie dough according to the recipe on page 105. Wrap both airtight and refrigerate overnight.

The next morning, laminate the dough according to the recipe. Chill for at least an hour, then, on a lightly floured work surface, roll the dough to a 10 x 25 in [25 x 63.5 cm] rectangle. Use a pizza wheel or a flat knife to trim a little less than ½ in [1 cm] from each side of the rectangle for tidy edges. Spread the filling evenly across the rectangle. Measure intervals of 4 in [10 cm] along both of the long sides. Cut to join each of these intervals to make six rectangles. Cut each rectangle along the diagonal to make twelve triangles.

To shape the croissants, take one triangle and, in the middle of the base (the short side), cut a 1 in [2.5 cm] notch. Roll up the croissant, stretching the tip as you roll to create a bit of tension. Place the croissant on a baking sheet lined with parchment paper with the tip of the roll on the underside. Repeat for each triangle, making two sheets of six croissants, 2 in [5 cm] apart. Brush with egg wash, then let rise for 2½ hours at room temperature, until puffed and soft.

Shortly before the croissants are risen, preheat the oven to 350°F [180°C] with the convection setting turned on. When the croissants are fully risen, brush a second time with egg wash, then bake for 25 to 30 minutes, until golden brown.

To top, drizzle or brush with glaze and sprinkle with chopped nuts and candied orange peel.

Serve the same day or store airtight at room temperature for a couple days.

Baba au Rhum

Baba Ponczowa

If you want to start a fight with a French person, tell them that baba au rhum is Polish. The emblematic French dessert of mini brioche soaked in rum syrup is the work of the Polish King Stanisław I's pastry chef. The king, exiled in France in the early eighteenth century, legendarily rejected a dry yeasted babka, or kouglof, the Alsacienne yeasted Bundt similar to Poland's yeasted Easter baba (see page 149), so the pastry chef soaked it in sweetened alcohol to make it more appealing. All were delighted, and the cake made its way through the royal courts of France until eventually a descendant of that very Polish pastry chef, Nicolas Stohrer, went on to open the famed Stohrer Patisserie, one of the oldest continually running pastry shops in Paris.

The baba au rhum found today in Poland, the baba ponczowa, is made in a mini-Bundt or savarin shape. If you don't have mini-Bundt pans, a donut pan or muffin tin will also work.

NOTE: If the tops of your baked babas are too round and won't sit still on your plate when flipped upside down, trim a coin sized sliver straight off the rounded bottoms to stabilize them, or serve them on their side, cut in half, with cream in the middle.

MAKES 12 small Bundt babas or 18 donut-sized babas

DOUGH

1 batch Placek Dough (page 101)

EGG WASH

1 egg and 3 Tbsp [45 g] whole milk, whisked until smooth

SYRUP

2 cups [400 g] sugar
2 cups [475 g] water
2 star anise pods (optional)
3 cardamom pods (optional)
1 cinnamon stick (optional)
5 Tbsp [75 g] rum or walnut liqueur

TOPPING

3½ oz [100 g] whipping cream
2 tsp confectioners' sugar
Candied fruit, chopped small

Prepare your placek dough according to the recipe on page 101 through the bulk proof. Once the dough is fully risen, butter and flour your pans. Use wet hands (to minimize sticking) to press the air out of the placek dough, then re-wet your hands to pinch off small portions and fill each pan about halfway. Alternatively, and arguably more tidily, fill a pastry bag fitted with a wide round tip and pipe the dough into the molds. Either way you fill the molds, brush the tops of the babas with egg wash, then let them rise for about 1 hour, or until they've risen almost to the top of the molds.

Shortly before you're ready to bake, preheat the oven to 350°F [180°C] with the convection setting turned on. Brush the top of each baba with egg wash a second time, then bake for about 15 minutes, or until golden brown. Allow the babas to cool for about 10 minutes, then turn them out of their molds and allow to cool on a rack.

(At this stage, you can freeze the babas airtight until you're ready to use them, or store them airtight at room temperature for up to 3 days.)

cont'd

Make the syrup. In a medium saucepan, bring the sugar and water, and star anise, cardamon, and cinnamon stick (if using), to a low boil without stirring, allowing the sugar to dissolve. Simmer for about 3 minutes, then remove from the heat and add the rum. Allow the syrup to cool, then strain out the spices (if used).

Once the syrup is cooled, prepare the whipped cream. In the bowl of your stand mixer fitted with the whisk attachment, beat the whipping cream and confectioners' sugar on high until you have stiff peaks.

To assemble the babas, dip each baba in syrup until soaked through, then set top-side down on a cooling rack. Pipe or spoon a dollop of whipped cream onto each, and decorate with tiny chopped candied fruit. Serve immediately.

Bilberry Tropéziennes

Jagody Tropézienne

Every summer when the wild bilberry—jagody—season rolls around, a trend has developed among Polish bakeries to not just churn out the classic streusel or glaze-topped Jagodzianki (page 139), but also to load up just about any pastry you can imagine with the berries: stuffed French croissants, pavlovas, donuts, cheesecakes. This is my submission to the trend, a bilberry-topped tarte Tropézienne. A midcentury darling of the south of France, famously beloved by Brigitte Bardot, this dessert just happened to be invented by Polish pastry chef Alexandre Micka. Micka's original tarte Tropézienne had no fruit, just a simple cream flavored with orange blossom water, sandwiched between layers of brioche, but here we go a step further.

NOTE: Just as with the Jagodzianki (page 139), bilberries can be replaced by wild blueberries. They're very close cousins. In this recipe, frozen berries will work fine. This is best served immediately after assembling, but the individual components can be prepared in advance.

MAKES 12 to 14 tarts

DOUGH

1 batch Chałka Dough (page 98) or Challah Dough (page 100)

EGG WASH

1 egg and 2 Tbsp [30 g] whole milk, whisked until smooth

BILBERRY FILLING

1¾ cups [225 g] bilberries or wild blueberries (fresh or frozen)
3 Tbsp [40 g] sugar
1½ tsp cornstarch
2 tsp lemon juice
2 tsp lemon zest

CREAM FILLING

½ batch Stiff Budyń with Agar Agar (page 342)
8 oz [230 g] whipping cream
1 Tbsp sugar
2 tsp fleur d'oranger (optional)

TOPPING

¾ cup [150 g] pearl sugar

The day before you plan to make the Tropéziennes, prepare your chałka or challah dough according to the recipe on page 98 or page 100 and follow the instructions for a chilled overnight proof in the fridge. At the same time, prepare your budyń according to the recipe on page 342 and chill overnight.

The next day, when you're ready to bake, turn your dough out onto a lightly floured work surface, then use your bench knife to divide the dough into portions of about 2 oz [55 g]. Press each dough portion to degas, then form into a tight ball (see page 22). Allow the balls to rest smooth-side up, loosely covered with plastic wrap or a damp tea towel, for about 15 minutes. After the dough has rested, use a rolling pin to flatten each ball into a disk, about ¾ in [2 cm] thick. Arrange the disks evenly on two baking sheets lined with parchment paper, at least 1 in [2.5 cm] apart, then brush with egg wash. Allow to rest for 2½ hours, until light and puffed and a finger pressed into the dough springs back slowly.

While the buns rise, prepare the bilberry filling. In a small mixing bowl, mix the berries, sugar, cornstarch, lemon juice, and zest. Set aside for 1 hour. After the berries sit, they will be in a puddle of their own juice. Transfer the mixture to a small saucepan and bring to a low bubble over medium heat, stirring continually. Allow to simmer for 3 to 5 minutes until the juice visibly thickens but still runs. Remove from the heat and set aside to cool.

cont'd

Shortly before the dough has risen fully, preheat the oven to 350°F [180°C] with the convection setting turned on.

Brush each bun a second time with egg wash and sprinkle generously with pearl sugar. Bake for 20 minutes, or until the buns are golden brown. Remove from the oven and let the buns cool completely.

Once your buns are cool, you can wait until you're ready to serve them to assemble your tarts. When you're ready to serve, prepare the cream filling. In the bowl of your stand mixer fitted with the whisk attachment, whisk the budyń until smooth. While mixing on low speed, drizzle in the whipping cream and sugar. Add the fleur d'oranger (if using). Once incorporated, increase the speed to high and beat until you have a stiff whipped cream. This will take at least 5 minutes. Note that once the cream is finished, it can be stored in the fridge for up to a day, or you can assemble the Tropéziennes immediately.

Cut each bun in half like a hamburger bun. Use a spoon or a pastry bag with a fat round tip to spread or pipe a thick layer of cream on the bottom half of each bun. You can create a little depression in the cream with a spoon, or simply pipe a donut shape. Spoon blueberry filling into the middle of the cream, then top each bun with its upper half. Serve immediately.

Spiced Meat Rolls

Paszteciki z Mięsem

There's a city in the northwest of Poland, just over the border from Germany, called Szczecin that specializes in paszteciki z Mięsem, savory sausage roll–style filled buns, and when you live in Berlin, like I do, that's enough reason for a weekend trip. I've heard this voyage pooh-poohed by Polish friends who insist Szczecin is culturally just an extension of Germany—after all, it fell within the German border before the war. Though I'm guessing the residents of Szczecin would disagree, and so would the paszteciki, which never appear on the German side. This might be one of those rare cases of a hard culinary border. In Szczecin, you can find just about every kind of paszteciki imaginable, filled with cabbage, potatoes, buckwheat, cheese, and meat. The city has its own style of deep-fried paszteciki, but more common around Poland is this baked version stuffed with spiced meat.

MAKES 21 paszteciki

DOUGH

1 batch Chałka Dough (page 98) or Challah Dough (page 100)

FILLING

¾ cup plus 1 Tbsp [200 g] kefir, yogurt, or buttermilk

⅓ cup plus 2 Tbsp [50 g] dry bread crumbs

3 Tbsp [40 g] olive oil

3 onions, minced

5 garlic cloves, minced

2 tsp kosher or sea salt

2 tsp ground black pepper

⅛ tsp ground cinnamon

⅛ tsp ground nutmeg

1 Tbsp nigella seeds

1 tsp garlic powder

1 lb [500 g] ground meat

1 egg, beaten

3 Tbsp [8 g] chopped parsley

EGG WASH

1 egg and 3 Tbsp [45 g] whole milk, whisked until smooth

TOPPING

Flaky sea salt

Coarsely ground black pepper

FOR SERVING

Full-fat sour cream

Prepare your chałka or challah dough according to the recipe on page 98 or page 100 and allow to rise either overnight in the fridge or at room temperature for about an hour.

While the dough rises, prepare the filling. In a medium mixing bowl, mix the kefir and bread crumbs and allow to soak for about 10 minutes. Meanwhile, heat the olive oil in a small skillet over medium heat, then sauté the onions, garlic, and salt until translucent. Add the pepper, cinnamon, nutmeg, nigella seeds, and garlic powder, and sauté for another couple of minutes before removing from the heat. In a large mixing bowl, mix together the meat with the sautéed onion mixture, the egg, the bread crumb mixture, and the parsley until well-mixed. Use your hands if it's easier.

Once the dough is fully risen, shape the paszteciki. Turn it out onto a lightly floured work surface and roll it into a 14 x 18 in [35.5 x 46 cm] rectangle. Fold in each long side by one third to make guide lines to divide the dough into three long rectangles,

cont'd

then cut along the guidelines with a flat knife or a pizza cutter. Spoon an even line of filling down the center of a rectangle the long way.

Brush one long side of the rectangle with water—this will act as glue to seal and hold the roll together—then fold the un-brushed side over the filling to meet the brushed side. Use a fork or your fingers to press the dough together, then roll the filled part of the roll over this seam to hide it. Repeat for the other two rolls. Cut each tube into seven rolls, making twenty-one rolls total. (You can also make these smaller and have more bite-sized rolls for parties.) Line two baking sheets with parchment paper and arrange the paszteciki evenly at least 1 in [2.5 cm] apart. Brush with egg wash and set aside to rise for 2 to 2½ hours, until the dough is light and puffed and a finger pressed into the dough springs back slowly.

Shortly before the dough has risen, preheat the oven to 350°F [180°C] with the convection setting turned on. Brush each bun a second time with egg wash, then sprinkle with a little flaky salt and pepper. Bake for 25 to 30 minutes, or until golden brown.

Serve immediately with sour cream, or store airtight in the fridge for up to 3 days, warming in a toaster oven before serving.

Sauerkraut and Mushroom Rolls

Paszteciki z Kapustą i Grzybami

One of the tastiest Polish culinary combinations is kapustą z grzybami—cabbage and mushrooms. It's a common savory filling in pierogies and stews or just enjoyed on its own. Here it makes its way into paszteciki. The use of sauerkraut gives these a characteristic and craveable salty-sour hit, while the mushrooms add an earthy umami. I like to make these as a meat-free party snack or starter, with a little sour cream for dipping.

NOTE: The dough and filling for this recipe can be made the night before the day you wish to bake and chilled in the fridge, or it can be prepared directly.

MAKES 24 paszteciki

DOUGH

1 batch Chałka Dough (page 98) or Challah Dough (page 100)

FILLING

2 Tbsp [30 g] olive oil

1 large shallot, minced

1 lb [455 g] mixed mushrooms, finely diced (about 5 cups)

1 Tbsp kosher salt

2 tsp coarsely ground black pepper

12 oz [340 g] sauerkraut, drained and finely chopped (about 3 cups)

1 Tbsp all-purpose flour

EGG WASH

1 egg and 1 egg yolk, whisked until smooth

TOPPING

Flaky sea salt

Caraway seeds

Prepare your chałka or challah dough according to the recipe on page 98 or page 100 and allow to rise either overnight in the fridge or at room temperature for about an hour. While the dough rises, prepare the filling. In a large skillet, bring the olive oil to a sizzle over medium heat. Sauté the shallots until translucent and beginning to brown, then add the mushrooms. Add the salt and pepper and sauté the mixture, stirring as needed, until the mushrooms have lost most of their water and have begun to brown. Add the sauerkraut and flour and mix together. Continue to cook for another couple minutes, then remove from the heat and allow to cool.

Once the dough is fully risen, shape the paszteciki. Turn it out onto a lightly floured work surface and roll it into a 14 x 18 in [35.5 x 46 cm] rectangle. Fold in each long side by one third to make guide lines to divide the dough into three long rectangles, then cut along the guide lines with a flat knife or a pizza cutter.

Spoon an even line of filling down the center of a rectangle the long way. Brush one long side of the rectangle with water—this will act as glue to seal and hold the roll together—then fold the un-brushed side over the filling to meet the brushed side. Use a fork or your fingers to press the dough together, then roll the filled part of the roll over this seam to hide it. Repeat for the other two rolls.

cont'd

Use a flat-edge knife or bench knife to press straight down to cut eight even paszteciki from each roll. Set them on two baking sheets lined with parchment paper, twelve on each. Brush with egg wash, then set aside to rise for 2 to 2½ hours, until light and puffed and a finger pressed into the dough springs back slowly.

Shortly before the paszteciki have finished rising, preheat the oven to 350°F [180°C] with the convection setting turned on. Before baking, brush the paszteciki with egg wash a second time and sprinkle with flaky sea salt and caraway seeds. Bake for about 20 minutes, or until golden brown.

Serve immediately, or store airtight in the fridge for up to 3 days, warming in a toaster oven before serving.

Chanterelle and Smoky Cheese Danishes

Danisze z Kurkami i Oscypkiem

From the first days of autumn, the forest-lined roads that cross Poland become dense with folding beach chairs; baskets of yellow, orange, and brown mushrooms; and the old men and women who foraged them earlier that morning. There are porcinis and saffron milk caps and simple boulotes, but the gold standard is the chanterelle—*kurki* in Polish. At once meaty, nutty, and buttery, it's easily the most sought-after wild mushroom, a veritable woodland jackpot. During the foraging season, contemporary bakeries have started showcasing wild mushrooms on classic drożdżowe or puff pastry bases. Here, I combine chanterelles with a smoked sheep's cheese, oscypek, typical of the Tatra mountains. You can substitute smoked Gouda, cheddar, or provolone.

NOTES: If chanterelles are not available, brown button mushrooms, morels, and porcinis will all work. If you don't want to make the labor-intensive półfrancuskie dough, this filling works wonderfully with the challah and chałka dough style of savory Danishes (page 130).

MAKES 10 Danishes

DOUGH

1 batch Półfrancuskie Dough (page 105)

EGG WASH

1 egg and 3 Tbsp [45 g] whole milk, whisked until smooth

SAUCE

3½ Tbsp [50 g] unsalted butter
6 Tbsp [50 g] all-purpose flour
2 cups plus 2 Tbsp [500 g] whole milk
1 tsp kosher salt
2 tsp ground black pepper
⅔ cup [50 g] shredded smoky cheese

FILLING

3 Tbsp [40 g] unsalted butter
2 Tbsp [30 g] olive oil
5 garlic cloves, roughly chopped
4 to 5 cups [500 g] whole chanterelles, washed, dried, and roughly chopped if very large
2 to 3 tsp kosher salt
Ground black pepper

TOPPING

1 handful flat-leaf parsley, finely chopped
⅔ cup [50 g] finely grated smoky cheese

Prepare the base dough for the półfrancuskie dough according to the recipe on page 105 and allow to chill overnight in the fridge. The next morning, laminate the półfrancuskie dough (page 106). Chill for at least an hour, then get to work shaping your Danishes.

On a lightly floured work surface, roll out your dough to a 17 in [43 cm] square with a thickness of about ⅛ in [3 mm]. As you roll, run your hands under the dough from time to time to allow the dough to contract and relax, then continue rolling. Once the rectangle is the correct size and you can run your hands under it without it contracting, use a pizza wheel or a flat knife to trim a little less than ½ in [1 cm] from each side of the rectangle. This will make tidy edges for the next step. Use a ruler to measure out 1½ in [4 cm] intervals along two opposite sides of the dough, then use the ruler as a guide to join the marks to cut out about ten long strips.

cont'd

Place one hand on each end of a strip and roll the ends in opposite directions to twist up the strip like a rope. Then, starting from one end, roll the rope up in a loose spiral and place on a baking sheet lined with parchment paper. Shape the rest of the Danishes, placing each about 2 in [5 cm] apart on two baking sheets lined with parchment paper. Brush with egg wash, then set aside to rise for 2½ hours at room temperature, until light and puffed and a finger pressed into the dough springs back slowly.

While the Danishes are rising, make the sauce. In a medium saucepan on low heat, melt the butter. Add the flour and whisk until it's a thick, even paste. Continue whisking for a couple minutes until the paste starts to bubble. Continuing to whisk, add the milk one third at a time. Once the milk is incorporated and there are no chunks of the butter paste, add salt and pepper and increase the heat to medium. Continue whisking for about 5 minutes as the mixture starts to simmer and thicken. When the sauce is thickened, remove from the heat and stir in the shredded cheese. Set aside.

Next, make the filling. Heat the butter and olive oil in a large skillet over medium-high heat until a piece of garlic sizzles when tossed in. Put in all the garlic and sauté for a few minutes until starting to brown, then add all the mushrooms, salt, and pepper and give it a stir. Let the mushrooms cook until all the water has come out and then mostly evaporated, stirring occasionally. Stir the cooked mushrooms into the sauce, and then cover and set aside until ready to use.

About a half hour before the pastry has fully risen, preheat the oven to 350°F [180°C] with the convection setting turned on. Once the pastry has fully risen, give it one more egg wash, then scoop a generous portion of the mushroom filling onto the center of each. Bake for about 20 minutes, or until the pastry is golden brown. Finish with a generous sprinkle of parsley and grated cheese.

Serve hot or reheat in the oven later the same day, holding off the parsley and cheese topping until ready to serve.

Loaded Potato Knishes

Knysze Ziemniaczane

In 1974, the newly released book of the great Yiddish novelist and master of the short story Isaac Bashevis Singer was reviewed by one Alan Lelchuk. Bashevis Singer, a rabbi's son raised in Warsaw, had a particular knack for describing and memorializing pre-war Poland—from bakers' daughters flirting over yeasty baskets of rolls, to the smells and sounds, both foul and sensual, of Krochmalna Street, the chaotic heart of the Jewish ghetto, to the smoke- and schmalz-filled salons where artists and bundists met to argue over their vibrant, difficult world. The book Mr. Lelchuk reviewed was *Shosha*, a love story set on the eve of the German invasion of Warsaw. In his search to properly convey his admiration of Mr. Singer's writing, to give a compliment to that uncanny ability to transport the reader into the heart of old Poland, Lelchuk says this:

"The aroma from potato knishes and chickpeas with beans is real."

And really, potato knishes—baked mashed potato dumplings with salty onions—permeate much of the diaspora of Polish Jews, appearing even as a sexual innuendo in midcentury Borscht-belt comedy and song. A popular New York City street food, it's imbued with comfort and nostalgia, perfect for party snacks or a picnic.

MAKES 18 medium knishes

DOUGH

3 cups [375 g] all-purpose flour
1 tsp double-acting baking powder
½ tsp kosher salt
⅓ cup [75 g] sunflower oil or any neutral oil
1 egg
½ cup plus 2 Tbsp [150 g] room-temperature water
1 tsp dark soy sauce or tamari

FILLING

3 lb 5 oz [1.5 kg] small to medium potatoes (waxy varieties work well here)
3 to 4 Tbsp [45 to 60 g] olive oil
3 or 4 medium yellow onions, halved and cut into thin strings (3 cups [325 g])
1 garlic clove, finely diced
1½ tsp kosher salt
2 tsp ground black pepper
2 tsp red wine vinegar or apple cider vinegar
14 oz [400 g] full-fat sour cream
1¾ cups [150 g] shredded cheddar cheese
¼ cup [10 g] chopped flat-leaf parsley

EGG WASH

1 egg, beaten

Begin by mixing the dough. In a medium mixing bowl, whisk together the flour, baking powder, and salt until combined. In the bowl of your stand mixer, whisk together the sunflower oil and egg to emulsify, then add the water and soy sauce and whisk until even. (The soy sauce will mimic the umami flavor of schmaltz.) Add the dry ingredients to the oil mixture, then, using the dough hook attachment, mix on low speed until just combined. Increase the speed to medium and mix for 10 minutes. The final dough will be quite loose and supple and slightly tacky. Coat your hands with a bit of oil to handle the dough and move it to a lightly oiled medium mixing bowl. Fold the dough under itself a few times to give it tension and form into a smoother ball shape, then cover airtight and let it rest in the fridge for 1 hour or up to a day.

While the dough rests, make the filling. Bring a large pot of salted water to a boil, then add your potatoes, whole. Boil until soft, then drain the water and run cold tap water over the potatoes until they're cool enough to handle. The skins should peel off easily with your hands or a small paring

cont'd

knife. In a large mixing bowl, give the potatoes a rough mash, and set aside.

In a medium skillet, heat the olive oil over medium-high heat until a piece of onion sizzles when thrown in the pan. Add the onions, garlic, salt, and pepper, and give a quick stir, coating the onions in oil and spices. Allow the onions to brown, stirring occasionally as needed. Once the onions are translucent and browned, add the vinegar and give them a quick stir, deglazing any bits stuck to the pan. As soon as the vinegar has evaporated, remove the pan from the heat and allow the onions to cool for about 15 minutes.

After the onions have cooled, add them to the mashed potatoes along with the sour cream, cheese, and parsley, and mix until combined. Preheat the oven to 350°F [180°C] with the convection setting turned on, then start shaping your knishes.

Remove the dough from the fridge and generously flour both your work surface and the dough. Roll the dough into a very thin square, running your hands occasionally under the dough to allow it to rest and contract before continuing to roll. If the dough rips a tiny bit, don't worry, it'll be fine. Once your square is about 23 in [58 cm] long on each side, use a flat knife or pizza cutter to trim a little less than ½ in [1 cm] from each side of the square to create tidy ends and divide it into three long rectangles. Divide the filling evenly between each rectangle, laying it down the middle of each rectangle, forming it into a fat sausage of filling, leaving 1 or 2 in [2.5 to 5 cm] of dough unfilled at the end of each rectangle. Then, like you're folding a burrito, fold up the short uncovered ends of the dough, cover the filling on each dough rectangle, and fold each long side of dough up and over the filling, overlapping by about 1 inch [2.5 cm]. Turn the roll seam-side down on your work surface, then slice the roll at eight even intervals—these are your knishes. Pick up a knish and, on one of the open sides, pinch together the dough to seal—this is your bottom. Place it sealed-side down on a baking sheet lined with parchment paper, about 1 in [2.5 cm] apart, then press down a bit and shape into a fat round with a little open window of potato filling. Repeat for the rest of the knishes, making two pans of nine. Brush with egg wash, then bake for 30 minutes, or until golden brown.

Serve hot or cold with an extra helping of sour cream or some spicy mustard. Any extra knishes can be refrigerated for up to 4 days or frozen for up to 2 months and reheated in a warm oven.

Dżenneta's Tatar Goose and Pumpkin Turnovers

Tatarskie Bielasze

Dżenneta Bogdanowicz lives in the tiny village of Kruszyniany in Podlasie, far western Poland, where tidy wooden houses and a modest, green-painted wooden mosque are surrounded by the ancient Białowieża Forest, a mythical place roamed by moose, wolves, and Europe's last wild bison who cross back and forth across the Belarusian border. Kruszyniany is home to a community of Poland's Tatars, and it's there that Dżenneta runs her restaurant, Tatarska Jurta, with the aim of sharing and preserving the distinct Polish Tatar cuisine on which she was raised. The Tatar minority in Poland has been around for about six hundred years, since the early fifteenth century when mercenary soldiers came from Crimea to help the Polish Lithuanian Union, the alliance of the Kingdom of Poland and the Grand Duchy of Lithuania, in the fight against the Teutonic Germans. When the kingdom ran out of cash to pay the Tatars for their services, they instead offered land as payment and the Tatars stayed. There are just shy of two thousand Polish Tatars today, and Dżenneta's community is about five hundred strong, but, though small, the food culture is one of the brightest in Poland, with a strong tradition of savory meat baking.

While filling your plate with steamed dumplings and sour cream at Tatarska Jurta, Dżenneta will tell you that Tatar cooking takes its influences from the entirety of Asia. From Turkey and the Middle East come the labor-intensive borek-style goose-stuffed pierekaczewnik and sweet diamond-shaped halwa. From Ukraine and Russia come the fried czebureki meat patties; from Uzbekistan and Kyrgistan come manty, the cheese or meat steamed dumplings; and from India, the flaky, spiced meat–filled samsa, or samosa. All this is mixed with the more Polish-style fermented vegetable salads and quick vinegar pickles. Tatar foods are spiced primarily with black pepper, hot paprika, onions, and nigella seeds. It's a very meat-heavy cuisine, starring beef, veal, or poultry like goose, duck, and turkey; the Tatars are Muslim, so the Polish tendency toward pork is out of the question.

Goose and pumpkin, as is used here, is a favorite traditional flavor combination in Tatar cooking, but for this recipe, the goose can be swapped out for turkey, duck, or ground beef. These bielasze are made from a classic yeast dough, and the filling requires no pre-cooking, as it steams inside the dumpling during baking. The end result is a gorgeously crispy then juicy bite. The bielasz can be made as one long roll, or as individual dumplings shaped into half-moons or circles. Here we make the small half-moons, which Dżenneta calls "baby bielasze."

NOTE: This yeasted dough does not have a final proof after shaping, which creates the unique crunch.

MAKES 18 bielasze

cont'd

DOUGH

1 batch Chałka Dough (page 98)

FILLING

3 cups [350 g] finely diced pumpkin (I prefer hokkaido or butternut squash for a richer, slightly sweet flavor)

1 medium yellow onion, finely diced (⅔ cup [100 g])

12½ oz [355 g] finely diced goose, turkey, or duck meat, or ground beef

1½ tsp kosher salt

1 tsp hot paprika

1 tsp ground black pepper

EGG WASH

1 egg, beaten

TOPPING

Nigella seeds, sesame seeds, and/or sunflower seeds

Prepare your chałka dough according to the recipe on page 98, through the bulk proof. If making these for a party, I like to prepare the dough a day in advance and let it rise and chill in the fridge until I'm ready to use it.

Shortly before you're ready to bake, preheat the oven to 350°F [180°C] with the convection setting turned on. In a medium mixing bowl, mix together the pumpkin, onion, meat, salt, paprika, and pepper, making sure everything is evenly coated in spices.

Turn your dough out onto an unfloured work surface and divide it into eighteen portions of just under 2 oz [50 g] each. Flatten each portion of dough to degas and then shape into a tight ball (see page 22). Cover loosely with a damp tea towel or a piece of plastic wrap, then let them rest smooth-side up for 10 minutes to relax.

Once the dough has rested, use a rolling pin to roll a ball of dough into a large flat circle, about 5 in [13 cm] across. I don't find the need to flour the dough, but if yours is sticking a little bit, use a tiny bit to make it easier. Don't use too much or you'll find it difficult to seal the dumplings. Place a few tablespoons of the filling on one half of the circle, leaving about a ½ in [1 cm] border of dough. Fold the unfilled half of the dough over the filled half to create a half-moon shape, then press to seal the edges. To seal the edges even better, fold and press the bottom side of the edge over the top bit by bit to create a twisted or pleated edge. This helps prevent the steam from popping open your dumplings while baking. Place the shaped dumpling on a baking sheet lined with parchment paper and repeat for the rest of the dumplings, spacing them about 1 in [2.5 cm] apart. This recipe makes two sheet pans of dumplings. Brush the tops with egg wash, then sprinkle with seeds, and bake for 30 minutes, until golden brown and crispy. It's fine to let one pan rest while the other bakes. They might just be a little fluffier in texture.

These are best served hot from the oven or at room temperature the same day, but can be frozen for up to 2 months and reheated in a warm oven.

/3

CIASTKA: SLAB CAKES, LAYER CAKES & BUNDTS

There's a Polish expression, from which this book gets its name, about the country's baking tradition and especially about its cake: *Dobre dobre, nie za słodkie—good, good, not too sweet.* It's a bit tongue-in-cheek and self-aware, but it's true. The Polish preference in cakes is for the gently sweet, not the overwhelmingly so. My cousin Deborah remembers her grandmother's coffee cake fondly: "You know, it really wasn't very sweet. It's unlike the American cakes we would eat." This doesn't mean Polish cake culture is tepid—it's the opposite. It's a bakery tradition heavy on both everyday snacking cakes and more elaborate cream and sponge cakes loaded with decorative puddings, fruits, and glazes. Even a small cukiernia—a sweet-shop bakery—can regularly have cases loaded with ten or twenty different kinds of cake to cater to the country's afternoon tea and snack habit.

The most classic Polish cakes are large slabs, baked in rectangular molds and piled with seasonal fruit and kruszonka (streusel). As commonly baked at home as in coffee shops and bakeries, these simple cakes let the jammy sweet and sour of the baked fruit and sugary streusel star. The bases of these cakes are massively varied, from thin kruche or short dough, to softer sour cream- or yogurt-based coffee cake batter, to fluffy yeast dough. Beyond the slab cakes are the Bundts, made with moist and crumbly starch- and sour cream–enriched batter or a light, panettone-style brioche dough. So many of the cakes you find in classic East Coast American coffee shops—crumb cake, marble cake, coffee cake—have roots in these Polish cakes.

In addition to the everyday slab and Bundt cakes are the more dazzling layer cakes and roulades. Often inventions of the post-war era and having taken on a mist of nostalgia and kitsch, these cakes tend to have the worst reputation, as those resplendent bakery cases are commonly filled with factory-made versions. Their layers of dry sponges, processed jams, and artificial creams are a product of the shortages and food ethics of the communist era. Yet, it's these very cakes that contemporary, artisan bakeries—from Warsaw to Wrocław—are playing with the most, updating them to reflect changing food values in a return to the quality of both the bakery and the home kitchen.

This chapter has a bit of both the old world and the new wave, with delicious results.

SHORTCRUST DOUGH

Ciasto Kruche

This classic short dough makes a cookie-like crust for all kinds of slab cakes such as szarlotka and sernik as well as simple cookies and rugelach variations. What makes it different from other short doughs is that the Polish version tends to use egg yolks in addition to or instead of whole eggs for extra fat and crumb, as well as a bit of sour cream.

NOTE: Occasionally a recipe will call for only a half batch of kruche dough. In this case, you can wrap the second half airtight and store frozen for up to 3 months. Thaw overnight in the fridge, then use.

MAKES about 2¼ lb [1 kg] of dough

1 Tbsp [15 g] full-fat sour cream
1 egg
1 egg yolk
1 tsp vanilla extract
4 cups [500 g] all-purpose flour
1 tsp [6 g] kosher salt
1 cup plus 5 Tbsp [300 g] cold unsalted butter, cubed
1½ cups [180 g] confectioners' sugar, sifted

In a small mixing bowl, whisk together the sour cream, egg, egg yolk, and vanilla until smooth and no streaks of sour cream remain.

In the bowl of your stand mixer fitted with the paddle attachment, mix the flour and salt together on low speed just to combine, then add the butter and mix until sandy and no visible chunks remain. Continuing to mix on low speed, add the sugar, and mix until incorporated. Pour in the egg mixture in a slow stream and continue to mix until the dough comes together into a solid mass, 1 to 2 minutes. Remove the dough from the bowl, form it into a thick disk, and wrap airtight. Chill for 1 hour or up to a week before using. In the freezer, this will last for up to 3 months.

VARIATION: CHOCOLATE SHORTCRUST DOUGH
Replace 50 grams of flour with 50 grams of cocoa powder (so in total: 3½ cups plus 1 heaping tablespoon [450 g] all-purpose flour and ½ cup plus 1 heaping tablespoon [50 g] cocoa powder). Mix in the cocoa powder with the flour and salt. This chocolate dough adds a lot of extra chocolate flavor and a nice color contrast. Use this dough anywhere you'd use plain kruche dough.

RISEN SHORTCRUST DOUGH

Ciasto Półkruche

Półkruche or "half" kruche dough is a lighter short dough than the basic kruche dough thanks to the addition of baking powder. The resulting texture is more crumbly, halfway between a cake and a cookie. Several Polish cakes use this dough as a base or shredded into a streusel-like crumb topping.

MAKES about 2¼ lb [1 kg] of dough

1 Tbsp [15 g] full-fat sour cream
1 egg
1 egg yolk
1 tsp vanilla extract
4 cups [500 g] all-purpose flour
2 tsp [6 g] fleur de sel or 1 tsp kosher salt
1½ tsp double-acting baking powder
1 cup plus 5 Tbsp [300 g] cold unsalted butter, cubed
1½ cups [180 g] confectioners' sugar, sifted

In a small mixing bowl, whisk together the sour cream, egg, egg yolk, and vanilla until smooth and no streaks of sour cream remain.

In the bowl of your stand mixer fitted with the paddle attachment, mix the flour, salt, and baking powder on low speed until homogenous. Add the butter and mix until the dough is sandy and no visible chunks remain. Add the sugar and mix until incorporated. Pour in the egg mixture in a slow stream and continue to mix on low speed until the dough comes together into a solid mass, 1 to 2 minutes. Remove the dough from the bowl, form it into a thick disk, and wrap airtight. Chill for 1 hour or up to a week before using. In the freezer, this will last for up to 3 months. To use, simply defrost in the refrigerator overnight.

VARIATION: RISEN CHOCOLATE SHORTCRUST DOUGH

Replace 50 grams of flour with 50 grams of cocoa powder (so in total: 3½ cups plus 1 heaping tablespoon [450 g] all-purpose flour and ½ cup plus 1 heaping tablespoon [50 g] cocoa powder). Mix in the cocoa powder with the flour and salt. This chocolate dough adds a lot of extra chocolate flavor and a nice color contrast. Use this dough anywhere you'd use plain półkruche dough, such as on the base of Pinched Cake (Pleśniak, page 221) or any sernik (cheesecake).

Bundt Cake

Babka Piaskowa

Here, we make the world's most perfect Bundt cake. Bundt is typical not just in Poland but around Eastern and Central Europe. Soft, moist, and crumbly, Bundt babka is a Polish Easter staple and forms the basis of many variations on coffee and streusel cakes. But I'm burying the lede because I'd hate to put you off this. *Piaskowa* means sandy—a name that reflects its crumbly texture. Don't worry, no one's eating sand, it's just bad marketing. The inclusion of cornstarch and sour cream make this a soft and moist cake with exactly the right coffee-cake heft while being just a bit airier than a pound cake. This dreamy cake can be adapted to any flavor profile you like—drizzle with Cointreau, zest it up with lemon and poppy seed, mix in fruits. But try it first just as it is—with a sprinkle of confectioners' sugar and maybe a dollop of sour cream.

MAKES 1 Bundt cake

FOR THE PAN

1 tsp unsalted butter
½ cup [70 g] dry bread crumbs

BATTER

6 eggs
2 egg yolks
1 tsp vanilla extract
7 oz [200 g] full-fat sour cream
2⅓ cups plus 1 Tbsp [300 g] all-purpose flour
½ cup plus 1 Tbsp [100 g] cornstarch
1 tsp double-acting baking powder
1 tsp baking soda
1 tsp kosher salt
1½ cups [350 g] unsalted butter, cubed and at room temperature
2 cups [400 g] granulated sugar

FOR SERVING

Confectioners' sugar, for dusting

Preheat the oven to 350°F [180°C] with the convection setting turned on. Butter a Bundt pan, coat it in the bread crumbs, and set aside. This creates a nice nonstick exterior without the visible white spots you can get from flouring a pan.

Begin by making the batter. In a small mixing bowl, whisk together the eggs, egg yolks, vanilla, and sour cream until smooth, then set aside.

In the bowl of your stand mixer fitted with the paddle attachment, mix the flour, cornstarch, baking powder, baking soda, and salt on low speed until combined. Add the butter and allow it to incorporate into the flour, increasing the speed to medium and mixing until you have a thick and fluffy batter, 2 to 3 minutes. Reduce the speed to low and add the sugar, mixing until just incorporated, about a minute. Continuing to mix on low, add the egg mixture one third at a time, beating briefly between incorporations. Once all the egg mixture is incorporated, run a spatula along the bottom of the bowl to check for unmixed bits, then beat for another minute on medium speed, until any final bits are incorporated and the batter is smooth and fluffy.

Pour the batter into the Bundt pan and bake for 45 minutes, or until a cake tester comes out clean. Allow to cool before inverting the babka onto a serving plate. Sprinkle with confectioners' sugar, then serve or store airtight at room temperature for up to a week.

This can be stored frozen for up to 3 months and thawed at room temperature.

Marble Cake

Ciasto Marmurkowe

There isn't so much to say about marble cake. While you'll find it in just about every Polish cake shop, this simple chocolate-and-vanilla cake isn't truly Polish—it's a classic cake that's popular the world over whose roots are likely in the Austro-Hungarian baking tradition. So, here's a digression: In the 1980s, the children's book author Carol Chapman wrote a story called *The Tale of Meshka the Kvetch*, illustrated by Arnold Lobel. Meshka is an old woman who lives in a Polish shtetl. Meshka has a tendency toward complaining—kvetching—until one fated day she wakes up and all the things that she complains about start coming true. Her feet hurt like two melons? They turn into melons. Her son is so lazy he sits in his bed reading like a bump on a pickle? He turns into a pickle. Only by learning to be grateful and not complain does Meshka's curse reverse itself. Now, the little chocolate and vanilla cat you see in the picture—that's Meshka too. She's named after Meshka the Kvetch. And she sits around so lazy all day like a loaf of marble cake, we think she might just turn into one.

NOTE: This recipe fits a large 9 x 5 in [23 x 13 cm] loaf pan or a large Bundt pan. If you want to make a smaller loaf, just cut the recipe in half and make sure you leave 1 in [2.5 cm] between the batter and the top of the pan.

MAKES one 9 x 5 in [23 x 13 cm] loaf or one large Bundt

4 eggs
1 egg yolk
5⅓ oz [150 g] full-fat sour cream
1 tsp vanilla extract
1¾ cups plus 1 Tbsp [225 g] all-purpose flour
⅓ cup plus 1 Tbsp [75 g] cornstarch or potato starch
¾ tsp double-acting baking powder
¾ tsp baking soda
1 tsp kosher salt
1 cup plus 5 Tbsp [300 g] unsalted butter, at room temperature
1½ cups [300 g] sugar
⅓ cup [25 g] cocoa powder
3 to 3½ Tbsp [45 to 50 g] boiling water
1½ Tbsp [20 g] cold unsalted butter, cut into small batons

Preheat the oven to 350°F [180°C] with the convection setting turned on. Line the bottom of a 9 x 5 in [23 x 13 cm] loaf pan with parchment paper but leave the sides unlined. This will help the cake cling to the sides and form a nice domed top.

Begin by making the batter. Whisk together the eggs, egg yolk, sour cream, and vanilla in a medium mixing bowl until smooth, then set aside.

In the bowl of your stand mixer fitted with the paddle attachment, mix the flour, cornstarch, baking powder, baking soda, and salt on low speed until even. Add the butter and allow it to incorporate into the flour, increasing the speed to medium and mixing until you have a thick and fluffy batter, 2 to 3 minutes. Turn the speed to low and add the sugar, mixing until just incorporated, about 1 minute. Add the egg mixture one third at a time, beating briefly

cont'd

on low speed between incorporations. Once all the egg mixture is incorporated, run a spatula along the bottom of the bowl to check for unmixed bits, then beat for another minute on medium speed, until you have a fluffy and smooth batter.

Mix together the cocoa powder and boiling water in a medium mixing bowl until smooth, then add about 1¾ cups [340 g] of the batter and gently fold until the mixture is homogeneous.

To assemble the cake, layer the batter in the pan vanilla–chocolate–vanilla–chocolate–vanilla for a total of three alternating layers of vanilla and two of chocolate. At one end of the pan, insert a knife or chopstick in the batter almost to the bottom and squiggle the length of the pan to create the marbling effect. Finally, arrange the pieces of butter in a continuous line down the length of the top of the cake—this will help it to split exactly in the middle. Bake for about 45 minutes, or until a cake tester comes out clean. When the cake is completely cool, slide a knife around the edges to release it, then invert to remove it from the pan.

Serve immediately or store airtight at room temperature for up to a week. This can be stored frozen for up to 3 months and thawed at room temperature.

Szarlotka

Shortcrust Apple Cake

"In my house we never baked bread," Łukasz Szlapa, a humble Krakowiak aerospace engineer and hobbyist bread baker, told me. "But we did bake szarlotka. It's one of my first memories around food, the smell of baking apples, turning deep brown and caramelized in the szabaśnik, the ever-warm baking part of my grandmother's piec kaflowy, the enormous, old, tiled stove that kept the whole house warm in her Beskidy village just south of Kraków." There's almost no Polish family without a szarlotka recipe—a short-crust apple pie with either a crumble or a second layer of pastry and occasionally a meringue topping. After all, the autumnal climate and its wonderful glut of apples suits it. Here we keep things classic with a slightly sour apple filling, the sweetness coming from a thick layer of crumble on top. Bake it and think of a little house with a big, tiled stove in the middle of the forest.

NOTE: Łukasz recommends using the early ripening papierówka apples, also called paper apples or white transparent apples. Cortland, Granny Smith, or any other tart baking apple will work as well.

MAKES one 13 x 9 in [33 x 23 cm] cake (8 to 12 slices)

DOUGH
1 batch Półkruche Dough (page 191)

TOPPING
Double batch Streusel (Kruszonka, page 346)

FILLING
3 lb 5 oz [1.5 kg] apples, peeled, cored, and cut into 1 in [2.5 cm] cubes
¾ cup [150 g] sugar
Juice of 1 lemon

Prepare the półkruche dough and streusel according to the recipes on pages 191 and 346, then chill both for at least 1 hour.

While your dough and streusel chill, prepare the filling. In a large pot, toss together the apples, sugar, and lemon juice. Cover and simmer over low heat, stirring occasionally, for about 20 minutes, or until the apples have softened and half turned into sauce. Set aside to cool for about 30 minutes.

While the apple filling cools, preheat the oven to 350°F [180°C] with the convection setting turned on and line a 13 x 9 in [33 x 23 cm] baking dish with parchment paper.

To prepare the base of the szarlotka, roll out your dough on a lightly floured work surface into a rectangle about the size of the pan. Trim the edges to make a tidy rectangle, then gently lift the dough and place it in the pan. Press the dough to fit all the way to the edges, then prick it all over with a fork. Chill the dough for 20 minutes. Blind-bake for 15 minutes, or until it is no longer shiny, rather matte, and just beginning to turn golden brown.

Once the base is blind-baked, remove it from the oven. Pour in all the apple filling and top with the streusel. Return it to the oven and bake for another 35 to 40 minutes, until the streusel is golden brown and the filling bubbles.

Allow to cool completely, then slice in squares and serve as is or with a dollop of whipped cream. If you like a delicious hot mess, don't wait until it's cool, just dig in right away. Store the cooled cake airtight at room temperature for 2 to 3 days or refrigerated for up to 5 days.

NON-TRADITIONAL VARIATION:
Add 1 cup [120 g] slivered almonds in the streusel to give this an extra dimension of crunch and nuttiness.

Szarlotka II

Jewish Apple Pie

I didn't eat apple pie growing up—but I thought I did. After all, we made it in a pie plate. My mom kept me in the dark about this until I was in grade school. Then I learned the thing we called apple pie wasn't apple pie at all. It was szarlotka. How she managed to pull the wool over my eyes in New England, the heart of apple country, I'll never know. Either way, when I did finally try pie, it was a terrible disappointment compared to our szarlotka, which, unlike pie, is succulent and sweet with loads of soft and tart baked apples nestled in custardy cake. And really, this is more cake than pie, made in a pie plate or a springform pan spread with thick batter that leaks between the apples. It's a kind of Jewish apple cake, and it need make no apologies for not being pie, though I'll always think of it that way.

NOTE: In my home we always made this with vegetable shortening, but for the sake of flavor, this recipe switches the shortening out for butter.

MAKES one 9 in [23 cm] szarlotka

2 lb 3 oz [1 kg] tart and firm apples, such as Granny Smith, Braeburn, or Cortland (8 to 10 medium apples)

3 Tbsp [40 g] unsalted butter, at room temperature

2¼ cups [450 g] sugar

4 eggs, at room temperature

2 tsp vanilla extract

½ tsp kosher salt

2 cups [250 g] all-purpose flour

¾ tsp ground cinnamon

Line the base of a 9 in [23 cm] springform pan with parchment paper, then butter the sides and coat with sugar. Preheat the oven to 400°F [200°C] with the convection setting turned on.

Peel, core, and slice the apples into 1½ to 2 in [4 to 5 cm] chunks. Gently pile the apples into the pan, all the way to the top. No need to pack them tightly.

In the bowl of your stand mixer fitted with the paddle attachment, cream the butter and 2 cups [400 g] of the sugar on medium speed until fluffy. Continuing to mix, add the eggs one at a time, then increase the speed to medium-high. Beat for about 5 minutes, until the batter turns a pale yellow. Reduce the speed to low and add the vanilla and salt. Finally, add the flour and continue to mix on low speed until your batter is smooth. It will be thick but pourable.

Pour the batter over the top of the apples in the springform pan, covering the top entirely. Use a spatula to smooth the batter to the edges of the pan. If it doesn't seem like enough batter, don't worry! It will sink down among the apples as it bakes. In a small bowl, mix together the remaining sugar and cinnamon, then sprinkle evenly over the szarlotka. Bake the szarlotka for 15 minutes at 400°F [200°C], then lower the heat to 350°F [180°C] and continue to bake for another 45 to 55 minutes. The top will be a rich tan color and a knife inserted into the middle will come out clean but wet from the apples. If the top starts to get too dark, cover loosely with aluminum foil for the remainder of the bake. Remove from the oven and allow to cool completely before sliding a knife around the edge of the cake and undoing the springform sides.

Serve at room temperature with vanilla ice cream or store covered in the fridge for up to 5 days, serving cold or reheating in the oven.

Shortcrust and Fruit Snacking Tart

Kruche z Owocami

This is one of the essential cake styles in the Polish compendium of crust-fruit-streusel bakes. As the name suggests, this cake has a base of kruche—or shortcrust—dough. It can be made with just about any fruit that's in abundance during the season and finished off with a heavy hand of kruszonka. This recipe uses apricots for a bright orange, tangy bar cake, but I give options for two other seasonal fruit fillings: rhubarb and gooseberry. You can also use a double portion of the cherry or apple fillings on pages 334 and 336.

MAKES one 13 x 9 in [33 x 23 cm] cake (about 12 slices)

DOUGH

½ batch Kruche Dough (page 190), chilled

STREUSEL

1 batch Streusel (Kruszonka, page 346)

APRICOT FILLING

5 cups [780 g] diced pitted fresh apricots
⅔ cup [130 g] sugar
Juice of ½ lemon
1¼ Tbsp [13 g] cornstarch
1 tsp vanilla extract

FOR SERVING

Confectioners' sugar, for sprinkling

Prepare the kruche dough and streusel according to the recipes on pages 190 and 346, then chill both for 2 to 4 hours while you prepare the apricot filling.

In a medium mixing bowl, combine the apricots, sugar, and lemon juice and set aside to macerate for 2 to 4 hours.

Preheat the oven to 350°F [180°C] with the convection setting turned on. Line a 13 x 9 in [33 x 23 cm] baking dish with parchment paper.

On a lightly floured work surface, knead your cold dough a few times to make it a bit more supple so it doesn't crack while rolling. Roll the dough out into a rectangle about the size of the pan, then trim the edges to tidy. Gently lay the dough into the pan, pressing it out to fit perfectly. Prick all over with a fork, then chill for 20 minutes in the fridge.

Once chilled, blind-bake your crust for 15 to 20 minutes, until the surface is no longer shiny and is just starting to get golden. Remove from the oven but keep the oven at temperature.

While the crust bakes, make the filling. While the apricots were sitting in sugar and lemon juice, the sugar and acid will have sucked juice out of the fruit. Mix in the cornstarch until no lumps are visible. Pour the fruit and juice mixture into a medium saucepan and bring it to a simmer on medium-low heat, stirring to prevent sticking. Simmer for about 5 minutes, or until the juice thickens up into a loose gelatinous texture. Remove from the heat and stir in the vanilla.

cont'd

Pour the filling into the crust, top with a layer of streusel, and bake for about 25 minutes, until the filling bubbles and the streusel is golden brown. Cool fully before cutting to allow the fruit filling to set, then dust with confectioners' sugar and cut into squares.

Serve immediately or store airtight at room temperature for several days.

VARIATIONS:

RHUBARB FILLING

17½ oz [500 g] rhubarb, cubed
¾ cup [150 g] sugar
2 Tbsp [30 g] lemon juice
1½ Tbsp [13 g] cornstarch
1 tsp vanilla extract or seeds from ½ vanilla pod

GOOSEBERRY FILLING

17½ oz [500 g] gooseberries, gently crushed
¾ cup [150 g] sugar
2 Tbsp [30 g] lemon juice
1 tsp vanilla extract or seeds from ½ vanilla pod
1½ Tbsp [13 g] cornstarch

Follow the same steps to prepare these fillings as for the apricot filling.

Loaf Crumb Cake with Fruit

Piaskowe Ciasto z Owocami

This is an easy fruit crumb cake, thrown together in an hour. Similar to the crumb cakes you'd find in American bakeries or anywhere across central Europe, it's a great vehicle for any fresh seasonal fruit and berries, or frozen fruit in the winter. It's the kind of simple, moist, not-too-sweet snacking cake you can leave in your kitchen to cut in slices for morning coffees, afternoon teas, and after-dinner treats. Make in a loaf pan, or double the recipe for a 9 in [23 cm] square baking pan.

MAKES one 9 x 5 in [23 x 13 cm] loaf

BATTER

1⅓ cups [165 g] all-purpose flour

1½ tsp double-acting baking powder

½ tsp kosher salt

5 Tbsp [70 g] unsalted butter, at room temperature

⅔ cup [130 g] sugar

2 eggs, at room temperature

½ cup [120 g] thick, full-fat, Greek-style yogurt, or full-fat sour cream

1 tsp vanilla extract

TOPPING

2 cups [240 g] berries, cherries, or chopped stone fruits, washed and dried

1 Tbsp sugar

1 batch Streusel (Kruszonka, page 346)

½ cup [60 g] confectioners' sugar (optional)

Preheat the oven to 350°F [180°C] with the convection setting turned on. Line the bottom of your loaf pan with parchment paper and set aside. Leave the sides of the pan unlined. This will help the batter cling to them as it rises.

Begin by making the batter. Whisk together the flour, baking powder, and salt in a medium mixing bowl. Cream the butter and sugar in your stand mixer fitted with the paddle attachment. Add the eggs one at a time and mix on low speed. Scrape down the sides of the bowl, then add the yogurt and vanilla and mix until even. Add the dry ingredients and mix until you have a smooth batter, about 2 minutes.

Pour the batter into your prepared pan. There should still be a couple empty inches until the top of the pan. Bake for 25 to 30 minutes, until golden brown and a crust has formed but there's still a bit of wiggle to the cake. As quickly as possible, remove the cake from the oven and top with an even layer of the fruit, then sprinkle with the tablespoon of sugar, and finally add a layer of streusel. Return to the oven and bake for another 20 minutes, or until the streusel starts to turn golden and a cake tester comes out clean. Allow the cake to cool, then dust with confectioners' sugar (if using) and cut into slices.

Serve immediately or store airtight at room temperature for several days.

Lekach

Extra-Soft Earl Grey Honey Cake

There's a bit of a battle for the best dessert of Rosh Hashana, the autumnal Jewish new year. In keeping with the tradition of eating apples and honey to ensure a sweet year ahead, the two dueling cakes are apple cake and honey cake. Honey cake, or lekach, has similar origins to the honey-based Polish pierniki, or gingerbreads. When it's done right, this cake is soft, rich, and spicy. Unfortunately, it's mostly done wrong and so it rarely wins out against its rival, apple cake. But really, it can be the most extraordinarily tender loaf cake. I'm team lekach, and this is my recipe, drizzled with a honey and bergamot-y Earl Grey glaze. It will stay moist for a week and might just change hearts and minds.

MAKES one 9 x 5 in [23 x 13 cm] loaf cake (10 to 12 slices)

CAKE

1½ cups plus 2 Tbsp [200 g] all-purpose flour
1 cup [100 g] light rye flour
1 tsp baking soda
½ tsp double-acting baking powder
1 tsp ground cinnamon
½ tsp kosher salt
2 eggs
½ cup plus 1 Tbsp [135 g] strong brewed Earl Grey tea
½ cup plus 1 Tbsp [135 g] orange juice
1 tsp vanilla extract
½ cup plus 1½ Tbsp [135 g] sunflower oil
3½ Tbsp [75 g] honey
¾ cup [150 g] granulated sugar
¼ cup [50 g] light brown sugar
3 Tbsp [25 g] slivered almonds or unsalted shelled pumpkin seeds

GLAZE

¾ cup plus 1½ Tbsp [100 g] confectioners' sugar
1½ tsp honey
1½ tsp strong brewed Earl Grey tea

Preheat the oven to 350°F [180°C] with the convection setting turned on. Line the bottom of a loaf pan with parchment paper but leave the sides unlined. This will help the cake cling to the sides to form the nice domed top.

Begin by making the batter. In a medium mixing bowl, mix together the all-purpose flour, rye flour, baking soda, baking powder, cinnamon, and salt. In the bowl of your stand mixer fitted with the paddle attachment, beat together the eggs, tea, orange juice, vanilla, sunflower oil, honey, granulated sugar, and brown sugar on medium speed until smooth and emulsified, about 2 minutes. Add the dry ingredients one third at a time, scraping down the sides of the bowl between additions and incorporating each addition on low speed until just smooth and no dry pockets remain, being careful not to overmix.

Fill the loaf pan, being sure to leave about 1 inch [2.5 cm] of space from the top of the pan. Sprinkle with the almonds, then bake for about 45 minutes, or until a cake tester comes out clean. Allow to cool for about 30 minutes, then slide a butter knife around the sides of the pan to release the cake and turn it out onto a cooling rack.

To make the glaze, mix the confectioners' sugar, honey, and tea until smooth. When the cake is cool, pour or drizzle the glaze over the top. This is best done by setting the cake on a cooling rack over the sink, so drips go straight down the drain and don't pool around the sides of the cake.

Store in an airtight container at room temperature and serve all week. If you'd like to freeze this cake, hold off on the glaze and wrap airtight. It can keep for up to 3 months frozen, then thaw at room temperature and glaze for serving.

Hanna's Apple Cake

Hanna Geller is something of a professional balabusta. She's a London-born-and-based recipe developer, writer, and food educator, but of equal importance, she is in possession of what might be the most well-traveled apple cake recipe in the history of the twentieth century. Really, it's her grandmother Lisl's recipe, and to fully appreciate this cake, you have to hear her story.

It starts in Poland, as you might guess. If you look hard enough in the ruins of the Lublin ghetto, you can still find the partial storefront of Oma Lisl's family corset shop. It was there in Lublin that Lisl was born in 1920 and started her life, speaking Polish and Yiddish, and making frequent trips to Warsaw to visit the rest of the family. As was the case for so many Polish Jews, the good times didn't last long and over the course of the next twenty years, the family moved around almost nonstop, first for economic opportunities and then, after Kristallnacht in 1933, as refugees. The journey took them from Lublin to Vienna to Paris, and then in 1938, they caught one of the last boats out to Casablanca. From Morocco, the family sailed to Montevideo, Uruguay, where they would all work in a sausage factory for a year and a half before gaining entry to the United States and ending up in New York in 1941. Lisl's travels wouldn't end there. She met a young rabbi from Texas and moved there with him. Throughout all of this, the family kept their recipes, adapting cakes and kugels with the ingredients available in whatever country or region they landed.

Hanna describes Oma Lisl as a tiny, endearing woman, always in a housecoat, who never, ever sat down for a meal, instead hovering and serving, shoving food from one person's plate to another's. "She'd run after you with a banana. And there was always a cake and cookies on the counter. Never a whole of anything—the freezer was full of half cakes and single slices, waiting for an emergency. She once talked her way into a movie theater where my mother and father were on a date. They heard her calling out to them with a picnic basket full of food. Feeding people was her love language."

And so, after her granddaughter Hanna got married, Oma Lisl gave her this recipe for her first Rosh Hashana as host. The cake itself has a crunchy top of caramelized sugar and an almost sticky, moist interior that keeps its softness for days. Hanna has adapted Oma Lisl's recipe ever so slightly. Soft brown sugar and olive oil bring a more contemporary taste while keeping the original cake's wonderful texture.

MAKES one 9 in [23 cm] cake

14 oz [400 g] cored and peeled firm apples (4 to 5, such as Braeburn or Royal Gala)
1 Tbsp [15 g] lemon juice
1 cup [220 g] olive oil
1¼ cups [250 g] caster sugar
¼ cup [50 g] soft brown sugar
3 eggs
1 tsp vanilla extract
2½ cups [300 g] all-purpose flour
1 tsp baking soda
½ tsp double-acting baking powder
1½ tsp ground cinnamon
½ tsp kosher salt
Demerara sugar, for sprinkling

cont'd

Preheat the oven to 340°F [175°C]. Grease a 9 in [23 cm] springform pan or angel food cake pan and line the bottom with parchment paper.

Peel, core, and thinly slice the apples. Place in a medium mixing bowl and toss with the lemon juice (the acid in the lemon juice will prevent browning).

In the bowl of your stand mixer fitted with the paddle attachment, combine the olive oil, caster sugar, brown sugar, eggs, and vanilla and beat for 3 to 5 minutes, until thick and completely emulsified. Meanwhile, in a medium bowl, combine the flour, baking soda, baking powder, cinnamon, and salt and stir together. In your stand mixer, continuing to mix on low speed, add the dry mixture to the wet mixture until just mixed with no dry bits. (You can also do this part by hand with a rubber spatula to ensure you don't overmix.)

Once the batter is combined and thick and no dry pockets of flour remain, assemble your cake, pouring batter and layering apples in stages. Place half of the batter in the bottom of your pan, then cover with half of the apple slices. Cover this with the second half of the batter, then arrange the second half of the apple slices over the top in a pretty spiral. Sprinkle the top with demerara sugar and bake for 70 to 75 minutes, until the cake is firm to the touch and a tester comes out clean. Cool completely before sliding a butter knife around the edge of the springform pan, then releasing it and slicing.

This cake is best the second day and can last up to 5 days at room temperature sealed airtight.

Chocolate and Whipped Cream Warsaw Cake

Wuzetka

Wuzetka is a double-tiered midcentury creation named after, of all things, the WZ (Wschód-Zachód, or East-West) highway that runs through Warsaw. The highway was built shortly after the war and, as legend has it, a cukiernia along the new route invented the cake. As such, wuzetka is a signature Warsaw bake but also widespread throughout the country. It's a chocolate sponge filled with a layer of jam and cream, soaked in alcohol, and topped with a rich ganache. Since its inception this cake has remained popular, and today's new wave of pastry chefs have upped the softness of the sponge and ditched the old-school, artificial gelatin-based cream fillings in favor of whipped mascarpones and sour creams and have swapped industrial jams for varieties of thick homemade compotes. Notable contemporary versions include the wuzetka with gushy cherry compote at Cukiernia Kukułka on Warsaw's Mokotowska Street, and the cherry and fresh blackberry wuzetka loaf at the now-closed Wuzet Cukiernia in Wrocław. Here I use whipped sour cream and blackberry jam for a light tang to balance the rich chocolate sponge, which is soft enough to skip the liqueur soak if you prefer to keep it light.

MAKES one 13 x 9 in [33 x 23 cm] cake (8 to 12 slices)

CAKE

2⅓ cups plus 1 Tbsp [300 g] all-purpose flour
¾ cup plus 2 Tbsp [70 g] cocoa powder
1 tsp double-acting baking powder
1 tsp baking soda
1 tsp kosher salt
2 eggs
1¾ cups [360 g] caster sugar
⅔ cup [150 g] sunflower oil
½ cup plus 2 Tbsp [150 g] brewed coffee, cooled
½ cup plus 2 Tbsp [150 g] water
2 tsp vanilla extract
7 oz [200 g] full-fat sour cream

FILLING

17½ oz [500 g] whipping cream, cold
1 cup [120 g] confectioners' sugar
1 tsp vanilla extract
17½ oz [500 g] mascarpone or full-fat sour cream, cold
½ cup [120 g] cherry liqueur, cherry vodka, rum, or cherry juice (optional)
¾ cup [250 g] black cherry jam

GANACHE

7 oz [200 g] bittersweet chocolate, finely chopped, or chocolate chips
2½ Tbsp [35 g] unsalted butter
7 oz [200 g] heavy cream

TOPPING

8 to 12 fresh or maraschino cherries

Preheat the oven to 350°F [180°C] with the convection setting turned on. Grease a 13 x 9 in [33 x 23 cm] baking dish, then line the bottom with parchment paper and flour the sides.

Begin by making the batter. Whisk together the flour, cocoa powder, baking powder, baking soda, and salt in a medium bowl. In the bowl of your stand mixer fitted with the paddle attachment, beat the eggs and sugar on medium-high speed until light and fluffy, about 5 minutes. Turn the speed to low and add the sunflower oil in a thin drizzle, then increase the speed to medium-high and beat for another couple minutes. Lower the speed again and

cont'd

add the coffee, water, and vanilla until just mixed. Finally, on low speed, add the dry ingredients and sour cream in stages, alternating one-third portions until fully mixed. Once no lumps of flour or sour cream are visible, pour the batter into the pan. Bake for about 30 minutes, or until a cake tester comes out clean. Allow the cake to cool, then slide a knife around the edges and invert the pan onto a tray to release the cake. Chill the cake in the freezer for 1 hour to stiffen but not freeze fully. This will make it easier to cut into two halves. Meanwhile, chill the (clean) bowl of your stand mixer and the whisk attachment in the fridge or freezer.

Shortly before the cake is fully chilled, make the filling. In the chilled bowl of your stand mixer fitted with the whisk attachment, whip the cream, confectioners' sugar, and vanilla on medium-high speed until stiff. Lower the speed and add the mascarpone, spoonful by spoonful, until fully incorporated. Scoop one eighth of the whipped cream into a small bowl. Cover the smaller portion of whipped cream and refrigerate until serving.

Remove the chilled sponge from the freezer. Use a large serrated bread knife to slice off the domed top of the cake to flatten, then make a second horizontal cut through the middle to divide the cake into two thinner layers. Remove one layer and set onto a baking sheet lined with parchment paper or a serving dish.

Use a pastry brush to brush the plated cake layer with cherry liqueur or juice (if using), then spread the cherry jam evenly on top and layer the whipped cream from the large bowl on top of this. Place the top layer of the sponge on the cream and brush this top layer with the liqueur (if using).

Trim the sides of the cake with a serrated knife to make a flat and even rectangular cake. Now it's ready for its ganache topping.

To make the ganache, put the chocolate and butter in a heatproof bowl. Bring the cream to steaming in either a covered saucepan or the microwave, then pour over the chocolate and butter. Stir the ganache until smooth and shiny, then pour over the top of the cake, covering the entire cake in a thin layer.

Put the whole cake in the fridge to chill the ganache, about 20 minutes. Serve immediately or store covered airtight in the fridge for up to 3 days. When ready to serve, cut the cake into twelve even squares. Clean the knife between cuts to get tidy edges. Fit a pastry bag with a star-shaped tip and fill with the remaining whipped cream. Garnish the cake slices with a spritz of whipped cream and a cherry.

Chocolate Roulade with Coffee Cream

Rolada Czekoladowa

Factoring geography into eating was a lesson that took me a long time to learn. No seafood in a landlocked country, etcetera. When I was twenty-one, well before I'd taken this to heart, I was living in Kathmandu, one of the overlooked great bakery capitals of the world. One weekend I rode a motorcycle up to a picturesque hilltop village hours away from anything, including the wonderful city bakeries. In the town's teashop was a lone slice of Swiss roll, almost plastic in its perfection. Giving no consideration to context (where could this improbable Swiss roll have come from, and how long had it been there?), I ordered it. There was not enough tea in the world to wash away the taste of that dry, greasy, flavorless cake. It's a memory that still haunts my mouth. It put me off roulade cakes for at least a decade. But that was my fault. If I'd thought about geography for even a moment, I'd have spared myself. That cake had been sitting at least 100 miles from the nearest bakery for god-knows-how-long and staved off molding by what could only be unnatural means. So, where should you go if you want to eat a good roulade cake? Poland, of course—one of the great centers of rolled-cake culture. It's easy to count ten different flavors of roulades to a bakery, each better than the next: coffee, chocolate, fruit, berry, coconut, egg liqueur—you name it. Polish rolled sponge cakes are a *thing*, and they're very good.

MAKES 1 roulade (serves 10)

EGG WHITES

2 egg whites
¼ tsp white vinegar
2 Tbsp [25 g] granulated sugar

BATTER

⅓ cup [25 g] cocoa powder
¼ cup plus 2 tsp [70 g] hot brewed coffee
3 eggs
2 egg yolks
⅔ cup [130 g] granulated sugar
1 tsp vanilla extract
½ tsp kosher salt
¼ cup [40 g] all-purpose flour

FILLING

3½ oz [100 g] whipping cream, cold
1 tsp vanilla extract
7 Tbsp [50 g] confectioners' sugar
1½ tsp instant espresso powder
7 oz [200 g] mascarpone, cold

Line a 13 x 9 in [33 x 23 cm] baking pan or jelly roll pan with parchment paper and preheat the oven to 400°F [200°C] with the convection setting turned on.

Whip the egg whites. Add the egg whites and vinegar to the bowl of your stand mixer fitted with the whisk attachment. On medium speed, beat until soft peaks start to form, then add the sugar a spoonful at a time. Once all the sugar is incorporated, increase the speed to high and beat until stiff peaks form. Transfer the whipped egg whites to a small mixing bowl. Note: There's no need to wash the bowl of your stand mixer at this point.

To make the batter, in a small bowl, mix together the cocoa powder and coffee until smooth. In the bowl of the stand mixer fitted with the whisk attachment, add the eggs, egg yolks, sugar, vanilla, and salt. Beat on high speed until pale yellow and fluffy. Turn off the mixer, and use a spatula to stir in the cocoa mixture. Once evenly incorporated, add the flour

cont'd

and stir in with a spatula. Gently fold in the whipped egg whites one quarter at a time until no lumps are visible.

Pour the mixture into your lined pan and bake for 15 minutes, or until the cake is puffed and a cake tester comes out clean. Remove from the oven and cover immediately with a clean tea towel. After about 20 minutes, invert the pan, tea towel and all, onto a cooling rack. Carefully remove the parchment paper, then gently roll up the cake from one of the short sides, tea towel and all. This will prevent the cake from sticking to itself.

While the cake cools, prepare the filling. In the bowl of your stand mixer fitted with the whisk attachment, whip the cream and vanilla until soft peaks form. Add the confectioners' sugar and espresso powder a little at a time, mixing on low until fully incorporated. Continue to beat, increasing the speed to high, until you have a stiff whipped cream. Add the mascarpone one quarter at a time, and beat until the mixture becomes stiff again.

Once the cake is fully cool, unroll it and spread the cream on the cake, leaving about 1 in [2.5 cm] on both short sides of the cake unfilled. This will help prevent over-filling. Gently roll up the cake, starting from an unfilled edge.

Either slice and serve immediately or wrap up tightly in parchment paper or plastic wrap and refrigerate for up to several days, until ready to serve.

Pinched Cake

Pleśniak

About pleśniak, a friend told me this: "Everyone bakes pleśniak. Even people who don't bake bake pleśniak." So it's only logical that everyone has an opinion about how pleśniak should be made. A friend from Warsaw said it must be made with blackberries. Another said his grandmother made it with gooseberries. My downstairs neighbor in Berlin, Katarzyna, said it can only be made with red currants, nothing else. Each person said their piece with the certainty of dogma. I think it's Małgosia Minta, the book's photographer, who got it right, though. "It's a clean-out-the-fridge cake. Get rid of all the preserves you have leftover from the winter. Any fruit that's overflowing from the garden." Pleśniak unappealingly translates to *mold cake*, for the moldy-looking combination of meringue and dough. Fortunately, this cake is also called *skubaniec*, which means pinched cake, from the pinched-off pieces of dough topping the cake. Maybe all that is to say that this cake is whatever you want it to be.

NOTE: Often this cake is made with a chocolate dough or a mix of chocolate and vanilla dough. Here I use only vanilla dough, but feel free to substitute part with the Risen Chocolate Shortcrust Dough (page 191).

MAKES one 9 in [23 cm] square cake (8 to 12 slices)

CRUST

1 batch Półkruche Dough (page 191)
1½ Tbsp [15 g] dry bread crumbs

FRUIT FILLING

10 cups (about 3 lb [1.4 kg]) berries (blackberries, raspberries, blueberries, red or black currants, gooseberries, quartered strawberries)
⅓ cup plus 2 Tbsp [90 g] sugar
Juice of ½ lemon
3 Tbsp [30 g] cornstarch

MERINGUE

¼ cup plus 2 Tbsp [75 g] sugar
1 Tbsp cornstarch
4 egg whites
1 tsp lemon juice

Prepare the półkruche dough according to the recipe on page 191 and chill for 1 hour or up to several days before using.

To prepare the fruit filling, mix the berries, sugar, and lemon juice in a bowl and set aside for about 1 hour, until the juice has leaked out.

Line the bottom of a 9 in [23 cm] square baking pan with parchment paper. Divide the dough into two portions, one of two thirds and the other one third. Wrap the one third in plastic wrap and refrigerate until ready to use. On a lightly floured work surface, give the larger portion of the dough a brief knead to return it to elasticity, then gently roll out to the size of the pan. Gently transfer the dough to the pan and press to fit. Prick all over with a fork, then chill for 20 minutes in the fridge.

While the dough chills, preheat the oven to 350°F [180°C] with the convection setting turned on.

Once the dough has chilled, blind-bake it 15 to 20 minutes, until it puffs, no longer looks greasy, and starts to turn golden brown. Remove it from the oven.

While the base of the cake bakes, prepare the meringue. In a small mixing bowl, mix the sugar and cornstarch. In the bowl of your stand mixer fitted with the whisk attachment, beat the egg whites on medium to high speed until they start to get foamy. Still beating, add the lemon juice and a spoonful of sugar-starch mixture. Continuing to beat, add the sugar-starch mixture a spoonful at a time until it's all gone. Keep beating until a stiff and shiny meringue has formed. The whole process start to finish takes about 5 minutes.

cont'd

To assemble the cake, sprinkle half of the bread crumbs over the blind-baked base. Drain your macerated fruit in a sieve, then toss the fruit with the cornstarch, and spoon in an even layer over the crust. Spoon the meringue over the fruit, smoothing with a spatula in a thick, even layer. Finally, remove the remaining third portion of dough from the fridge and pinch off small pieces, about 1 in [2.5 cm], to roughly cover the meringue layer.

Bake for about 25 minutes, until the top of the meringue has puffed and the dough pieces are golden brown. Remove from the oven and allow to cool completely before slicing.

This cake can keep, chilled and wrapped airtight, for up to 3 days.

Napoleonka

Cream Slice

Napoleonka wasn't quite born Polish—it's a one-layered variation of a French mille-feuille, whose own origins are Italian. Still, this flake-and-cream slice cake can be found in just about every cukiernia in Poland. They vary in quality from lovingly handmade pastry to powdered-pudding mediocrity, but when it's good, it's very good. There's some controversy as to whether this cake should be called *napoleonka* or *kremówka*, but the one thing everyone agrees on is that in his youth, Pope John Paul II ate eighteen slices in one sitting. For this reason, some people call it *kremówka papieska, pope's cream cake*. For the sake of secular cake-eating, let's stick to *napoleonka*.

NOTE: I like to prepare my pastry and filling the night before serving for easy assembly. Napoleonka often has gelatin added to the cream for extra stability. I prefer to use agar agar powder for the same effect, keeping this dessert vegetarian. Instead of the Francuskie dough, you can use two large sheets of ready-made puff pastry.

MAKES one 13 x 9 in [33 x 23 cm] cake (12 slices)

PASTRY

1 batch Francuskie Dough (page 240), chilled

FILLING

Double batch Stiff Budyń with Agar Agar (page 342), chilled

2 egg whites

1 Tbsp granulated sugar

TOPPING

3 Tbsp [25 g] confectioners' sugar

Prepare the Francuskie dough according to the recipe on page 240 and chill for at least 2 hours.

While the dough chills, prepare the filling. Make one double batch of stiff budyń according to the recipe on page 342, but don't chill. In the bowl of your stand mixer fitted with the whisk attachment, whip the egg whites with the sugar to soft but not stiff peaks. In a heatproof bowl, fold the egg whites into the warm budyń filling, then cover the surface of the mixture with plastic wrap and chill in the fridge until set, at least 2 hours or overnight.

While the filling cools, bake the pastry. Preheat the oven to 350°F [180°C] and line two baking sheets with parchment paper. On a lightly floured surface, roll the dough to about 27 x 19 in [68 x 48 cm], then trim about ½ in [1 cm] off each side to make a tidy rectangle. Divide the dough into two 13 x 9 in [33 x 23 cm] rectangles. Arrange one rectangle on each of your baking sheets and prick all over with a fork. Place one rectangle in the refrigerator. Bake the other rectangle for 25 minutes, or until golden brown and crispy. Remove the baked pastry from the pan and set on a cooling rack. Repeat for the second rectangle of pastry.

Once the pastry is cooled, cut one of the sheets into twelve even rectangles. The best way to cut this is with a large, sharp knife pressed straight down or gently sawing with a bread knife. This will be your top layer. Precutting now will be easier than cutting the top layer after assembly since napoleonka is filled with a semi-soft cream.

When you're ready to assemble, use a whisk to whip the stiffened budyń filling until you have a smooth and thick cream with no chunks. Place the uncut sheet of baked pastry on a tray lined with parchment paper. Spread the uncut sheet of pastry with a thick, even layer of the filling, then top with the cut pastry pieces in an even rectangle. Use an offset spatula to even out the filling around the edges. Wrap the whole thing tightly in plastic wrap, then return to the fridge to set until serving, at least 1 hour. This will keep refrigerated for up to 3 days stored airtight. When ready to serve, dust with confectioners' sugar, then use a sharp knife to cut into squares, using the pre-cut top pastry as your guide.

Layered Biscuit and Sour Cream Cake

Marcinek

I had to drive clear across Poland to try this cake. Marcinek is a many-layered biscuit and sweetened sour cream cake claimed as a regional delicacy by the town of Hajnówka. Hajnówka is the last stop before you hit the thick Białowieża Forest and the Belarusian border. On my way, I found a room for the night in the culinarily named Knyszyn (Knish) Forest. Over breakfast, the only other guest, an off-road motorcycle enthusiast and IT specialist, told me what he knew about Hajnówka. "It's the center of that other religion. Not Catholic. The other one." "Orthodox?" I offered. "Yes, that." I asked him about the marcinek cake. "Never heard of it. Watch out your phone doesn't go onto the Belarusian network. You'll have to pay a lot of money." An hour of driving on small roads and ten prismacolor painted wooden Orthodox churches later, I was in Hajnówka. The internet had promised five different bakeries offering the cake but I could find only one, the Cukiernia Emma, a miniature outlet the size of a galley kitchen in a parking lot behind several apartment blocks. It was closed. Given the eight-hour drive I'd pulled off in fewer than two days and the glowing fridge case full of marcinek cakes inside, I stuck around, hoping someone would show up. When finally my luck turned and a smiling old woman in a bibbed apron came rushing downstairs, she already knew what I was there for. "Marcinek," she said as a statement. "You," and pointed at me. She sliced off a thick square of cake, wrapped it in paper, and asked me what else I'd like. "You want kwas," she answered for me, waving a hand at a shelf of sweet fermented bread juice in giant brown plastic bottles. "It's Lithuanian."

The marcinek cake was excellent. Icebox style, it was incredibly moist, just a bit sour, and lightly sweet. I'm still trying to figure out what to do with all the kwas.

NOTE: This cake should be made at least a day before serving so that the cream can soak in and soften the layers.

MAKES one 9 in [23 cm] cake (12 slices)

BISCUIT LAYERS

- 8 cups [1 kg] all-purpose flour
- 1½ tsp baking soda
- 2 tsp kosher salt
- 1 cup plus 5 Tbsp [300 g] unsalted butter, cubed and at room temperature
- 1 cup plus 2½ Tbsp [230 g] granulated sugar
- 4 eggs, at room temperature
- 2 tsp vanilla extract
- 10½ oz [300 g] full-fat sour cream

FILLING

- 21 oz [600 g] whipping cream
- ¾ cup plus 1 Tbsp [100 g] confectioners' sugar
- 2 tsp almond extract
- 12½ oz [350 g] mascarpone
- 5½ oz [150 g] full-fat sour cream

Preheat the oven to 350°F [180°C] with the convection setting turned on. Measure two pieces of parchment paper to fit two baking sheets. Using a pencil and plate or a base of a cake form, trace two circles onto each paper, then flip over. Set aside.

Begin by mixing the biscuit dough. In a medium mixing bowl, whisk together the flour, baking soda, and salt. In the bowl of your stand mixer fitted with the paddle attachment, cream the butter and sugar

cont'd

for about 5 minutes on medium speed, until light and fluffy. Turn the speed to low and add the eggs one at a time, allowing for each to incorporate before adding the next. Scrape down the sides of the bowl with a spatula as you mix. Still on low speed, add the vanilla, then one third of the flour mixture. Once no dry pockets of flour are visible, add one third of the sour cream, then continue alternating the flour and sour cream until they are all gone and a homogenous dough has formed. The dough will be thick and a tiny bit stretchy. Scrape the dough out into a new bowl, then cover airtight and chill in the fridge for an hour until stiffened.

While the dough chills, wash, then chill the bowl of your stand mixer and the whisk attachment in the fridge.

Once the dough is chilled, on a lightly floured work surface, divide the dough into fifteen even portions of about 4½ oz [130 g] each and form into balls. Using a floured rolling pin, roll out one ball into a thin disk 8 in [20 cm] across. Place the dough disk on one of the circles you've traced on the paper. Stretch it to fit and trim with a knife or pizza cutter to even out the edges into as perfect a circle as you can manage. Repeat for the second disk. Use a fork to prick holes over the entirety of each disk, then bake for 10 minutes, until starting to turn golden. While those disks are baking, prepare the second sheet. Alternate like this until all your disks are baked. If you need to save space, you can stack them on top of each other on a cooling rack while they're still warm from the oven.

Once all the disks are baked and cooled, prepare the filling. In the chilled bowl of your stand mixer fitted with the whisk attachment, whip the cream, confectioners' sugar, and almond extract on high speed until a stiff whipped cream has formed, then lower the speed and add the mascarpone and sour cream on low speed. Once everything is incorporated, increase the speed to high for 1 minute.

Remove one quarter of the whipped cream and put it in a separate bowl, cover airtight, and refrigerate until ready to use. This will be the portion to cover the outside of the cake.

On your preferred serving dish, place a spoonful of cream, then one biscuit disk. Spread a generous amount of cream on top of the disk, thick enough that no biscuit is visible and going all the way to the edges. Place the next biscuit on top and then repeat, spreading the filling and layering until the thirteenth biscuit has been used (save the last two biscuits for later). Wrap the cake in plastic wrap, put a small pan weighted with a soup can on top of the cake, and refrigerate overnight.

The next day, remove the plastic wrap, then spread the remaining whipped cream on the outside of the cake. If the cream has deflated a bit, simply whip again until stiff. Using a food processor or crushing by hand, grind the two remaining biscuit disks into fine crumbs, then sprinkle all over the top of the cake.

Slice and serve with your favorite berries. The cake will keep for several days, covered, in the fridge.

Zackary Leon Furst's Golden Raisin Mead Cake

This is a story of one cookie and two cakes. I met Zackary Leon Furst, the former head chef at Melbourne's celebrated Bar Liberty, on a late summer evening at a Warsaw restaurant. He was deep into a monthlong trip through Poland to track both his heritage flavors and inspiration for his menu. The grandchild of wartime immigrants from Kraków and Zakopane, his cooking is strongly influenced by Polish cuisine, adapted for the modern gastronomic wine bar, and takes advantage of the accessibility of traditional Polish ingredients—honey, buckwheat, smoked meats—in Australia.

More than eighty years ago, his grandparents, Babcia Zdzisława and Dziadek Lech, escaped the country on the eve of the German invasion with the help of the Red Cross, meeting each other and falling in love in a Russian refugee camp. From there, they traveled to another camp in Russia, then to Uganda, then on to India. They finally made it to Australia, where Dziadek Lech worked on the train line from Perth to Kalgoorlie. The whole journey took four years until the family finally settled in the town of Wodonga in rural Victoria. There, two generations later, Zackary grew up eating and cooking with his babcia the traditional pierogies, honey biscuits, and rosół (chicken soup) of her home country—heavy stuff for the 105°F [40°C] heat of Australia. When Zackary trained and began working as a chef, he made a point of always having a cake on his menu, and found himself chasing the nostalgic taste of his babcia's honey biscuits. When he tracked down her recipe book, he found not just the honey biscuits but her piernik (gingerbread cake) recipe. He combined her piernik spice mix with the flavor of her honey biscuits and created a light, contemporary cake, using the honey his brother makes as a beekeeper.

Despite Polish and Central European cuisine being a minority influence in the Melbourne food world—proximity to Asia and more broad Western European migration bringing the primary food influences—Zackary has found that diners delight in his elevated dishes with the less common Polish flavor palate. This cake is no exception.

NOTES: This cake is a little involved—it's coming from a fine dining world. But if you're up for a project, you'll be richly rewarded. I like to make the cake, raisin jam, and pudding component of the cream filling in advance, and then assemble to serve. If you can't find mead, replace it with 2 Tbsp [25 g] water, 4 tsp [25 g] honey, and 1 Tbsp [15 g] rum or bourbon.

MAKES one 6½ x 4½ in [16.5 x 11 cm] cake (about 8 slices)

cont'd

CAKE

2¾ cups plus 2 Tbsp [360 g] all-purpose flour
1½ tsp double-acting baking powder
1 tsp baking soda
1 tsp kosher salt
3 Tbsp plus ½ tsp [25 g] ground fennel seed
3 Tbsp plus ½ tsp [25 g] ground anise seed
2½ tsp ground cinnamon
2 tsp ground cloves
¾ tsp ground black pepper
¾ tsp ground nutmeg, plus more to serve
3 eggs
½ cup [100 g] sugar
1 cup plus 1 tsp [225 g] sunflower oil
1 cup [340 g] pourable honey
1 cup [240 g] whole milk

MEAD CREAM

1 egg
4 tsp [12 g] cornstarch
1 Tbsp all-purpose flour
¾ cup plus 1 Tbsp [200 g] whole milk
3½ Tbsp [50 g] mead (see Notes)
3 Tbsp [60 g] honey
1 Tbsp unsalted butter

GOLDEN RAISIN JAM

1 cup [140 g] golden raisins
¼ cup plus 1 Tbsp [75 g] water
1 Tbsp sugar

HONEY SYRUP

7 Tbsp [100 g] warm water
1 Tbsp honey
Pinch of kosher salt

FOR ASSEMBLING

3½ oz [100 g] whipping cream
Ground nutmeg, for finishing

Preheat the oven to 350°F [180°C] with the convection setting turned on, and line the bottom of a 13 x 9 in [33 x 23 cm] baking pan with parchment paper.

Begin by making the batter. In a medium mixing bowl, whisk together the flour, baking powder, baking soda, and salt. In the bowl of your stand mixer fitted with the paddle attachment, combine the fennel, anise, cinnamon, cloves, pepper, nutmeg, eggs, and sugar and beat on high speed for about 3 minutes. Continuing to beat, add in the sunflower oil and honey in a thin stream until fully combined. Reduce the speed to low and add the flour mixture and milk, alternating about one third of each until fully incorporated, scraping down the sides of the bowl between additions. Once the mixture is smooth and no dry pockets of flour remain—being careful not to overmix—pour the batter into the prepared pan. Bake for about 40 minutes, or until a cake tester comes out clean. Set aside to cool. Once cool, slip a knife around the edges of the pan to release, then turn out onto a cooling rack.

While the cake cools, make the mead cream. Whisk together the egg, cornstarch, and flour in a large heatproof bowl. In a saucepan, combine the milk, mead, and honey and warm over low to medium heat until steaming. Pour the hot milk into the egg mixture in a thin stream, whisking constantly to temper the egg. Once all the liquid has been incorporated into the egg mixture, return it to the saucepan on medium-low heat. Whisk constantly until the mixture starts to thicken and bubble, continuing to whisk vigorously for another 3 minutes after it starts to bubble and before removing it from the heat. Immediately after removing it from the heat, add the butter and stir until melted and the mead cream is smooth. Pour the mead cream into a heatproof bowl, cover with plastic wrap directly on the surface, and refrigerate until fully cool, about 1 hour.

Meanwhile, wash and chill the bowl of your stand mixer and the whisk attachment in the fridge.

While the mead cream cools, prepare the raisin jam. In a small covered saucepan, bring the raisins, water, and sugar to a low simmer for about 15 minutes. Once the raisins are plump and some of the water has boiled off, use an immersion blender or food processor to purée the mixture into a smooth paste. Set aside.

Finally, make the honey syrup. In a small heatproof bowl, whisk together the water, honey, and salt, then set aside.

Once the mead cream is cool and the raisin jam and honey syrup are made, you're ready to assemble your cake. Prepare your cake layers by using a serrated knife to trim off the domed top, then cut the whole cake in half the short way to make two even rectangles. Place one layer on a serving dish, then brush with honey syrup and spread with a layer of raisin jam.

In the chilled bowl of your stand mixer fitted with the whisk attachment, pour in the whipping cream in a thin stream while whisking on high speed. Continue whisking for about 5 minutes, until you have a stiff whipped cream. Fill a pastry bag with the whipped cream and snip a diagonal tip. Cover the layer of raisin jam with swirls of cream, top with the second layer of cake, and brush this with honey syrup, then cover with another layer of cream swirls. (If you don't want the fuss of a pastry bag, simply spread on the cream with a spatula or spoon.) Finish with a sprinkle of nutmeg.

Serve immediately, cut into narrow rectangles, or store in the fridge for several hours before serving.

Minta's Gingerbread Loaf Cake

Dirty Piernik

A traditional Polish piernik loaf cake, the staropolski, is, like the Pierniki Toruńskie (page 253), a labor of planning ahead. The dough ages in the cold for at least a month, sometimes two, and if we're being honest, the cake is often dry and rarely delicious. But if the Christmas season isn't about loaf cakes that we feel ambivalent about but last forever, what is it about? Well, maybe it can be about something similar but a little bit different.

For one Polish girl, Małgosia Minta, planning ahead to make a staropolski piernik is out of the question. It's not her fault, it's just who she is—a scatterbrain, a luftmensch. She inherited this trait from her mother and her grandparents before her, just as she inherited their piernik recipe. She suggests you think of this as a very valid alternative to a staropolski piernik but for people with ADHD or at least very busy lives. It comes together quickly and will stay moist and soft for up to a week, thanks to the incorporation of a whole jar of powidła (plum butter).

Though I've just thrown a lot of shade at traditional staropolski piernik cakes, if you ever want to taste the rarest of birds—a moist and perfectly aged staropolski piernik—visit the Dej Piekarnia in Warsaw's Stare Bielany district during the month of December.

MAKES one 9 x 5 in [23 x 13 cm] loaf

CAKE

9 Tbsp [125 g] unsalted butter
1 cup plus 2 tsp [250 g] whole milk
¼ cup plus 1 Tbsp [70 g] demerara sugar or granulated sugar
¾ cup [250 g] Plum Filling (page 333)
4 eggs
2⅓ cups plus 1 Tbsp [300 g] all-purpose flour
1 batch [40 g] Gingerbread Spice (page 341)
1 Tbsp grated orange zest (optional)
2 tsp baking soda
½ tsp kosher salt
1 cup [180 g] chopped dates
1 cup [120 g] chopped walnuts
2 Tbsp [25 g] finely chopped Candied Orange Peel (page 332) (optional)
1 to 2 Tbsp [15 to 30 g] cold unsalted butter, cut into small batons

TOPPING

1 batch Chocolate Glaze (page 350)
½ cup [60 g] slivered almonds, candied fruit, star anise, or red peppercorns for decorating (optional)

Preheat the oven to 350°F [180°C] with the convection setting turned off, and line the bottom of a loaf pan with parchment paper, leaving the sides of the pan unlined. This will help the cake climb the sides and form a domed top.

Begin by making the batter. In a medium saucepan, warm the butter, milk, and sugar over low heat, stirring occasionally, until the butter is melted the sugar is dissolved. Remove from the heat and allow to cool until just warm or room temperature. Add

cont'd

the plum filling to the mix and whisk well, then add the eggs one by one until you have a homogenous purple mixture.

In the bowl of your stand mixer fitted with the paddle attachment, mix together the flour, gingerbread spice, orange zest (if using), baking soda, and salt for a minute on low speed, just until even. Pour the plum filling mixture into the dry ingredients and continue to mix on low speed until you have a smooth, medium-thick batter with no dry pockets of flour. Mix for another 2 minutes, then add the dates, walnuts, and candied orange peel (if using) and mix for a minute to incorporate. Pour the batter into the prepared loaf pan and arrange the pieces of butter in a continuous line down the middle of the cake. This will help the cake rise and split exactly along the middle as they melt.

Bake for 45 minutes, or until a cake tester comes out clean. If the top begins to get too dark as it bakes, cover with aluminum foil for the remainder of the bake. Once baked, allow to cool for at least 30 minutes before sliding a knife around the edges of the pan to release the cake.

Once the cake is fully cool, prepare your chocolate glaze according to the recipe on page 350. Place the cake on a cooling rack over the sink, then drizzle the glaze on top, allowing it to run down the sides. Top with any decorations you like, then allow the cake to chill in the fridge or on a cold balcony (as in Poland in the winter) to set the glaze.

Serve or store in an airtight container at room temperature for up to a week.

45
Made in Poland

/4

CIASTECZKA: COOKIES, SMALL-BITES & WAFERS

There's a common Polish cookie called ciasteczka z maszynki: machine cookies. Machine cookies are simple butter shortbreads with a distinct, ridged, rectangular form. They get their name and shape from the hand-cranked meat grinder with which they're made. Until the last decade or so, a metal meat grinder that attached like a vise to a kitchen counter was a standard home appliance. Still is, in many homes of a certain vintage. To make the cookies, a thick short dough—Ciasto Kruche (page 190)—is cranked through the press and a molded die affixed to the end. The dough is pushed out like sausage meat and cut off in segments before being baked up crispy. It's a funny method—at least, I think so. It also reveals something about a lot of typical Polish cookies: Even when they're made at fancy pastry shops and bakeries with organic flours and whole grains, they're often very retro.

Maybe one of the unifying characteristics of Polish cookies is that, like the cakes, rarely are they overly sweet. Instead, they're little bites just sweet enough to serve to a visitor or to show appreciation to a friend, with their form and cuteness being at least half the point. Flavors lean toward the classic: jam, poppy seed, gingerbread spice, and nuts. Often, homes in Poland have a cupboard shelf or cookie tin dedicated to cookie storage. My friend Adam says that, in his grandmother's house, cookies somehow magically appeared, and no one ever saw where she got them from. The cookies just seemed to live forever in her cupboard, never running out, always refilling, often getting stale in the meantime. He now keeps a cookie cupboard in his own home: "You must," he says.

Many people told me that, until recently, cookie making from scratch was a regular weekend activity in the Polish home, with the yield kept in a tin all week, the process repeated the following weekend. But alongside the homemade, there's also another cookie culture for the more time-pressed: ciasteczka na wagę or by-weight cookies. By-weight cookies are a communist-era phenomenon that has persisted to present day. Made in larger factory bakeries and packed up in cardboard boxes with a perforated rip-off cover, they're sold at market stands and old-style cake shops. Concerning ciasteczka na wagę, a woman in Warsaw told me: "A lot of us have bad memories of these. They're made with terrible ingredients, terrible fats, no butter or flavor. I can taste how bad they are when I close my eyes." These by-weight cookies come in at least thirty different varieties, maybe more. Every time I think I've seen them all, I see a new variety. Diamonds, crescents, disks, crunchy, soft, flat, and puffy. Even if they tend to underwhelm a lot of people, the homemade versions of these cookies are often wonderful. It all comes down to ingredients and freshness.

The following chapter is a survey of the seemingly endless variety of Polish cookies.

SOUR CREAM FRENCH DOUGH

Ciasto Francuskie

This dough is very similar to a classic cream cheese dough—also called a dairy dough—that in American baking forms the base of rugelach and many other flaky pastries. Like dairy dough, this is a 1:1:1 proportion of butter, dairy, and flour and is basically a modified puff pastry that is a standard both in Polish and Jewish baking. Use this sour cream French dough for fruit turnovers, jam pockets, pies, and more. It's incredibly versatile and can be substituted for the Półfrancuskie (page 105) in most places for a flakier and crispier result. For best results, keep your butter and dairy very cold. As the name suggests, here we use sour cream, which does double duty of adding a touch of acidic flavor and simultaneously keeping the dough's color if you plan to keep it in the fridge for longer than a day.

NOTE: This dough can be made by hand or with a food processor and chills for a minimum of 3 hours or up to 3 days in the fridge. Store frozen for up to a month and thaw overnight in the fridge before using.

MAKES about 2¼ lb [1 kg] of dough

1 cup plus 1½ Tbsp [250 g] unsalted butter
4 cups [500 g] all-purpose flour
½ tsp kosher salt
¼ tsp double-acting baking powder
1 cup [240 g] full-fat sour cream
1 tsp lemon juice

Cut the butter into ½ in [1 cm] cubes and place in the freezer for 20 minutes.

IF MIXING BY HAND, whisk together the flour, salt, and baking powder in a large mixing bowl. Add ¾ cup [180 g] of the sour cream and whisk until the texture is loose, sandy, and shaggy. Add the frozen butter and toss until the butter is fully coated in flour. Turn the mixture out onto a work surface and, using your rolling pin, roll out the dough until the butter is in ragged strips. Try to do this with as few passes of the rolling pin as possible, so as not to heat up the dough. The dough will be very shaggy and not fully formed at this point. Scoop it all up and return it to the mixing bowl. Add the remaining ¼ cup [60 g] sour cream and the lemon juice and mix this in by hand just until the dough starts to come together. Turn the dough back out onto the work surface and knead it just a couple times to bring it together. Then form it into a disk and wrap airtight. Chill for 2 hours or up to 3 days, until ready to use.

IF USING A FOOD PROCESSOR, pulse the flour, salt, and baking powder until evenly distributed, then blitz the dry ingredients with ¾ cup [180 g] of the sour cream until sandy. Add the frozen butter and blitz until shaggy with some tiny bits of butter still visible. Add the remaining ¼ cup [60 g] sour cream and the lemon juice, then blitz until a crumbly mass forms. Remove the dough from the food processor and press it into a disk. Wrap airtight and chill for 2 hours or up to 3 days, until ready to use.

Rose and Almond Jewel Rugelach

Rogaliki z Różą i Migdałami

Tiny and pretty, these little rose jam–stuffed rugelach are found in Poland with or without an almond paste filling. The flavor combination is one I was surprised to find in Poland and one that I'd never seen in American rugelach. Rather, I'd always associated rose and almond with a Moroccan corne de gazelle or a Persian love cake, not a Polish or Ashkenazi cookie, but I had to track these down after my friend Dominika told me about eating these with tea on Jewish holidays in Poland. And sure enough, when I looked, there they were, sold by weight at market bakery stands, small and jewel-like, a very special gem in the world of rugelach.

NOTE: I make these with kruche dough for its sugar cookie texture, as well as its malleability, which allows for extra filling to be stuffed inside. If you prefer a flakier dough, the Sour Cream French Dough (page 240), rolled very thin, can also be used.

MAKES 24 small cookies

DOUGH

½ batch Kruche Dough (page 190)

FILLING

¾ cup plus 1½ Tbsp [95 g] almond meal

¾ cup plus 2 tsp [95 g] confectioners' sugar, sifted

1 tsp almond extract

1 egg white

½ cup [150 g] Rose Paste (page 344)

EGG WASH

1 egg, beaten

TOPPING

2½ Tbsp [30 g] granulated or demerara sugar

1 cup [120 g] confectioners' sugar, sifted

Prepare your kruche dough according to the recipe on page 190 and chill for 1 to 2 hours, until very stiff.

While the dough chills, prepare your almond paste. In a food processor or a stand mixer fitted with the paddle attachment, pulse the almond meal and confectioners' sugar until even. Add the almond extract and egg white and pulse briefly until a thick paste has formed.

Preheat the oven to 350°F [180°C] with the convection setting turned on. Divide your dough into three even portions. Form each portion into a disk, giving each a brief knead so that it doesn't crack while rolling. On a lightly floured work surface, roll out one disk to an about 9 in [23 cm] circle. Trim the edges with a knife or pizza cutter, then divide the disk like a pie into eight even wedges. Put about ½ tsp of almond paste and ½ tsp of rose paste in the center of the wide outer edge of each wedge, about ½ in [1 cm] from the top.

Fold in the filling from the wide top of the triangle (opposite the point) so it doesn't leak out while baking. To do this, first fold in the two sides of the top of the wide base of the triangle to meet each other on top of the filling, then roll the wide base of the triangle over these folded sides and the filling to encapsulate the filling completely. Finally, press

cont'd

to seal in the filling in a half-moon shape, then continue to roll up the cookie in the same direction, all the way to the tip of the triangle, forming a crescent. Use your fingers to gently pinch the ends of the rugelach and shape into a slight half-moon. Repeat with the remaining dough and filling. Place the rugelach about 1 in [2.5 cm] apart on a baking sheet lined with parchment paper. Use a pastry brush to egg wash each rugelach, then sprinkle with granulated sugar.

Bake for about 15 minutes, or until golden brown. Remove from the oven and allow to cool for about 5 minutes. While still warm, toss in confectioners' sugar.

Eat immediately or store in a cookie tin for up to a week.

American-Style Rugelach with Apricot and Chocolate

Rogaliki, or rugelach, spread worldwide with the emigration and refugee waves of Jewish bakers from Poland in the last century. Made in mini-croissant shapes or sliced snails, as in this recipe, rugelach changed according to the available ingredients and the tastes of wherever they went. Rugelach that went to Israel became softer, richer, and syrup-soaked, mirroring the Levantine sweets of the region. Rugelach that went to America also mirrored the new culture and became . . . whatever they wanted to be. The American style is generally a flaky cookie made with a cream cheese dough—here we'll use our Sour Cream French Dough (page 240) for a similar effect. Whether rugelach are classic jam rolls or more contemporary and loaded with sprinkles and chocolate, they all owe something to their forebears in Poland. These use apricot lekvar and chocolate filling for an extra decadent bite.

MAKES 21 cookies

DOUGH

1 batch Francuskie Dough (page 240)

FILLING

5¼ oz [150 g] bittersweet or couverture chocolate, finely chopped

7 Tbsp [100 g] unsalted butter

¼ cup plus 2 tsp [35 g] confectioners' sugar, sifted

¼ cup [20 g] cocoa powder

¼ tsp ground cinnamon

½ cup [130 g] Apricot Filling (page 333)

EGG WASH

1 egg and 3 Tbsp [45 g] whole milk, whisked until smooth

TOPPING

2 to 3 Tbsp [30 to 40 g] demerara sugar

Prepare the Francuskie dough according to the recipe on page 240 and chill for at least 2 hours.

Immediately after you've made the dough and set it to chill, prepare your chocolate filling. This will give it enough time to cool. Melt the chocolate and butter in a double boiler or a bowl in your microwave in short bursts and stir until smooth. Stir in the confectioners' sugar, cocoa powder, and cinnamon. Set aside to cool for an hour or two, until thickened into a spreadable paste. Do not refrigerate to accelerate this process—it will make the filling too hard to spread.

Once the dough is chilled, shape your rugelach. Lightly flour your work surface and your dough, then roll it out to a very thin (⅛ in [3 mm]) about 16 x 14 in [40.5 x 35.5 cm] rectangle. Trim the edges, then fold and unfold it in thirds the long way to create a guide to cut the dough into three long rectangles. Spread a thin layer of chocolate filling on each long rectangle, leaving each long side with about a ½ in [1 cm] empty portion. This will help you roll up the rugelach without the filling gushing. Spread with a very thin layer of apricot filling (jam will also work here in a pinch, but it has a tendency to gush). Roll up each rectangle into a long tube, then set on a tray seam-side down and chill in the freezer for at least 20 minutes.

Preheat the oven to 350°F [180°C] and line two baking sheets with parchment paper. After the rolls have chilled, cut them into 1½ in [4 cm] snails and place on the baking sheets upright like wagon wheels about 1 in [2.5 cm] apart. Brush with egg wash and sprinkle with demerara sugar.

Bake your rugelach for 25 minutes, until golden brown.

Store in a cookie tin for up to a week.

Jam and Poppy Seed Sponge Sandwiches

Baletki

If you don't have people in your life who will tell you when you have poppy seeds stuck in your teeth, find some before you make these. These aren't so much cookies as teeny tiny cakes, as dainty as their name, *baletki—little ballet shoes*. A simple biscuit sponge, baletki are made texturally surprising with tart raspberry jam and a load of poppy seeds that toast in the oven and pop in your mouth. Dip these in coffee—the sponge soaks up liquid for a hint of the espresso-soaked savoiardi biscuits in tiramisu.

MAKES about 24 sandwiches

SPONGE

3 Tbsp [40 g] granulated sugar
⅓ cup [40 g] confectioners' sugar
3 eggs, at room temperature and separated
¼ tsp kosher salt
1 tsp vanilla, lemon, or almond extract
1 tsp grated lemon zest (optional)
⅔ cup [80 g] all-purpose flour
¾ cup [100 g] poppy seeds

FILLING

¼ to ½ cup [80 to 160 g] raspberry jam

Preheat the oven to 350°F [180°C] and line two baking sheets with parchment paper.

Begin by making the batter. In a small mixing bowl, whisk together the granulated and confectioners' sugar. In the bowl of your stand mixer fitted with the whisk attachment, beat the egg whites and salt on medium-high speed until stiff peaks form, about 4 minutes. Turn the speed down to medium and add the sugar mixture one spoonful at a time. Once all the sugar is in, turn the speed back up to medium-high and beat for another 2 minutes, or until the meringue becomes silky and shiny. Mixing on medium speed, add the egg yolks one at a time. The batter will now be a very pale yellow. Finally, add your flavor extract and lemon zest (if using) and mix on low speed until just incorporated.

Turn off the mixer and remove the bowl from the machine. Using a spatula, gently fold in half of the flour and then the other half, continuing to fold until the batter is smooth.

Evenly spoon 1 Tbsp dollops onto the baking sheets about 1 in [2.5 cm] apart, using your finger to push the batter off the spoon. You should have about twenty-four dollops on each pan. Pick up one pan with two hands and hold it about 4 in [10 cm] above your work surface, then allow it to drop straight down. This will help slam larger air bubbles out of the cookies. Repeat for the second pan.

Generously sprinkle each cookie with poppy seeds, then bake one tray on the middle rack for about 10 minutes, until the cookies are golden brown. Repeat with the second tray. Allow the cookies to cool before removing them from the parchment paper.

Once cool, spoon about a teaspoon of jam onto the flat side of half the cookies, then press each with an unfilled cookie like a sandwich until the jam spreads to the edges.

Serve immediately, or store in an airtight container for up to several days.

Pressed Shortbread “Machine Cookies”

Ciasteczka z Maszynki

I know you’ve been looking for a way to repurpose your countertop meat grinder into the multi-tool cookie press that it is—who hasn’t? These crank-pressed butter cookies, ciasteczka z maszynki, are much like other pressed shortbread cookies like those blue tin Danish butter cookies or the sort of whipped Italian shortbreads you can buy by the pound, but machine cookies are a bit crumblier and come in a flat-ribbed shape. This is one of the few places I suggest you go full-on old-school and use vanillin or vanilla sugar for the authentic taste, but vanilla extract is also nice.

NOTE: I know you probably don’t have a meat grinder at home. A manual cookie press or stand-mixer attachment with a long ridged form will work just fine.

MAKES about 36 cookies

1 batch Kruche Dough (page 190), at room temperature

Prepare the kruche dough according to the recipe on page 190. Either skip the chilling stage and go directly to pressing your cookies, or make it in advance and chill, then let it come to room temperature when you’re ready to press and bake your cookies.

Preheat the oven to 350°F [180°C] with the convection setting turned on. Line two baking sheets with parchment paper.

Fill a cookie press with the dough and press out about 2½ in [6 cm] cookies and arrange them 1 in [2.5 cm] apart on the baking sheets. Bake for 12 to 15 minutes, or until they start to turn golden brown.

Store in a cookie tin for up to 2 weeks.

Rustic Chocolate Macaroons

Marcepanki

Just at the border of Poland and Germany lies the divided town of Frankfurt an der Oder and Słubice. Frankfurt an der Oder is the German half, Słubice is the Polish half. The split is a result of redrawn borders post–World War II. The two halves are separated by the river Oder and couldn't be more different. All day, Germans cross back and forth on the bridge to do their shopping on the Polish side where the cigarettes are cheaper and the food is better. I can't blame them—I do the same thing. Mostly though, I cross the bridge to go to one particular bakery and cake shop. This cukiernia sells just about every cookie, cake, and bread there is, and in the corner is a large freezer stocked with boxes of homemade pierogies to take home. The best thing this bakery makes, though, is the chewy, deeply chocolate marcepanki, rustic almond-based sandwich macaroons. Like the city, these two halves are separated by a river. A river of dark chocolate ganache.

MAKES 20 to 24 cookies

DOUGH

1¾ cups [210 g] confectioners' sugar, sifted
1 cup plus 3 Tbsp [140 g] almond meal
½ cup [40 g] Dutch-process cocoa powder
Pinch of salt
2 egg whites
1 tsp lemon juice
1 tsp vanilla extract

FILLING

4 oz [115 g] semisweet chocolate, chopped into small pieces, or chocolate chips
3½ Tbsp [50 g] heavy cream
8 to 10 prunes, chopped (optional)

TOPPING

Confectioners' sugar, for dusting

Preheat the oven to 350°F [180°C] and line two baking sheets with parchment paper.

Begin by making the dough. In a medium mixing bowl, whisk together the sugar, almond meal, cocoa powder, and salt.

In the bowl of your stand mixer fitted with the whisk attachment, beat the egg whites and lemon juice on high speed until stiff peaks form. Whisk in the vanilla, then turn off the mixer.

Switch to either the paddle attachment or hand-mixing with a wooden spoon and add the dry ingredients, one third at a time, until no dry pockets remain and a thick, sticky batter has formed.

Using wet hands to prevent sticking, roll out 1 in [2.5 cm] balls of dough and place 2 in [5 cm] apart on the baking sheets. Bake for 10 to 12 minutes, until the cookies have puffed and the surface has cracked. They will still be soft at this stage. Remove from the oven and set aside to cool.

While the cookies cool, make the ganache filling. Place the chocolate in a small heatproof bowl. In a small saucepan, heat the cream over medium heat until steaming. Pour the hot cream over the chocolate and stir until melted and silky. Cool at room temperature until thickened, 15 to 20 minutes.

Spoon a generous teaspoon of ganache onto the flat side of half the baked cookies, add a few pieces of chopped prunes (if using), then cover each with an unfilled cookie like a sandwich. Sprinkle or roll in confectioners' sugar, then serve.

Store airtight and refrigerated for up to a week, or make ahead then freeze and thaw at room temperature for 2 hours before serving.

Soft Iced Toruń Gingerbread

Pierniki Toruńskie

The city of Toruń in Western Poland is famous for a very oddly shaped soft piernik—gingerbread. They're called *Katarzynki*, but that name is trademarked by the town's gingerbread factory. To me, Katarzynki look a bit like two-headed mutant snowmen, but regardless of what your gingerbread Rorschach tells you, they're worth a bake.

Centuries ago, Toruń was an important and rich stop on the Hanseatic trade routes that went between Western Europe and Asia, hence it had a lot of that old-timey signifier of wealth and travel: spices. The huge amount of expensive spices in these cookies was the ultimate seventeenth-century food flex, and while today's gingerbread doesn't connote the same status it once did, the city keeps up its beloved tradition.

These pierniki are special for a few reasons. They're aged—either on the front end or the back, the dough or the baked cookie. The long process comes from the days of using potash, an ash derivative, to leaven the gingerbread, as potash needed time to activate and release its leavening powers. Nowadays, baking soda and baking powder make this irrelevant, as the cookie is gonna rise one way or the other. But it wasn't just about rising—the aging allows the spices and softness to develop well. Some people make the dough about a month in advance and store it chilled before rolling out and baking. I prefer to bake them directly, then seal the cookies in an airtight container with an apple for about a week, then glaze. The sweet base of these cookies is honey, as opposed to the brown sugars and molasses of Western Europe and North America, and the flour is 50 percent rye, which gives them extra chew, softness, and longevity. If you don't have the wild-looking Katarzynki cookie cutter, don't worry: These also come in hearts and circles.

MAKES 18 to 20 cookies

DOUGH

½ cup plus 2½ Tbsp [220 g] pourable honey
2 eggs
3 Tbsp [45 g] full-fat sour cream
3 Tbsp [40 g] sunflower oil
2½ cups [250 g] light rye flour
2 cups [250 g] all-purpose flour
1 batch Gingerbread Spice (page 341)
1 Tbsp baking soda
1 tsp kosher salt

GLAZE

1 batch Thin Glaze (Lukier, page 348)
1 batch Chocolate Glaze (page 350)

Begin by making the dough. In a medium mixing bowl, whisk together the honey, eggs, sour cream, and sunflower oil. In the bowl of your stand mixer fitted with the paddle attachment, combine the rye flour, all-purpose flour, gingerbread spice, baking soda, and salt and mix for a minute on low speed, just until all ingredients are even. Pour the liquid mixture into the dry ingredients and mix until you have a thick batter with no remaining streaks of flour, about 2 minutes.

cont'd

At this point, you can shape and bake your cookies immediately, or wrap your dough in plastic wrap then seal airtight and chill in the fridge for up to 2 months.

Either way, when you're ready to bake your cookies, preheat the oven to 350°F [180°C] with the convection setting turned on and line two baking sheets with parchment paper.

On a lightly floured work surface, roll out the dough until it's a little less than ½ in [1 cm] thick. Cut out your cookies using 2 to 3 in [5 to 7.5 cm] cookie cutters and place them 1 in [2.5 cm] apart on the baking sheets. Reroll the remaining dough to make more cookies until it's all gone. Bake each tray for about 10 minutes, until the cookies are puffed, beginning to brown, and still a bit soft. Remove from the pan and allow to cool completely on a cooling rack.

After the cookies have cooled, you have two options. If you're baking from aged dough, you can glaze and serve the cookies immediately. If you're baking the cookies directly, put them in a large cookie tin or airtight container with an apple and set somewhere cool for about a week to soften and gain moisture before topping and serving.

When your cookies are soft enough and you're ready to glaze for serving, prepare your glazes according to the recipes on page 348 and page 350, then dip the cookies in the glazes, turning them over to get both sides covered, and allow to set on a cooling rack.

Serve or store in a cookie tin for up to 2 weeks.

Decorated Christmas Gingerbread

Pierniczki

My in-laws are Czech, not Polish. But they do live about an hour from the border, and there's an enormous amount of international overlap with pastries and cookies in their region. When I first got married and was eager to impress my very sweet mother-in-law, I had the idea of bringing gingerbread for their Christmas cookie platter. Czechs, like Poles, make elaborate plates of tiny Christmas cookies and share and swap among family members. I made what was, to me, an impressive ginger-bread: spicy and crunchy. When I brought the cookies, though, the family took bites and looked at me with a kind of pity reserved for a very sweet idiot. "They're good," they said, "but they're crunchy." That was when my mother-in-law took me to the balcony and showed me boxes and boxes of cookies that had been absorbing moisture and softening for months and developing the flavor of the spices. One person's stale is another person's soft. For a truly authentic Polish gingerbread experience, do like my Czech mother-in-law and let these age in the cold for at least a week or up to a month before eating.

NOTE: If you want to hang these on ribbons on your Christmas tree, skip the aging process, as that can make them too delicate to hang. Use a toothpick to make a hole in the top of each cookie before baking.

MAKES 40 cookies

DOUGH

1 egg
1 egg yolk
1½ Tbsp [30 g] honey
1 Tbsp full-fat sour cream
1 tsp vanilla extract
3 cups plus 3 Tbsp [400 g] all-purpose flour
1 cup [100 g] light rye flour
1 batch Gingerbread Spice (page 341)
1 tsp kosher salt
1 tsp double-acting baking powder
1 cup plus 5 Tbsp [300 g] cold unsalted butter, cubed
1½ cups [180 g] confectioners' sugar, sifted

FOR DECORATING

1 batch Royal Icing (page 349)

Begin by making the dough. In a small mixing bowl, whisk together the egg, egg yolk, honey, sour cream, and vanilla until smooth.

In the bowl of your stand mixer fitted with the paddle attachment, mix the all-purpose flour, rye flour, gingerbread spice, salt, and baking powder for a minute on low speed, just until all the ingredients are combined. Continuing to mix on low speed, add the butter and mix until you have a sandy texture and no chunks of butter are visible. Add the confectioners' sugar a little at a time and mix until incorporated. Pour in the egg mixture in a thin stream and mix until a thick dough has formed and no dry pockets remain, about 2 minutes. Form the dough into a disk and wrap airtight. Chill for 2 hours or up to a week. (This dough can be frozen for several months and thawed overnight in the fridge before using.)

cont'd

When you're ready to bake, preheat the oven to 350°F [180°C] with the convection setting turned on and line two baking sheets with parchment paper. Allow the dough to warm up at room temperature for about 20 minutes, then give it a brief knead, just enough so that it doesn't crack when rolling.

On a lightly floured surface, roll the dough out to ¼ in [6 mm] thickness. Use cookie cutters to cut out your cookies in whatever shape you like and place them 1 in [2.5 cm] apart on the baking sheets. Reroll the remaining dough to make more cookies until it's all gone. Bake for 10 minutes, or until just starting to brown. Allow to cool on a cooling rack, then place in an airtight container or cookie tin with an apple. Store in a cool location for 1 week to a month, until the cookies are soft.

When ready to serve, prepare the royal icing according to the recipe on page 349. Either dip cookies in the glaze or pipe on designs using a pastry bag and fine-point tip. If the icing is too liquid for piping, let it sit for 20 minutes and it will thicken up.

Once all your cookies are decorated, let them dry on a cooling rack until the royal icing has set and hardened.

Store in a cookie tin for up to 3 weeks.

Tim Mazurek's Mazurek

That Tim Mazurek had never made a mazurek made no sense at all. "The funny thing is, my name is obviously a dessert, and I never really investigated that. Every six months to a year, someone in the food world will write to me and say, you know your name is a pastry?" The beloved food writer of *Lottie + Doof*, known for his sensitive and thorough approach to recipes, Tim was raised in a Polish American family in Chicago. "We had our little bakery," he says, "and it's still there. Every week someone would go. I grew up with that as my primary exposure to Polish baking and dessert culture." As an adult, developing recipes, he'd never approached mazurek, but lately he's been going through a phase of fussy-looking, elaborate desserts. It felt like a good time to try.

But maybe it isn't so nonsensical that Tim hadn't touched his namesake pastry until now. If there's a hard-to-pin-down Polish pastry, it's mazurek. A decorative Easter cookie-cake with few rules other than beauty, it's generally made with a shortcrust or kruche base, a filling—almond paste, jam, walnut paste, and chocolate spread are all valid—an elaborate pattern of bakalie—dried fruits and nuts—and jams, candies, flowers, and whatever other pretty things you have on hand. The decoration resembles the folk art–style painting common on old wooden houses or fireplaces of stylized flowers and patterned geometry, like Fabergé eggs. "I was surprised to see how unstandardized [mazurki are]," Tim says. "There are themes that reappear, but the decoration seems to be what they most have in common. And even that seems to vary wildly." Tim's observation is backed up by Irena Głowacka's seminal 1972 cookbook *Pieczenie Ciast i Ciasteczek (Baking Cakes and Cookies)*. The baking manual has no fewer than twenty mazurek recipes—mazurek with lemons, mazurek with dried plums, mazurek with nuts and honey, mazurek with apples, mazurek with chocolate, mazurek with poppy seeds, and more.

When Tim set about to develop his own mazurek recipe for this book, he played with everything from dulce de leche—kajmak—to white chocolate–raspberry ganache—before settling on a simple jam and glaze filling on an Easter egg shape because it felt like the simplest and best base for the real priority—the decorations. "It's short pastry with toppings. People can play with it a million ways." So follow along with Tim's recipe, or substitute any number of the fillings from chapter 6 of this book.

NOTE: You can also use the Lukier recipe on page 348 for the glaze.

MAKES 1 large mazurek

cont'd

DOUGH

2 egg yolks

2 Tbsp [30 g] full-fat sour cream

1 tsp vanilla extract

2⅓ cups plus 1 Tbsp [300 g] all-purpose flour

½ cup plus 2 Tbsp [75 g] confectioners' sugar

½ tsp kosher salt

¾ cup [170 g] unsalted European-style butter, cold and cut into ½ in [1 cm] cubes

FILLING

⅓ to ½ cup [100 to 160 g] raspberry jam

GLAZE

1½ cups [180 g] confectioners' sugar

2 tsp light corn syrup, honey, or golden syrup

1 Tbsp refined coconut oil, melted

1 tsp lemon juice

½ tsp vanilla extract

Couple of drops of almond extract

Pinch of kosher salt

2 to 5 Tbsp [30 to 75 g] whole milk

FOR DECORATING

Almonds, seeds, dried fruit, poppy seeds, candied fruit, flowers

Begin by mixing the dough. Whisk together the egg yolks, sour cream, and vanilla in a small mixing bowl until smooth. Mix the flour, confectioners' sugar, and salt in a food processor or stand mixer fitted with the paddle attachment, then add butter bit by bit, pulsing or mixing on low speed until sandy and no chunks of butter remain. Add the egg mixture and continue pulsing or mixing until the dough comes together. Form the dough into a compact disk and wrap airtight, then refrigerate for at least 1 hour or up to 5 days before using.

When you're ready to use the dough, allow it to rest at room temperature for about 15 minutes until pliable enough to roll. Unwrap the dough. Break off one fifth of the dough and set it aside for decorations. On a well-floured work surface, or between two floured sheets of parchment paper, roll the larger portion of dough into a large oval or egg shape, about ¼ in [6 mm] thick. Use a flat knife or pizza cutter to trim the edges and cut into your final shape, then slide the dough onto a baking sheet lined with parchment paper. Roll out the remaining portion of dough into long, thin ropes and twist to form a decorative border for your egg shape. The dough will be too delicate to make twists long enough to go around the whole egg, so this can be broken into three to four twists and pressed together where they meet. Any messy edges can be hidden with decorations. Brush the edge of the egg shape with water, then gently set the twisted border around the egg. Any extra dough can be rolled and cut into leaf shapes with a paring knife or stamped out with cookie cutters. These can be placed around the twisted edge as decorations.

Chill the shaped mazurek for at least an hour in the fridge. Shortly before baking, preheat the oven to 350°F [180°C] with the convection setting turned on. Prick the entire flat middle of the mazurek with a fork, then bake for 15 to 20 minutes, until no longer shiny and starting to turn golden. If the center puffs up, just press it down gently. Remove from the oven, spread evenly with a thin layer of the raspberry jam, then return to the oven for another 10 minutes, or until the jam has started to bubble and the pastry is fully golden brown. Remove from the oven and let it cool completely.

To make the glaze, combine the confectioners' sugar, corn syrup, coconut oil, lemon juice, vanilla, almond extract, and salt and whisk until smooth, adding the milk one spoonful at a time until you have the desired thickness. It should be thin enough to pour but thick enough to still be a bit opaque. Pour and smooth over the top of the cooled mazurek. Allow it to set briefly, then decorate (with nuts, fruits, etc.) as desired.

Store airtight at room temperature for up to 3 days.

Fruit Turnovers

Rożki z Jabłkami i Wiśniami

I did my bakery training in France, but the best chausson aux pommes (apple turnover) I ever had was at the Kwaśne Jabłko apple farm in Włodowo in Northern Poland. The farm specializes in indigenous varieties of apples, grown without chemicals, and they produce naturally fermented, low-intervention ciders. One summer, a young pastry chef from Poznań was working in their restaurant and created a delicate, flaky puff pastry with the most pleasingly sour filling I've ever had. While that sort of French-style chausson aux pommes makes its appearance in new Polish bakeries, the more local variety is this recipe, rożki z jabłkami, triangular turnovers with either apple or sour cherry filling.

NOTE: I like to prep the dough and filling the night before I'm going to bake, giving everything plenty of time to chill and making assembly and baking a short process, ready in no time for breakfast or tea.

MAKES 16 turnovers

PASTRY

1 batch Francuskie Dough (page 240)

FILLING

1 batch Apple Filling (page 336) and/or Cherry Filling (page 334)

EGG WASH

1 egg, beaten

TOPPING

Large crystal demerara sugar or any large-grain sugar

GLAZE

1 cup [120 g] confectioners' sugar, sifted

A few tsp lemon juice or the extra liquid from cherry filling

Prepare the Francuskie dough according to the recipe on page 240 and allow to chill for at least 2 hours.

While the dough is chilling, prepare the apple and/or cherry filling according to the recipes on page 336 and/or 334, then refrigerate while your dough finishes chilling.

When you're ready to assemble your turnovers, preheat the oven to 350°F [180°C] with the convection setting turned on and line two baking sheets with parchment paper.

To shape the rożki, on a lightly floured work surface, roll out the dough to a square a bit larger than 20 x 20 in [51 x 51 cm]. As you roll, slide your hands under the dough from time to time, allowing it to relax and contract before you continue rolling so that your final dough will hold its size without contracting. Use a flat knife or pizza wheel to trim the edges, then use a ruler to measure 5 in [13 cm] intervals along each side. Connect the intervals and cut sixteen even squares.

In the center of each square, spoon a couple tablespoons of whichever filling you chose to make. If using the cherry filling, drain off the liquid before filling. Dip a finger or pastry brush in water and lightly dampen the edges of one half of the pastry. Fold the other half of the pastry over the filling, corner to corner, to meet the dampened side, then use a fork to seal the edges well. Flip the pastry over, and use the fork to seal the edge from the other side. Arrange the pastries on a baking sheet 1 to 2 in [2.5 to 5 cm] apart, then prick through the center of the pastry a few times with a knife to create steam vents. Brush the top of each pastry with egg wash, then sprinkle with the demerara sugar.

cont'd

Bake for 20 to 25 minutes, until golden brown and some of the filling bubbles up. Let the turnovers cool on the pan while you make the glaze.

To make the glaze, mix the confectioners' sugar with as much lemon juice or cherry filling juice as needed to make a thick but pourable glaze. Drizzle over the cooled turnovers.

Store in an airtight container for up to several days.

Porzeczka
- czerwona
- biała
9 zł/op

Fried Angel Wing Cookies

Faworki

When I said I was writing this book, friend after friend asked, "Will there be faworki?" It's a simple but beloved cookie that is especially popular for Christmas and Carnival but is a year-round favorite and can be purchased in most traditional bakeries. In parts of the Polish diaspora, particularly in North America, these are called *chruściki* or *angel wings*. Despite being deep-fried, they're never greasy, owing to the addition of spirytus or high-proof vodka in the dough. Many other faworki-type cookies show up across Europe, from Italy to Sweden to the Lorraine region of France, each country varying the recipe according to its own traditions, whether through the addition of cardamom in Norway or dipping in berry jams in Hungary. In Poland, though, faworki need no pairing: They stand on their own.

MAKES 45 to 50 faworki

DOUGH

7 egg yolks
¼ cup plus 1 Tbsp [75 g] full-fat sour cream
¼ cup [50 g] sugar
1 Tbsp spirytus, vodka, kirsch, or śliwowica
1 tsp vanilla extract
½ tsp kosher salt
1½ Tbsp [25 g] sunflower or other neutral oil
2⅓ cups plus 1 Tbsp [300 g] all-purpose flour

FOR FRYING

8½ cups [2 L] sunflower oil

TOPPING

1 cup [120 g] confectioners' sugar

Begin by mixing the dough. In the bowl of your stand mixer, whisk together the egg yolks, sour cream, sugar, spirytus, vanilla, salt, and 1½ Tbsp sunflower oil until homogenous. Add the flour, switch to the dough hook attachment, and mix on medium speed for about 8 minutes, until the dough is soft and smooth. Use oiled hands to form the dough into a ball, then place in a lightly oiled bowl, covered with plastic wrap, for 30 minutes to allow the dough to relax.

After the dough has rested, turn it out onto a floured work surface and roll until it's so thin that you can see your hand behind it. As you roll, pause frequently to run your hands under the dough to allow it to relax and contract before continuing to roll. Re-flour the surface as needed to prevent sticking or tearing. Once the dough is thin enough and no longer contracts, allow it to rest for another 5 minutes.

After resting, use a pizza cutter or a sharp flat knife to cut the dough into 1 x 4 in [2.5 x 10 cm] strips. In the center of each strip, cut an about 1½ in [4 cm] vertical slit. Fold and pull one end of each strip through the center slit, creating a bow-like twist.

Once you've formed your faworki, heat up the frying oil in a medium saucepan or deep skillet to 350°F [180°C]. Once the oil is hot enough, fry the faworki in batches for about 2 minutes on each side, or until golden, bubbly, and puffed. Remove with a slotted spoon or spatula and let cool on a paper towel–lined cooling rack. Once all the faworki are fried, allow to cool and turn crispy, then dust generously with confectioners' sugar.

Eat immediately, or store in a cookie tin for up to a week.

Bow Tie Cookies

Eier Kichel

"Big Kichel could have been the name of one of Meyer Lanksy's enforcers."
—Journalist Matt Kronsberg on the kichel at Generoso's Bakery in Brooklyn

***Kichlach*, Yiddish for *cookies*, usually describes a range of airy and thin Ashkenazi egg cookies. While they can be sweet, savory, peppery, oniony, or something in between, they all have their origins in the shtetls of Eastern Europe. In these prewar Jewish villages, poppy seed kichel and pepper kichel were the rage. In America, the variety that thrived is sweet egg kichel. Rolled out in sugar before being twisted into a bow-tie shape, they're feather-light. The bite has a crisp start with a meltaway finish. You can eat ten at a time and 5 minutes later forget it ever happened. Ephemeral just might be the first word that springs to mind when you taste one, and in fact, some people just call them *nothings*. From a bakery science perspective, kichel are very closely related to Faworki (page 266), with the distinction of baking rather than frying. In keeping with so much Jewish baking, egg kichel forgoes all dairy, instead taking their richness from eggs and oil.**

MAKES 60 to 70 kichlach

DOUGH
3 eggs
7 egg yolks
6½ Tbsp [90 g] sunflower or other neutral oil
¼ cup [50 g] sugar
1 Tbsp schnapps, kirsch, or vodka
1 tsp vanilla extract
½ tsp kosher salt
2¾ cups [350 g] all-purpose flour

FOR ROLLING
2 cups [400 g] sugar

Begin by mixing the dough. In the bowl of your stand mixer, whisk together the eggs, egg yolks, sunflower oil, sugar, schnapps, vanilla, and salt until homogenous. Add the flour, switch to the dough hook attachment, and mix on medium speed for about 15 minutes, until it forms a very soft dough with a satiny shine that can be stretched thin without tearing. Use oiled hands to remove the dough from the bowl and form into a ball, then place in a lightly oiled bowl, covered, for 45 minutes to allow the dough to relax.

Shortly before the dough has finished resting, preheat the oven to 350°F [180°C] with the convection setting turned on and line two baking sheets with parchment paper.

When the dough has finished resting, cover your work surface with a thick layer of sugar and turn out the dough onto the sugar. Cover the top of the dough with another thick layer of sugar, then roll until the dough is about ¼ in [6 mm] thick. As you roll, periodically run your hands under the dough to allow it to relax so that the final dough doesn't contract and lose its dimensions. Once the dough is rolled, use a pizza cutter to cut the dough into rectangles, about 2 x 3 in [5 x 7.5 cm]. Place the pieces on the lined baking sheets about 1 in [2.5 cm] apart. Twist each dough strip once in the middle to create a bowtie shape. Let the shaped kichel rest for about 5 minutes, then bake for about 10 minutes, until each cookie is lightly golden and puffed. Allow to cool.

Eat immediately or store for up to a week in a cookie tin.

Polish American Jam Cookies

Kołaczki

Kołacz in Poland doesn't mean the same as _kołacz_ in Chicago. Kołaczki in Chicago and the American Midwest are tender and flaky folded jam cookies synonymous with Polish baking and a very big deal, especially around Christmas. Kołacz in Poland, on the other hand, is a kind of Silesian yeasted cake pastry, nothing to do with the American cookies. Really, the Chicagoan kołacz cookies just aren't much of a thing in Poland. They exist, sure. And as in America, they're mostly for Christmas. But, as one friend says, "They don't even really have a name here. I guess usually if we have to, they're called _rożki_, which just means _cones_ or _wraps_." It's a word so unspecific that it applies to any number of other foods—including the Polish version of Bugles chips. But maybe in Chicago, the diaspora really got it right—because these are so good they deserve a spotlight.

MAKES 18 cookies

1 batch Francuskie Dough (page 240)
¾ cup [240 g] Plum or Apricot Filling (page 333), or jam of choice
½ cup [60 g] confectioners' sugar

Make the Francuskie dough according to the recipe on page 240 and chill for at least 2 hours.

When you're ready to bake, preheat the oven to 350°F [180°C] with the convection setting turned on and line two baking sheets with parchment paper.

On a floured work surface, roll out the dough to a square about 20 x 20 in [51 x 51 cm] and ⅛ in [3 mm] thick. Trim the edges with a flat knife or a pizza cutter, then use a ruler to measure intervals of about 3¼ in [8 cm] along each side. Join these intervals to cut eighteen even squares.

Place a teaspoon of fruit filling in the center of each square. Fold one corner of the square over the filling, then dab this folded corner with water. This will act as glue for your dough. Fold the opposite corner over the folded one, stretching it a bit to overlap well. Press gently to seal. Place the cookies on the baking sheets about 2 in [5 cm] apart.

Bake one sheet of cookies for 15 to 20 minutes, until golden brown, keeping the other sheet of cookies in the fridge to chill. Remove the first sheet pan from the oven and bake the second sheet of cookies. Once all the cookies have cooled, dust with confectioners' sugar.

Eat immediately, or store for up to a week in a cookie tin.

Dominika's Rolled Waffles with Cream

Rurki z Kremem

Dominika Buck remembers her first rurki z kremem easily and fondly. When she was a small child at the ballet school in Wrocław's Plac Solny, she and the other students would run to a literal hole-in-the-wall after class, a one-door stand at the end of the building from which a woman sold whipped cream–filled waffles. Lines of small ballerinas, sometimes still in tutus, always with their hair in buns, waited with their pocket money until they got their reward for practicing. "It's the first sweet I remember eating outside of my home. The waffle is crunchy and the cream is like a cloud."

Despite the fond memories, Dominika did not grow up to be a ballerina, though the cream waffles are not to blame. Instead she became a designer and the owner of Warsaw's Bar Rascal, a wine bar and restaurant that coincidentally sits in the same building as Poland's national ballet school. There, to pair with her personally sourced natural wines, Dominika serves thoroughly contemporary small dishes that draw influence from both seasonal local products and classic Polish dishes, with a touch of her own personal story. In the summer months, Rascal makes these rurki z kremem, plating them with little piles of small but pungently aromatic wild strawberries or inky jagody (bilberries). "Rurki remind you of holidays, trips to the zoo. Walks on old town squares. It's a wonderful thing."

The key to getting the waffle tubes right is catching the waffles at just the right moment, when they're golden brown but still pliable. Once wrapped around a wooden dowel or cannoli form, they'll set crispy. "It's a small, detailed work to make these," Dominika told me, "like folding pierogi."

NOTE: You'll need an ice cream cone waffle iron or pizzelle maker to make these.

MAKES 20 rurki

WAFFLES

3 small egg whites [75 g], at room temperature

¾ cup plus 2 Tbsp [105 g] confectioners' sugar

¾ cup [90 g] all-purpose flour

¼ tsp kosher salt

4½ Tbsp [60 g] unsalted butter, melted and cooled, plus more for the waffle iron

WHIPPED CREAM

17½ oz [500 g] whipping cream

½ cup [60 g] confectioners' sugar

1 tsp vanilla extract

FOR SERVING

About 4 cups [500 to 600 g] wild strawberries or blueberries

Begin by making the waffle batter. In the bowl of your stand mixer with the whisk attachment, whisk the egg whites on high speed to stiff peaks. In a medium mixing bowl, whisk together the confectioners' sugar, flour, and salt. Pour in the melted butter in a slow stream, whisking as you go. Add the egg whites and fold in until the batter is smooth and no pockets of egg white remain.

Heat up your waffle iron or pizzelle maker and brush it very lightly with melted butter. Spoon about 3 Tbsp of batter in the middle of the iron. Close and cook until golden brown but still soft and flexible. Using a 1 in [2.5 cm] dowel or rolling pin, roll up the waffle into a tube, then slide it off onto a cooling rack. As the waffles cool, they'll become crunchy. Repeat until all the batter is used up.

cont'd

Once the waffles are finished, you can store them in an airtight container for up to a week before filling and serving.

When you're ready to serve, make the whipped cream. In the bowl of your stand mixer fitted with the whisk attachment, beat the whipping cream, confectioners' sugar, and vanilla on medium-high speed until the whipped cream is stiff. Fill a pastry bag with the whipped cream and snip off about ½ in [1 cm] from the tip. Pipe cream into each waffle and plate with a small pile of berries next to it.

Serve immediately. Eating this with your hands is encouraged.

MERCEDES-BENZ
Paweł Huelle
SINGER
MAP
WISŁAWA SZYMBORSKA

Dulce de Leche Wafer Cookies

Andruty z Kajmakiem

Andruty are a taste of Polish childhood. Part of the compendium of Polish waffle sweets, they're often one of the first cookies children learn to make on their own as they're really just a sweet filling spread between waffle layers. It's easy to find ready-made waffle layers in Polish supermarkets, but the from-scratch versions of these are far better, as the homemade waffles give them an extra toasty edge with a flavor not unlike a Dutch stroopwafel. Andruty can be made with a variety of fillings, from hazelnut paste to chocolate spread to jam, but kajmak—the thick caramel made from cooked sweetened condensed milk, the Polish equivalent of dulce de leche—is an unbeatable classic.

NOTE: You'll need an ice cream cone waffle iron or pizzelle maker to make these.

MAKES 16 cookies

WAFFLES

6 egg whites
1⅓ cups plus 2 Tbsp [180 g] all-purpose flour
1½ cups [180 g] confectioners' sugar
1 tsp vanilla extract
½ tsp kosher salt
13 Tbsp [180 g] unsalted butter, melted and cooled, plus more for the waffle iron

FILLING

17½ oz [500 g] Dulce de Leche (Kajmak, page 347)

Begin by making the waffle batter. In a medium mixing bowl, whisk together the egg whites, flour, confectioners' sugar, vanilla, and salt until smooth. Continuing to whisk, pour in the butter in a thin stream until fully incorporated.

Heat up your waffle iron or pizelle maker and brush lightly with melted butter. Spoon 3 Tbsp of batter into the middle of the iron, then close and cook until golden brown. Remove the waffle and place on a cooling rack. The waffle will become crispy as it cools. Repeat for the rest of the batter, making between 12 and 14 waffles.

Once the waffles are cool, use a spatula or flat knife to spread one waffle with a thin, even layer of dulce de leche. Stack another waffle on top and repeat until you've made a stack of six or seven waffles layered with dulce de leche. Repeat for a second stack of waffles. Once you have two stacks of waffles, cover with a baking pan weighted with a soup can or a stack of books and leave to set for about an hour. The cookies will soften as the dulce de leche soaks in.

Once set, chill in the freezer for about 20 minutes, then use a large flat knife to cut each waffle stack into eight even triangles, making sixteen even triangular cookies.

These are best eaten the same day but can be stored airtight in the fridge for a few days.

Molded Walnut Cookies

Orzeszki

I've been making orzeszki, walnut cookies made from paper-thin shortcrust filled with cocoa paste or dulce de leche, for years, ever since I found a set of their very particular metal molds at a flea market in Prague. And whenever I make them, the reactions come in strong from my friends across the former Eastern Bloc nationalities. "Gorishok! This is my childhood!" "Orech! I love them." "How did you make these oreshki?" "Save me some orzeszki! Are they with caramel or chocolate?" All real reactions from a Ukrainian, a Czech, a Russian, and a Pole, respectively. Molded walnut cookies, whether homemade in a stovetop mold or delicate tin oven forms, or bought by weight at bakeries, are an enduring communist-era favorite, still widely available in Poland and Eastern Europe. These orzeszki use a chocolate filling, but you can also use Kajmak (page 347).

NOTE: You will need a set of walnut molds to make these cookies, but they're cheap and easy to find on the internet. You'll want at least twenty molds; the more the better, as each cookie needs two halves.

MAKES 30 to 36 orzeszki

DOUGH

½ batch Kruche Dough (page 190), chilled, or ½ batch Tim Mazurek's Mazurek Dough (page 259)

1 to 2 Tbsp [15 to 30 g] sunflower or other neutral oil for greasing the molds

FILLING

1⅓ cups [150 g] ground walnuts

3½ Tbsp [50 g] unsalted butter, at room temperature

⅔ cup [80 g] confectioners' sugar

¼ cup [20 g] cocoa powder

1 tsp vanilla extract

¾ tsp kosher salt

TOPPING

Confectioners' sugar, for dusting (optional)

Prepare your kruche or mazurek dough according to the recipe on page 190 or 259, and chill for at least 1 hour.

Once the dough is almost finished chilling, preheat the oven to 350°F [180°C] with the convection setting turned on. Dip a paper towel or pastry brush in sunflower oil and very lightly oil the inside of the nut molds to prevent sticking. Break off a large pea-sized portion of dough, roll into a smooth ball, then press into each mold, coating the inside evenly, all the way up to the edges. Continue for all of your molds. Place the molds on a baking sheet open side-up (I prefer a pan with edges so they don't accidentally roll off while handling) and bake for about 12 minutes, until golden brown. Allow to cool, then gently turn each nut half out of its mold. Brush out any crumbs from the molds, brush again with a bit of oil, and repeat with the remaining dough until you have 60 to 72 nut halves.

While the cookies bake, make the filling. In a medium mixing bowl, combine the ground walnuts, butter, confectioners' sugar, cocoa powder, vanilla, and salt and mix with a fork until it comes together in a thick paste.

Once the cookie halves are all baked and cool, assemble the cookies. Pull off a portion of filling about the size of a small grape and roll it into an oval. Set it between two nut halves and press slightly to close, being careful not to crack the cookie and leaving a bit of filling visible. Repeat with the remaining filling and shells.

Eat immediately or store airtight in the refrigerator for up to 5 days. Dust with confectioners' sugar before serving, if desired.

Hamantaschen

Hamantaschen are one of the signature cookies of Central and Eastern European Jews. Baked for Purim—the holiday celebrated by retelling of the story of Queen Esther, who saved the Jews from the evil Haman back in ancient Persia—hamantaschen are said to look like Haman's ears, Haman's hat, or a vulva, depending on whom you ask. Whatever it is, the form is always the same. A triangular stuffed pocket, traditionally filled with powidła, poppy seed filling, or apricot lekvar. Older versions of these were often made with a yeasted dough, but the modern-day hamantasch is usually a sugar-cookie style. I like to make mine with this ground walnut short dough. The nut addition gives these just a bit more stability so that the cookies hold their shape while baking, but also a much deeper flavor profile than a plain short or kruche dough. This recipe also gives the option for a touch of orange zest in the dough, which my friend Dan, when he waxes nostalgic about flavors, insists, "somehow makes it taste more . . . Jewish?"

NOTE: The ground walnuts can be store-bought or made from whole walnuts blitzed in a food processor until they are the texture of sand. Toast your walnuts before grinding for an even richer flavor.

MAKES 24 hamantaschen

DOUGH

2 eggs
1 tsp vanilla extract
4 cups [500 g] all-purpose flour
½ tsp kosher salt
1 cup plus 1½ Tbsp [250 g] unsalted butter, cold and cubed
1⅓ cups [150 g] ground walnuts
1¼ cups [150 g] confectioners' sugar
½ Tbsp grated orange zest (optional)

FILLING

1 batch Poppy Seed Paste (page 337), Apricot Filling (page 333), or Plum Filling (page 333)

TOPPING (OPTIONAL)

Confectioners' sugar, for sprinkling
1 batch Chocolate Glaze (page 350; optional)

Begin by mixing the dough. In a small mixing bowl, whisk the eggs and vanilla until well beaten, then set aside. In the bowl of your stand mixer fitted with the paddle attachment, mix the flour, salt, and butter on low speed until sandy in texture and no visible chunks of butter remain. Add the ground walnuts, confectioners' sugar, and orange zest (if using) and mix until evenly combined. Continuing to mix on low speed, pour in the liquid mixture in a slow stream until the dough comes together into a solid mass, 1 to 2 minutes. Remove the dough from the bowl, form it into a thick disk, and wrap airtight. Chill in the fridge for 2 hours or up to a week before using. In the freezer, this will last for a month. To use from frozen, simply defrost in the refrigerator overnight.

When you're ready to bake, preheat the oven to 350°F [180°C] with the convection setting turned on and line two baking sheets with parchment paper.

On a lightly floured work surface, knead your dough briefly so it doesn't crack while rolling. Roll the dough out to about ⅛ in [3 mm] thickness. Use a 2½ to 3 in [6 to 7 cm] round cookie cutter or large water glass to cut out circles. Set the scraps aside to reroll and cut more circles.

Put about 1 Tbsp of filling in the center of each circle, then fold up the sides to make a triangle, leaving a visible opening in the middle, and pinch along the seams to seal. Repeat for the rest of the circles, arranging your shaped hamantaschen

cont'd

about 1 in [2.5 cm] apart on the baking sheets. Refrigerate the cookies for about 20 minutes, then bake for 12 to 15 minutes, or until the cookies are light golden brown and no longer shiny.

Serve plain, dust with confectioners' sugar, or make a chocolate glaze according to the recipe on page 350 and drizzle over the tops of the cookies before chilling for 20 minutes to allow the chocolate to set. The hamantaschen will last all week stored in a cookie tin at room temperature.

Laskowy Prażony
80 zł
100 zł
Nerkowce extra
65 zł
Migdały Prażone
65 zł
Nerkowce
60 zł
Migdały
55 zł
Pistacje extra
70 zł
Orzechy Polskie
50 zł

Almond Florentine-Style Cookies

Florentynki

Almond Florentine cookies are diamond-shaped crunchy shortbreads with a layer of slivered almonds. The almonds toast while they bake, adding an extra dimension of flavor. I like to serve these in place of biscotti with strong coffee, or even crumbled and served on top of ice cream. If you prefer a thicker cookie base, use a full batch of kruche dough rather than half, and bake the base just a bit longer. For variety, switch out the slivered almonds for chopped hazelnuts, walnuts, or even sesame seeds.

MAKES 24 small cookies

DOUGH

½ batch Kruche Dough (page 190), chilled

TOPPING

2 egg whites
½ cup [100 g] sugar
1 tsp vanilla extract
¼ tsp kosher salt
1½ Tbsp [15 g] all-purpose flour
1½ Tbsp [25 g] unsalted butter, melted
1⅔ cups [200 g] slivered or chopped almonds

GLAZE

¼ cup [60 g] apricot jam or simple syrup

Prepare the half batch of kruche dough according to the recipe on page 190, then wrap airtight and chill for at least 1 hour.

Once your dough is chilled, preheat the oven to 350°F [180°C] with the convection setting turned on and line a 13 x 9 in [33 x 23 cm] baking pan with parchment paper.

Once your dough is chilled, roll it out on a lightly floured surface into a rectangle just larger than the pan, about ⅛ in [3 mm] thick. Trim the edges to tidy, then gently set the dough into the pan and press to fit. Prick the entire surface of the dough with a fork, then chill in the fridge for about 20 minutes. Blind bake for about 10 minutes, until the top is no longer shiny and the cookie is starting to turn golden brown.

While the cookie base bakes, prepare the almond topping. In a medium mixing bowl or the bowl of your stand mixer fitted with the whisk attachment, beat the egg whites, sugar, vanilla, and salt until foamy. Add the flour and mix until smooth. Continuing to mix, add the butter in a thin stream until evenly incorporated. Fold in the almonds with a spatula.

Evenly spread the almond mixture over the surface of your blind-baked cookie base, then return it to the oven for about 15 minutes, or until the surface is starting to turn golden brown. Remove from the oven and use a pastry brush to spread on a thin layer of apricot jam. Return to the oven for 1 to 2 minutes to set. This last step will make your cookies shiny.

Allow the whole thing to cool completely, then remove it from the pan and slice diagonally into 1½ in [4 cm] wide strips by pressing down with a large, flat knife. Then cut vertically in 1½ in [4 cm] strips to create diamond shapes.

Eat immediately or keep in a cookie tin at room temperature for up to 2 weeks.

Seeded Florentynki

Florentynki are nut brittle–style cookies. Caramelized and crispy, they can be loaded with any kind of seed or chopped nuts, which get toasty and flavorful as they bake. Oddly enough, this is a cookie as popularly sold by weight from bakeries as it is in commercial snack packs at gas stations and convenience stores and marketed as health cookies. I'd be leading you astray if I promoted the vague dietary values of these cookies—I'm pretty sure there aren't any—but they are delicious.

MAKES 18 to 24 cookies

2 egg whites
½ cup [100 g] sugar
1 tsp vanilla extract
1 Tbsp almond meal
¼ tsp fleur de sel
1½ Tbsp [25 g] unsalted butter, melted
2½ cups [350 to 400 g] sunflower seeds, pumpkin seeds, sesame seeds, slivered almonds, or chopped hazelnuts, or a mix
2 tsp grated orange zest (optional)
1 cup [140 g] chopped dried apricots or golden raisins (optional)

Preheat the oven to 350°F [180°C] with the convection setting turned on and line two baking sheets with parchment paper.

In a medium mixing bowl or the bowl of your stand mixer fitted with the whisk attachment, beat the egg whites, sugar, vanilla, almond meal, and fleur de sel until foamy. Add the melted butter in a thin stream, continuing to whisk until smooth. Fold in the seeds, and orange zest and dried fruit (if using).

Spoon out the mixture in 1 to 2 Tbsp mounds—1 Tbsp for smaller cookies, 2 for larger—on the baking sheets, about 2 in [5 cm] apart. Use a spoon or spatula to flatten out the mounds, then use a round cookie cutter or inverted drinking glass to gently shape each cookie into a perfect circle. You can also skip that step to leave these more rough and rustic looking.

Bake for 15 to 20 minutes, until golden brown, then allow to completely cool before removing from the baking sheet.

These will last in a cookie tin at room temperature for up to a month.

/5

PTYSIE, BEZY & SERNIKI: CHOUX, MERINGUES & CHEESECAKES

This is the chapter where things get creamy, dreamy, and cloudlike. The Polish love of cheesecakes, meringues, and cream puff–style desserts is evidenced in every café, every bakery.

I was once teaching a baking class at the Bibliothèque Medem in Paris, the largest Yiddish library in Europe. While we were waiting for the oven to heat, the conversation turned to everyone's mothers' and grandmothers' baking, specifically the recipes they brought with them from Poland. "The cheesecake here is never the same, my mother always complained," said one older woman. "It's because you can't get the right cheese here," another interjected. This might have been the first time the words "You can't get the right cheese here" were ever uttered in France, but the woman voicing this was completely right. Polish cheesecakes, or serniki, are an important part of the origin story of the deep and dense New York–style cheesecakes popularized by Jewish bakeries and cafeterias, now beloved the world over. That said, a true Polish cheesecake is very different. Still creamy and gorgeous like their New York descendants, they're lighter, crumblier, and based on smooth, churned twaróg, or farmer's cheese. And it's this very cheese at the core of the cake that makes the difference.

In both traditional and contemporary Polish baking (but the latter, in particular), sweet twaróg fillings are essential to cake culture and yeasted pastries. There have been cheesecakes in Poland since at least the seventeenth century, supported by the strong dairy-farming culture, and now they come in dozens of varieties, with everything from chocolate crusts to fruit incorporations and bright galaretka (gelatin) tops. In contemporary Poland, twaróg cheesecakes now find themselves in a crowd of New York cheesecakes, Japanese cheesecakes, and, of course, the ever-popular burned Basque cheesecake. Despite the variety available, the two most classic, and, I think, delicious—the Kraków style and the Viennese style—remain ubiquitous and beloved.

Any good Polish supermarket will have many different kinds of twaróg: full-fat, half-fat, creamy, smooth, and "cheesecake" twaróg. The cheesecake twaróg is a relatively new kind, blended smooth with a higher proportion of cream cheese than actual twaróg, catering to the contemporary taste for a richer, creamier, more New York–style cake. Even today, some people consider this cheating, as it will often have added starch or stabilizers, though some of those same people will add instant pudding—budyń—to their twaróg for stabilization. In earlier days, cheesecakes were made with "three-times-ground" full-fat twaróg, which meant that the twaróg would be put through a countertop meat grinder three times to reach the desired smoothness.

The cheesecake recipes in this book are true twaróg cheesecakes, blended with cream cheese, cream, and sour cream. It's a lot of dairy, but it remains faithful to the unique texture of Polish cheesecakes. Because you might be baking from this book in an area without a Polish or Eastern European grocery nearby from which to buy twaróg, each recipe provides an option for ricotta cheese, the closest substitution.

Moving on to meringues: If you've read the recipes in chapters 2 and 3, you may have noticed that many Polish doughs, including enriched dairy doughs, cakes, and cookies, tend to use only the egg yolk. This leaves a bit of a glut of egg whites. Never ones to waste food, Poland's bakers have long repurposed egg whites into beza, or meringue. Tort bezowy, a layered meringue pavlova, predates what is often considered the conception of pavlova in Australia and New Zealand. Crunchy meringue cookies and soft, fluffy meringue layers on cakes like pleśniak and szarlotka also make use of the abundance of leftover egg whites. And of course, because this is Poland, the meringues are often paired with whipped dairy.

Finally in the land of creamy desserts is choux pastry, the cooked dough that turns into steamed puffs in the oven. Choux features in many Polish desserts—cream puffs (ptysie), layer cakes (karpatki), rustic eclairs (eklery), and cruller donuts (gniazda). With the exception of the donuts, these are all basically vehicles for sweet cream.

CHOUX PASTRY

Ciasto Parzone

Choux pastry is ubiquitous in Polish baking, though hardly unique to it. The hot water pastry has its origins in Italian and French baking. While often credited to the sixteenth-century royal court of Catherine de Medici, there's evidence of this sort of pastry dating back centuries further. Regardless of its start, choux eventually spread to the rest of Europe, including Poland. While choux pastry in its better-known French baking tradition is often used to form perfectionist and almost rigid-looking desserts, the Polish use of choux is generally a bit rougher and rustic, free-form rather than fussy. The end result is joyful and loose, and it forms the base of numerous Polish pastries, including the famous choux-and-cream Karpatka (page 314).

NOTE: Baked choux pastry can be made up to 2 days before filling and using, or frozen long-term. To revive the shells from shelf or freezer storage to freshness and crispiness, put them straight on the rack in a 350°F [180°C] oven for a few minutes, then cool before filling. Because choux pastry is very absorbent, it's best to fill your baked choux pastry shells shortly before serving unless you want a deliberately softened texture, as with karpatka.

Choux pastry can be fussy. Here are a few tips for getting it right.

- Respect the rest times for the dough.
- Bake without the convection setting. This will help the pastry dry out as it bakes.
- When baking, even though your choux pastries will puff and may look ready before the allotted baking time, keep baking until they're truly a rich golden brown. Taking them out of the oven too early will collapse them.
- Don't open your oven to check! Again, this can cause the pastries to collapse.

MAKES about 21 oz [600 g] of dough

1 cup plus 3 Tbsp [280 g] water
7 Tbsp [100 g] unsalted butter, cubed and at room temperature
1 Tbsp [15 g] sugar
¾ tsp [5 g] kosher salt
1⅓ cups plus 1 Tbsp [170 g] all-purpose flour
5 eggs

In a medium saucepan, bring the water, butter, sugar, and salt to a boil over medium heat. Remove from the heat and add the flour, stirring vigorously with a spatula to press out any lumps of flour and create a smooth paste. Once the dough is smooth, return the saucepan to the heat and continue to stir for about 3 minutes to dry out the dough—it's essential you don't skip this step. Once the dough is ready, it will be a smooth and solid lump, a thin film will form on your pan, and a thermometer inserted into the center will read between 175 and 185°F [80 and 85°C].

Transfer the dough to the bowl of your stand mixer and let it cool for about 15 minutes. Once the dough has cooled, begin mixing on low speed with the paddle attachment and add the eggs one at a time, allowing each to fully incorporate before adding the next one. The dough will come apart with each added egg but will come back together after a minute of mixing. Scrape down the sides of the bowl between additions. Once all the eggs are incorporated, increase the speed to medium for a minute or two until the dough is a smooth medium-thick batter. Cover the bowl with a tea towel and let it rest for about 30 minutes. The dough will then be ready to use! It will be thin enough to pipe from a pastry bag but thick enough to hold its shape. Bake according to the instructions in each individual recipe.

Meringue and Cream Layer Cake with Fruit

Tort Bezowy z Owocami

Tort bezowy—meringue cake—is a kind of layered pavlova. But while pavlova made its global debut in Australia, the country for which it is best known, in the 1920s, meringue cakes had already been circulating in Germany, the Austro-Hungarian empire, and Poland for at least several decades. And while meringue cakes are not exclusive to Polish baking, tort bezowy is widespread in Polish coffee shops and bakeries to the point of seeming so. The base is simple: thick rounds of crunchy-outside-chewy-inside meringue, whipped cream, and piles of fresh fruit. This particular version takes advantage of the height of red berry season in Poland, with strawberries, gooseberries, cherries, currants, and raspberries piled high, but you can adapt to whatever fruits are in season.

NOTE: I like to make the meringue layers the night before I plan to assemble the cake, as it gives them time to stabilize and dry out.

MAKES one 9 to 10 in [23 to 25 cm] cake

MERINGUE

7 egg whites, at room temperature
¼ tsp cream of tartar or 1 Tbsp lemon juice
1¾ cups [350 g] caster sugar
1 tsp vanilla extract

CREAM FILLING

10½ oz [300 g] whipping cream
10½ oz [300 g] crème fraîche
7 Tbsp [50 g] confectioners' sugar, sifted
2 tsp vanilla extract or seeds from ½ vanilla pod

TOPPING

Strawberries (stemmed and quartered), cherries (pitted and halved), gooseberries, currants, raspberries

Preheat the oven to 225°F [110°C] with the convection setting off. Line a baking sheet with parchment paper. Use the base of a 9 to 10 in [23 to 25 cm] round pan to trace two circles on the parchment, then flip it over. These are the guides for shaping your meringue layers. If two circles don't fit on one sheet, use two pieces of parchment paper on two separate baking sheets.

Begin by making the meringue layers. In the bowl of your stand mixer fitted with the whisk attachment, beat the egg whites and cream of tartar on medium-high speed until foamy, then begin adding your sugar slowly, 1 Tbsp at a time, pausing between each addition. The goal here is to dissolve the sugar as it beats, creating a very smooth final product. Once all the sugar has been incorporated, add the vanilla, then turn the speed up to high and beat until you have very stiff peaks. The meringue should be very shiny and hold its shape completely without flopping over.

Spoon or pipe your meringue into the two circles. Keep the shape rustic, or use a flat-edge knife to smooth out the edges. Bake for 2½ hours in the low-temperature oven, then turn the heat off but allow the meringues to continue drying out in the warm oven for another hour. (If your layers are on two separate sheets, bake them on different racks in the oven and switch positions halfway through. If doing it this way, you may need to give them a bit more time to dry out.) Allow the meringues to cool to room temperature before trying to remove them from their pans and peel off the parchment paper—they will be very delicate and the less handling, the better.

Meanwhile, clean and chill the bowl of your stand mixer and the whisk attachment in the fridge.

cont'd

When you're ready to assemble the cake, prepare the cream filling. In the chilled bowl of your stand mixer fitted with the whisk attachment, add the whipping cream and crème fraîche and mix on low speed until incorporated and smooth. Add the confectioners' sugar, then turn the speed to high and whip until thick and stiff, about 5 minutes. Lower the speed and add the vanilla, then mix until just incorporated.

To assemble the cake, set one meringue layer on a flat serving dish. Smooth two thirds of the cream filling on this layer and add a layer of red fruits. Set the second meringue layer on top of this, and spoon on the final one third of the whipped cream. Decorate with excessive piles of fruit.

Serve immediately or store in the fridge, covered, for up to 2 days.

Meringue and Cream Layer Cake with Grapefruit Curd

Tort Bezowy z Grejpfrutem

As one Polish pastry chef told me: There are no rules with tort bezowy. And so, in the spirit of no rules, this is a version to make in the middle of a Northern winter when there's little else but oranges and grapefruits around. I use a not-too-sweet whipped crème fraîche or sour cream for tang, but mascarpone can also be subbed in. A grapefruit curd adds a bit of extra zip and color, and pink-orange grapefruit slices glitter on top.

NOTE: I like to make the meringue layers the night before I plan to assemble the cake, as it gives them time to stabilize and dry out. The ideal meringue layer is crunchy on the outside, a bit moist and chewy on the inside.

MAKES one 12 x 10 in [30.5 x 25 cm] cake

MERINGUE

7 egg whites, at room temperature

¼ tsp cream of tartar or 1 Tbsp [15 g] lemon juice

1¾ cups [350 g] caster sugar

1 tsp vanilla extract

GRAPEFRUIT CURD

2 eggs

2 egg yolks

6½ Tbsp [100 g] grapefruit juice (1 pink grapefruit, juiced)

3 Tbsp [30 g] grapefruit pulp (spooned from grapefruit and juicer after juicing)

½ cup plus 1½ Tbsp [120 g] granulated sugar

7 Tbsp [100 g] unsalted butter, cubed and at room temperature

1 tsp vanilla extract

CREAM FILLING

10½ oz [300 g] whipping cream

10½ oz [300 g] crème fraîche

7 Tbsp [50 g] confectioners' sugar, sifted

2 tsp vanilla extract or seeds from ½ vanilla pod

TOPPING

Supremed grapefruit slices

Begin by preparing your meringue layers. Preheat the oven to 225°F [110°C] with the convection setting off. Line a baking sheet with a sheet of parchment paper, then fold and unfold the paper in half down the middle, so you have a guide line for your rectangular layers.

In the bowl of your stand mixer fitted with the whisk attachment, beat the egg whites and cream of tartar on medium-high speed until foamy, then begin adding your sugar slowly, 1 Tbsp at a time, pausing between each addition. The goal here is to dissolve the sugar as it beats, creating a very smooth final product. Once all the sugar has been incorporated, add the vanilla, then turn the speed up to high and beat until you have very stiff-peaked meringue. It should be very shiny and hold its shape completely without flopping over.

Spoon or pipe the meringue into large identical rectangles, one on each half of the parchment paper. Keep the shape rustic, or use a flat-edge knife to smooth out the edges. Bake for 2½ hours in the low-temperature oven, then turn the heat off but allow the meringues to continue drying out in the warm oven for another hour. Allow the

cont'd

meringues to cool to room temperature before trying to remove them from the sheet and peel off the parchment paper—they will be very delicate and the less handling, the better.

While the meringues bake, prepare the grapefruit curd. In a small mixing bowl, whisk the eggs and egg yolks until smooth. In small saucepan over medium heat, heat the grapefruit juice, pulp, and sugar until dissolved and just starting to simmer. Remove from the heat and pour the mixture slowly into the eggs, whisking constantly to temper them. Return the mixture to the saucepan and the heat and, still whisking, allow to simmer until thickened, a few minutes. Once thickened, remove from the heat and add the butter and vanilla. Stir until melted and smooth, then cover with plastic wrap touching the surface of the curd and refrigerate until cooled. You can make the curd in advance and store airtight and refrigerated for up to a month.

When you're ready to assemble the cake, prepare the cream filling. In the bowl of your stand mixer fitted with the whisk attachment, add the whipping cream and crème fraîche and mix on low speed until incorporated and smooth. Add the confectioners' sugar, then turn the speed to high and whip until thick and stiff, about 5 minutes. Lower the speed and add the vanilla, and mix until just incorporated.

To assemble the cake, set one meringue layer on a flat serving dish. Smooth two thirds of the cream filling on this layer, then add a layer of grapefruit curd, saving a few tablespoons for decoration. Set the second meringue layer on top, then spoon the final one third of the cream filling on this. Decorate with drops of grapefruit curd and supremed grapefruit slices.

Store covered and refrigerated until ready to serve, ideally the same day but leftovers will be good for up to 3 days.

Nutty Meringue Cookies

Beziki z Orzechami

There's a terrible bakery stand at Warsaw's Hala Mirowska market. Really awful. The cheesecakes are dry, the cookies ancient and careless. And don't even think about touching their cakes. But even a broken clock is right twice a day, and their beziki z orzechami—nut meringues—are wonderful. While these aren't the most common cookies—plain meringue cookies are more typical—they do show up enough to make them worth mentioning. Often made with walnuts, other nuts and dried fruit land in these as well. Here, for a little something special, hazelnuts and almonds are roasted with honey and salt before mixing with chopped dried apricots. Vary the recipe and swap the apricots out for dried cherries, cranberries, yellow raisins, or prunes, and swap the nuts for pistachios, walnuts, pecans, and so on.

NOTE: Pay attention to your oven settings to achieve the crunchy exterior and chewy interior that makes these so luscious.

MAKES 24 meringues

NUTS

2 to 3 Tbsp [40 to 60 g] pourable honey
2 cups [250 g] skinless raw hazelnuts
1¾ cups [250 g] raw almonds with skin
1½ tsp flaky sea salt

MERINGUE

3 egg whites, at room temperature
⅛ tsp cream of tartar or 1 tsp lemon juice
¾ cup [150 g] caster sugar
1 tsp vanilla extract
1½ cups [250 g] finely chopped dried apricots

Preheat the oven to 350°F [180°C] with the convection setting turned on.

Begin by roasting the nuts. In a medium heatproof bowl in the microwave or in a double boiler, warm the honey just enough that it becomes extra fluid. Mix the hazelnuts and almonds into the warmed honey and stir to coat them well. Spread the nuts on a baking sheet lined with parchment paper, then sprinkle evenly with the flaky salt. Bake for 10 to 15 minutes, or until they just start to tan and smell toasty. Remove from the oven and allow to cool. Once cool, give the nuts a rough chop and set aside.

Make the meringues. Lower the oven temperature to 210°F [100°C] with the convection setting still turned on and two racks positioned in the oven. Line two baking sheets with parchment paper, then prepare the meringue.

In the bowl of your stand mixer fitted with the whisk attachment, beat the egg whites with the cream of tartar on medium-high speed until they become quite frothy. Add about 1 Tbsp of the sugar and continue beating. Add the sugar a spoonful at a time over a few minutes as the meringue begins to rise and stiffen. Adding the sugar slowly helps ensure the sugar dissolves and you have a smooth meringue. Once the sugar is incorporated, reduce the speed to low and add the vanilla, then turn the speed to high and beat for another 5 minutes. At this point, you should have a very shiny, stiff-peaked meringue. Using a spatula, gently fold in the chopped nuts and apricots. Spoon out the mixture onto the prepared baking sheets in twenty-four dollops spaced 2 in [5 cm] apart.

Bake the meringues for 1 hour with the baking sheets on separate racks, swapping them halfway through. After 1 hour, turn the convection setting off to help dry out the exterior and bake for another 30 minutes. Turn off the oven and let the meringues sit in the still-warm oven for another 30 minutes. The exteriors will be crispy, the interiors slightly chewy.

Store the meringues in an airtight container for a couple weeks.

Coconut Macaroons

Kokosanki

Kokosanki, or coconut macaroons, trace their origins back to the medieval Arab empire, where egg white and sugar cookies were made with ground almonds. Traders brought these to Italy, and from there, the style of cookie spread around Europe. It was in the late nineteenth century when dried coconut had become more readily available that the French started swapping out the almonds for coconut, and the rest is history. Nowadays they're both a polarizing and inevitable Passover treat as well as a staple on Central and Eastern European Christmas cookie platters. My friend Ulka Minorczyk, a chef in Warsaw, says that what makes the Polish kokosanki special is the hot sugar syrup that's added to the meringue. The result is a light and delicate yet very moist macaroon that won't spread while baking.

MAKES 12 large macaroons

BATTER

½ cup [100 g] sugar
¼ cup [60 g] water
2 egg whites, at room temperature
1 tsp lemon juice
1 tsp kosher salt
1 tsp vanilla extract
1 Tbsp coconut oil, melted
4¼ cups [250 g] sweetened shredded coconut

GLAZE

1 batch Chocolate Glaze (page 350; optional)

Preheat the oven to 350°F [180°C] with the convection setting turned on and line a baking sheet with parchment paper.

Begin by making the batter. In a small saucepan, bring the sugar and water to a boil. As soon as the sugar has completely dissolved, turn off the heat. In the bowl of your stand mixer fitted with the whisk attachment, add the egg whites and lemon juice and whisk on high speed until just past the foamy stage. Continuing to whisk, slowly pour in the hot sugar syrup in a very fine stream. The egg whites will continue to mount until all the syrup is incorporated. Keep whisking until you have stiff, shiny peaks, about 5 minutes. Reduce the speed to low and add the salt, vanilla, and melted coconut oil just until incorporated, then turn off the mixer. Using a spatula, gently fold in the shredded coconut.

Using an ice cream scoop, scoop twelve macaroons about 1 in [2.5 cm] apart on the baking sheet. Bake for 12 to 15 minutes, until the tops and bottoms start to brown. Cool completely.

If you like, make the chocolate glaze according to the recipe on page 350. Dip the bottoms of the cooled macaroons into the glaze, then place back on the baking sheet and refrigerate for about 20 minutes to set the chocolate.

Store in a cookie tin at room temperature for up to a week.

Meringue Roulade

Rolada Bezowa

This is a showstopper of a dessert that isn't as hard to make as it looks. Meringue roulades are a cake shop staple, a big part of the meringue-and-cream universe. Think of this recipe as a base for an infinite variety of cream rolls. Berries, preserved fruit, jam, caramel, lemon curd, or chocolate spreads are simple additions that can adapt this to your taste. Garnish with fruit, leaves, dustings of cocoa powder, whatever you like. Here we keep it simple and classic with a sprinkling of raspberries.

MAKES 1 large roulade (serves 10 to 12)

MERINGUE

1 cup plus 1½ Tbsp [165 g] caster sugar
1¾ tsp cornstarch
4 egg whites, at room temperature
1 tsp white vinegar
1 tsp vanilla extract
½ cup [60 g] confectioners' sugar

FILLING

14 oz [400 g] whipping cream
2 Tbsp [20 g] confectioners' sugar
1 tsp vanilla extract
8¾ oz [250 g] mascarpone
3 cups [350 g] raspberries

Preheat the oven to 300°F [150°C] with the convection setting turned on and line a baking sheet with parchment paper.

Begin by preparing the meringue. While the oven preheats, mix together the caster sugar and cornstarch in a small bowl and set aside. In the bowl of your stand mixer fitted with the whisk attachment, beat the egg whites and vinegar on medium-high speed until they begin to get foamy. Continuing to whisk, add the sugar mixture 1 Tbsp at a time, allowing the meringue to beat for about half a minute in between each addition. Once the sugar is incorporated, reduce the speed to low and add the vanilla, then turn the speed to high and beat for another 5 minutes. At this point, you should have a very shiny, stiff-peaked meringue.

Using an offset spatula or spoon, spread the meringue on the prepared baking sheet in an even square, about 12 x 12 in [30.5 x 30.5 cm]. Bake for 25 minutes, or until the meringue has puffed and turned a light beige color. While the meringue bakes, wash and dry the bowl of your stand mixer, then chill it in the fridge along with the whisk attachment.

Once the meringue is baked, remove it from the oven and immediately cover it with a large piece of parchment paper, then put a second baking sheet or large cutting board on top. Holding the pans together—you will need to wear oven mitts—flip the whole thing over, then remove the original baking sheet. Now you're looking at the bottom of your meringue square. Gently remove the parchment paper it baked on, then generously dust its surface with the confectioners' sugar to prevent sticking during this next step. Beginning with the side

cont'd

closest to you, gently roll up your meringue and the paper it's now sitting on into a medium-tight roll. Set this aside to cool for about 30 minutes.

Shortly before the meringue is finished cooling, make the filling. In the chilled bowl of your stand mixer fitted with the whisk attachment, combine the whipping cream and confectioners' sugar and beat to soft peaks on high speed. Lower the speed just enough to add the vanilla, then the mascarpone spoon by spoon. Once the mascarpone is incorporated, keep mixing on high speed until the mixture thickens further. Separate out about 1 cup of the whipped cream and set it aside covered in the refrigerator for later.

To assemble the roulade, place the meringue on your desired serving dish, then gently unfurl the roll. Spread an even layer of the whipped cream across the whole thing except for a 1 in [2.5 cm] strip along the inside edge where you will start rolling the roulade. Next, arrange a layer of raspberries on top, leaving 1 in [2.5 cm] at the end of the roulade (the end that will be on the outside), without raspberries. Roll up the roulade (without the paper this time) starting from the unfilled end, gently but firmly enough to leave no air pockets. Position the seam on the underside, then slide the parchment paper out from under. Trim short slices off both ends to reveal the raspberry spiral. Fit a pastry bag with a wide star-shaped tip and fill with the reserved whipped cream, then pipe a swirl down the top of the cake. Refrigerate until ready to slice and serve, ideally the same day.

MALINKI
12 szt.

Coffee Meringue Triangles

Sokoły

This is, admittedly, a niche pastry. Like Wuzetka (page 215), sokoły are Warsaw specialties. Triangular meringues filled with a coffee butter-cream or whipped cream, their name means *falcon*, a reflection of their vaguely beak-like shape. Make these for a taste of retro Warsaw and a crisp-yet-creamy dessert.

MAKES 9 sokoły

MERINGUE

5 egg whites, at room temperature

½ tsp white vinegar

1¼ cups [250 g] caster sugar

1 tsp vanilla extract

BUTTERCREAM

2 Tbsp [15 g] instant espresso powder, plus more for dusting

10½ oz [300 g] whipping cream, chilled

10½ Tbsp [150 g] unsalted butter, at room temperature

1⅔ cups [200 g] confectioners' sugar

⅛ tsp kosher salt

Preheat the oven to 275°F [130°C] with the convection setting turned off and line two baking sheets with parchment paper.

Begin by preparing the meringue. In the bowl of your stand mixer fitted with the whisk attachment, beat the egg whites and vinegar on medium-high speed until they begin to get foamy. Continuing to whisk, add the caster sugar 1 Tbsp at a time, allowing the meringue to beat for about half a minute in between each addition to dissolve the sugar and make a smooth meringue. Once the sugar is incorporated, reduce the speed to low and add the vanilla, then turn the speed to high and beat for another 5 minutes. At this point, you should have a very shiny, stiff-peaked meringue.

Transfer the meringue to a pastry bag with a round tip, then pipe nine equilateral triangles, three rows of three, onto each baking sheet for a total of eighteen triangles. Use an offset spatula or a spoon to smooth out the tops so they're an even thickness. If you don't feel comfortable free-forming the triangles, cut out a guide from cardboard and trace it on your parchment paper, then flip over the parchment so you don't get pencil or pen lines on your baked meringue.

Put the pans in the oven and lower the heat to 200°F [100°C]. Bake until crispy but still white, about 1½ hours. The final meringue triangles should be crunchy all the way through. Turn off the oven and let the triangles sit in the still-warm oven for another 30 minutes. The meringue can be made up to a week in advance as long as they're properly dried out and stored airtight.

Once the meringue triangles are cooled, make the buttercream. In a small bowl, stir the espresso powder and cream to dissolve. In the bowl of your stand mixer fitted with the whisk attachment, beat together the butter and confectioners' sugar, slowly increasing the speed once the confectioners' sugar is incorporated. Continue to beat on high speed for a few minutes, until light and fluffy. Turn the speed to medium, add the salt, then incorporate the espresso cream in a slow drizzle. Increase the speed to high and beat for another 3 to 5 minutes, until you have a light and satiny buttercream.

Using a spoon, spatula, or a pastry bag fitted with a star-shaped tip, fill half the triangles with the buttercream. Top with the empty halves, dust with espresso powder, and serve.

Store covered airtight and refrigerated for up to 3 days.

Viennese Cheesecake

Sernik Wiedeński

The French region of Bourgogne is known for three things. First, the wine, second, *les charolais*—the famous beef cows—and third, the mines. In the 1950s came a postwar wave of economic migration when Poles arrived to work in the mines. While today it isn't unusual to come across a small *epicerie polonaise* among the rolling hills and stone houses of the region, the Polish influence is very subtle several generations in. My friend Peter Gierszewski, a natural winemaker in Mâcon and grandson of Polish miners, generously opened his grandmother's recipe book to me. Suddenly a man with whom I'd only drunk the Frenchest of wine around tables spread with the Frenchest of cheeses was showing off a recipe for a different kind of cheese—sweet sernik, his grandmother's cheesecake, simple and plain, translated to French and adapted to the available fresh French cheeses for her family.

With a base of finely ground twaróg, sernik Wiedeński has a perfectly creamy yet gentle, soufflé-like texture. Lighter than a New York cheesecake, sernik Wiedeński holds up without any bottom crust—though you can add one if you like—making it purely cheesecake and nothing else. Thickened with starch rather than wheat flour and baked low-and-slow with a steam tray makes this a custardy flourless cake of dreams.

NOTES: Always make this cheesecake the day before you wish to serve it to give it time to properly set. Because twaróg is not available in all regions, this recipe offers a version made with ricotta. For the best results, it's important to use full-fat versions of all the dairy in this cheesecake.

MAKES one 9 or 10 in [23 or 25 cm] cheesecake

TWARÓG FILLING

15 oz [425 g] full-fat twaróg
4½ oz [130 g] whipping cream
7 eggs, 4 separated
17½ oz [500 g] cream cheese
7 oz [200 g] full-fat sour cream
2 tsp vanilla extract
1 Tbsp lemon juice
1¾ tsp cornstarch
¾ cup [150 g] sugar (fine or granulated)

OR

RICOTTA FILLING

19½ oz [550 g] full-fat ricotta, drained if any excess water
7 eggs, 4 separated
17½ oz [500 g] cream cheese
7 oz [200 g] full-fat sour cream
2 tsp vanilla extract
1 Tbsp lemon juice
1½ tsp cornstarch
⅔ cup plus 1½ Tbsp [150 g] sugar (fine or granulated)

TOPPING

¼ cup [30 g] confectioners' sugar
Fresh fruit or berries (optional)

cont'd

Preheat the oven to 425°F [220°C] with a rack in the middle and the convection setting turned on. Put an old rimmed pan or casserole dish at the bottom of the oven to preheat. Line the bottom of a springform pan with parchment paper and set aside.

To prepare your cheesecake, blend the twaróg with the whipping cream in a food processor or in a mixing bowl with an immersion blender until very smooth, then set aside. (If using ricotta, you can skip this step.)

In the bowl of your stand mixer fitted with whisk attachment, whisk the 4 egg whites until stiff peaks form. Transfer the egg whites to a medium bowl and set aside. There's no need to wash the mixer bowl or whisk for the next step.

In the bowl of your stand mixer now fitted with the paddle attachment, combine the blended twaróg or ricotta with the cream cheese and sour cream and mix on low speed for a minute or two until smooth. Continuing to mix on low speed, add the 4 egg yolks and 3 whole eggs one at a time, mixing until fully incorporated, occasionally running a spatula around the sides and bottom of the bowl to be sure all the cheese is mixed in. Finally, add the vanilla, lemon juice, cornstarch, and sugar and mix on low speed until no lumps remain. Remove the bowl from the stand mixer and, using a large spatula, gently fold in the whipped egg whites one third at a time, until the mixture is smooth and no pockets of egg white remain. Pour the mixture into the prepared springform pan. There should be at least ½ in [1 cm] of space between the top of the mixture and the top of the pan.

Bring a kettle of water to a boil, then pour the boiling water into the pan in the oven. Immediately after pouring in the water, put the cheesecake on the rack above it and close the door. Lower the oven temperature to 400°F [200°C] and bake for 15 minutes. The surface of the cheesecake should just begin to puff. Lower the temperature to 275°F [130°C] and continue to bake for 35 to 40 minutes. When the cheesecake is done, it will have puffed significantly and be very light in color with a few golden brown spots on top. The cheesecake will have a very strong wiggle—this is OK. It will set as it cools. There may be some cracks around the edges, but these will disappear as the cheesecake cools and sinks.

Remove the cheesecake from the oven and allow it to cool at room temperature, still in the pan. Once cool, cover the pan with plastic wrap or a plate and refrigerate for at least 6 hours, ideally overnight. Before serving, slide a knife around the edge before releasing the sides of the springform pan. The cheesecake should be sturdy enough to slide onto a serving dish. Top with sifted confectioners' sugar and fresh fruit, if desired. Store leftover cake covered airtight in the fridge for up to a week.

Krakower Raisin Cheesecake

Sernik Krakowski

Sernik Krakowski, or Kraków-style cheesecake, is a dense, slab-style cheesecake with a pastry-lattice top and a creamy filling brightly flavored with alcohol-soaked raisins and bits of candied orange peel. Despite the nominal Kraków, it's found everywhere regardless of city. The sturdy crust means it can be cut into a bar-style dessert, easy for handheld snacking or a picnic, should you feel so inclined. Soaking the raisins in Cointreau rather than the traditional rum or kirsch complements the candied orange peel in the most divine way. Use any liqueur or distillate you have on hand, though, or simply soak in water if you prefer not to use alcohol. The final cake is traditionally topped with Lemon Lukier (page 348), a glaze of confectioners' sugar and lemon juice, for a final citrusy burst.

NOTE: Because twaróg is not available in all regions, this recipe also offers a version made with ricotta.

MAKES one 13 x 9 in [33 x 23 cm] cake (8 to 12 slices)

CRUST

1 batch Kruche Dough (page 190)
Egg, beaten, or heavy cream, for brushing

ADD-INS

½ cup plus 1 Tbsp [80 g] raisins
3 Tbsp [45 g] Cointreau
3 Tbsp [45 g] hot water
2 Tbsp [25 g] finely chopped Candied Orange Peel (page 332)

TWARÓG FILLING

15 oz [425 g] full-fat twaróg
4½ oz [130 g] whipping cream
17½ oz [500 g] cream cheese
7 oz [200 g] full-fat sour cream
4 eggs
3 egg yolks
2 tsp vanilla extract
1 Tbsp lemon juice
3 Tbsp [25 g] all-purpose flour
¾ cup [150 g] caster sugar

OR

RICOTTA FILLING

19½ oz [550 g] full-fat ricotta, drained if any excess water
17½ oz [500 g] cream cheese
7 oz [200 g] full-fat sour cream (18 to 20 percent)
4 eggs
3 egg yolks
2 tsp vanilla extract
1 Tbsp lemon juice
3 Tbsp [25 g] all-purpose flour
¾ cup [150 g] caster sugar

GLAZE

1 batch Lemon Glaze (Lemon Lukier, page 348)

Prepare your kruche dough according to the recipe on page 190 and chill for 1 hour or up to several days before using.

While the dough chills, mix the raisins with the Cointreau and hot water, then set aside to plump.

Once the dough has chilled, divide it in half and return one half, wrapped airtight, to the fridge. Grease a 13 x 9 in [33 x 23 cm] baking pan and line with parchment paper.

cont'd

Turn the dough out onto a lightly floured work surface and give it a brief knead to return it to elasticity, then roll it out into a rectangle just a bit larger than the base of the pan. Trim the edges to make a perfect rectangle. Gently transfer the dough into the pan and press to fit. Prick all over with a fork then chill for 20 minutes in the fridge.

Preheat the oven to 350°F [180°C] with a rack in the middle and the convection setting turned on. Blind-bake the crust for 15 minutes, until it puffs, is golden brown, and no longer looks greasy. Remove from the oven and set aside.

Increase the oven temperature to 425°F [220°C] and allow it to heat up while you make your filling. Blend the twaróg with the whipping cream in a food processor or in a mixing bowl with an immersion blender until very smooth. (If using ricotta, you can skip this step.) In the bowl of your stand mixer fitted with the paddle attachment, combine the blended twaróg or ricotta with the cream cheese and sour cream and mix on low speed for a minute or two, until smooth. Continuing to mix on low speed, add the 4 eggs and 3 egg yolks one at a time, mixing just until fully incorporated, occasionally running a spatula around the bottom of the bowl to be sure all the cheese is mixed in. Finally, add the vanilla, lemon juice, flour, and sugar and mix on low until smooth. Drain the soaking raisins and add these and the candied orange peel to the cheese filling and mix. Set aside.

On a floured work surface, give the second half of the chilled kruche dough a short knead to prevent it from cracking while rolling, then roll it out into a rectangle a bit larger than the pan. Using a flat-edge knife or a pizza cutter, cut the rectangle the long way into ½ in [1 cm] strips.

Return to the filling mixture and give it a final stir to pull any sunken raisins up from the bottom, then pour it into the pan on top of the blind-baked bottom crust. Lay four of the dough strips along the edges of the pan to frame the lattice. It's OK if the strips hang over the edges—this will actually give you some stability as you lay the rest of the lattice. Next, gently lay five or six strips diagonally and evenly spaced along the cheesecake, then five or six strips diagonally and evenly spaced in the opposite direction. Use a flat knife to trim any excess dough from the end of the strips so you have a tidy lattice, then brush the lattice with either cream or a beaten egg.

Put the cheesecake in the oven, lower the temperature to 400°F [200°C], and bake for 20 minutes. The filling should start to puff and brown around the lattice, and the lattice itself should begin to brown. At this point, lower the heat to 275°F [130°C] and continue baking for 35 minutes. When baked, the cheesecake base will still have a little wiggle and the pastry will be golden brown. Remove from the oven and allow to cool to room temperature, then chill in the fridge loosely covered for at least 6 hours or overnight, until you're ready to serve.

To serve, prepare your lemon glaze according to the recipe on page 348, making it thin enough to be transparent and pourable. Slowly pour all over the cheesecake to glaze, then allow the glaze to set for about 20 minutes.

Serve cut into bars or keep refrigerated in an airtight container for up to a week.

Karpatka

Layered Choux and Cream Cake

Karpatka is an airy pudding cake—like a giant cream puff based on two craggy choux pastry layers meant to look like the peaks of the Carpathian Mountains. If you really want to get into it, only 10 percent of the Carpathian Mountains are in Poland—Romania is the winner, coming in at 50 percent—but maybe this cake named after the range pushes the stats in Poland's favor. While karpatka can be round or rectangular, when cut in squares, the cake could be confused with Napoleonka (page 225), often on display right next to it in bakery cases. But while napoleonka uses a crispy puff pastry crust and thick budyń filling, karpatka uses a softer choux crust and silky mousseline—a light pudding buttercream.

MAKES one 9 in [23 cm] cake

MOUSSELINE FILLING

Double batch Pudding (Budyń, page 342)

14 Tbsp [200 g] unsalted butter, at room temperature

CRUST

1 batch Choux Pastry (page 290)

TOPPING

½ cup [60 g] confectioners' sugar

Prepare the pudding according to the recipe on page 342. Spoon it into a mixing bowl and cover the surface directly with plastic wrap. Refrigerate until the cream has cooled to room temperature. Don't let it get too cold or the final cream won't whip correctly. When it reaches 70°F [20°C], remove from the fridge.

While the pudding cools, prepare the choux pastry according to the recipe on page 290.

Preheat the oven to 425°F [225°C] and line the bottom of two 9 in [23 cm] springform cake pans with parchment paper. Fill one pan with two thirds of the choux and spread it out evenly with a spatula dipped in water to prevent sticking. In the second pan, spread one third of the choux. Put the pans in the oven, and immediately lower the heat to 400°F [200°C]. Bake for 40 to 45 minutes, or until both crusts are golden brown and hard and make a hollow sound when tapped. (It's OK if the pan with less choux gets crispier, this is the base of the cake, and the extra sturdiness is a plus.) Remove from the oven and use a toothpick to poke several holes in the crusts to vent the steam. Return the crusts to the oven (still at 400°F [200°C]) and allow to continue drying for 15 more minutes with the oven door open a crack. Remove from the oven and gently flip the crusts out upside-down onto a cooling rack. Use a toothpick to poke several holes in the underside of each to vent steam. Allow to cool completely.

While the crusts cool, make the filling. In the bowl of your stand mixer fitted with the paddle attachment, whip the butter on medium-high speed for about 2 minutes, until smooth. Reduce the speed to low and add the room-temperature pudding a few spoonfuls at a time, scraping down the bowl as needed. Once all the pudding is incorporated into the butter, increase the speed to medium-high and whip for 3 to 5 minutes, until the filling becomes paler, lighter, and a bit stiffer.

To assemble, place the smaller, crisper crust craggy-side up on a plate or cake stand and spoon out all of the filling, then cover with the second, taller crust and gently press down to set. Smooth the cream around the edges with a butter knife or offset spatula. Let the cake set in the fridge, covered, for at least 1 hour and store, refrigerated and airtight, for up to 4 days. Dust with a thick layer of confectioners' sugar before serving.

Lemon and Blackberry Karpatka

Karpatka Cytrynowa z Jeżynami

It's natural to think of karpatka as a winter cake, what with the snow-capped mountain look and all. While the basic version is made with a vanilla mousseline filling, as in the previous recipe, in a country ever seeking ways to use up an abundance of summer fruits, among other ingredients, karpatkas take on many twists. There are pistachio karpatkas, blueberry karpatkas, chocolate karpatkas—endless karpatkas, really. This karpatka uses lemony cream and blackberries, a favorite in the Polish summer, but you can adjust according to what fruits are in season and available. Ripe persimmon, red currants, and early season strawberries would all be beautiful in this. The homemade filling can also be replaced by a cup of compote or jam.

NOTE: I like to start this recipe the day before, preparing the blackberry filling and the lemon pudding (budyń) for the final cream. This allows both components to cool and set, making the next day's work much quicker and easier, especially if you're serving this the same day for a party.

MAKES one 9 in [23 cm] cake

BLACKBERRY FILLING

2½ cups [300 g] fresh blackberries
3 Tbsp [40 g] granulated sugar
1 tsp lemon juice
1 tsp grated lemon zest
1½ tsp cornstarch
2 tsp finely chopped fresh mint (optional)

LEMONY MOUSSELINE

2 eggs
4 egg yolks
3 Tbsp plus 1 tsp [30 g] cornstarch
2 Tbsp [20 g] all-purpose flour
7 Tbsp [100 g] lemon juice
4 Tbsp [25 g] grated lemon zest
2 tsp lemon extract
½ cup [100 g] granulated sugar
1½ cups plus 2 Tbsp [400 g] whole milk
3 Tbsp [45 g] unsalted butter, plus 14 Tbsp [200 g] unsalted butter, at room temperature, for whipping
2 tsp vanilla extract

CRUST

1 batch Choux Pastry (page 290)

TOPPING

½ to 1 cup [60 to 120 g] fresh blackberries
Lemon zest
Mint leaves, whole or cut into chiffonade (optional)
¼ cup [30 g] confectioners' sugar

Begin by preparing the blackberry filling. Mix the blackberries, sugar, lemon juice, and zest in a medium mixing bowl and allow to sit for about an hour, until the juices are released. Stir in the cornstarch until no lumps remain. In a small saucepan over medium-low heat, bring the mixture to a low bubbling simmer for a few minutes, stirring constantly until it just begins to thicken. Mix in the mint (if using), remove from the heat, and set aside to cool. Refrigerate airtight until ready to use, up to several days.

cont'd

Meanwhile, prepare the mousseline. This starts with the same process as making a pudding (budyń; page 342). Whisk together the egg, egg yolks, cornstarch, flour, lemon juice, lemon zest, lemon extract, and ¼ cup [50 g] of the sugar in a large heatproof bowl. Set aside.

In a saucepan over low to medium heat, warm the milk and the remaining ¼ cup [50 g] of sugar until the sugar is dissolved and the milk is steaming and just starting to simmer. Pour half of the hot milk into the egg mixture in a thin stream, whisking constantly to temper the eggs. This process prevents the eggs from scrambling. Return the mixture to the saucepan and medium-low heat. Whisk constantly until the mixture starts to thicken and bubble into a pudding consistency—don't look away! The change happens suddenly. Continuing to whisk vigorously, allow the pudding to bubble for 1 to 2 minutes before removing it from the heat. Add the 3 Tbsp [45 g] of butter and the vanilla, stirring until smooth and melted. Pour into a shallow bowl and cover directly with plastic wrap to prevent a skin from forming. Refrigerate until the filling has cooled to room temperature or about 70°F [20°C]. Don't let it get too cold or the final cream won't whip correctly. When the filling reaches the desired temperature, remove from the fridge until ready to use.

While the pudding cools, prepare the choux pastry according to the recipe on page 290.

Preheat the oven to 425°F [225°C] and line the bottom of two 9 in [23 cm] springform cake pans with parchment paper. Fill each pan with half the choux and spread it out evenly with a spatula dipped in water to prevent sticking. Put the pans in the oven, and immediately lower the heat to 400°F [200°C]. Bake for 40 to 45 minutes, or until both crusts are golden brown and hard and make a hollow sound when tapped. Remove from the oven and use a toothpick to poke several holes in the crusts to vent the steam. Return the crusts to the oven (still at 400°F [200°C]) and allow to continue drying for 15 more minutes with the oven door open a crack. Remove from the oven and gently flip the crusts out upside-down onto a cooling rack. Use a toothpick to poke several more holes in the underside of each to vent steam. Allow to cool completely.

While the crusts cool, finish the filling. In the bowl of your stand mixer fitted with the paddle attachment, whip the remaining 14 Tbsp [200 g] of butter on medium-high speed for about 2 minutes, until smooth. Reduce the speed to low and add the pudding a few spoonfuls at a time, scraping down the side of the bowl as needed. Once all the pudding is incorporated into the butter, increase the speed to medium-high and whip for 3 to 5 minutes, until the filling becomes paler, lighter, and a bit stiffer.

To assemble, place one crust craggy-side up on a plate or cake stand. Spoon out the filling, reserving about ¾ cup for the top of the cake, then spread on the blackberry filling. Top with the second crust, craggy-side up.

This can be refrigerated airtight for up to 3 days. When ready to serve, spread the reserved cream on top, then top with fresh blackberries, lemon zest, mint (if using), and a dusting of confectioners' sugar.

Whipped Cream Puffs

Ptysie

Ptysie are cream puffs made from choux pastry and usually filled with whipped cream, though occasionally with meringue. *Choux* is French for *cabbage*, a vegetable that bears a not dissimilar appearance to a choux puff. Adorably, the French term of endearment, *petit choux*, means *little cabbage*. The Polish name for cream puffs is *ptysie*. It's pronounced *pa-tee-shee-ye*, a derivative of the earlier Polish name of this pastry, *pti-szu*. Pti-szu. Ptysie. Petit Choux. Follow? And, just like in French, there's a nice Polish way of calling someone your sweetheart with choux: *mój ty ptysiu*.

NOTE: These can be made half-sized for a more bite-sized dessert.

MAKES 12 large or 24 small ptysie

1 batch Choux Pastry (page 290)
17½ oz [500 g] whipping cream
½ cup [60 g] confectioners' sugar, plus more for dusting
1 tsp vanilla extract

Prepare your choux pastry according to the recipe on page 290.

While the dough rests and before you pipe it, chill the bowl of your stand mixer and the whisk attachment in the fridge. Preheat the oven to 425°F [225°C] with the convection setting turned off. On two baking sheets lined with parchment paper, use a pencil to trace evenly spaced 2¾ in [7 cm] circles, six on each sheet. Flip the paper over. These circles will be your guides.

Prepare a large pastry bag with a large open star tip, then set it inside a tall glass or measuring cup with the sides of the pastry bag folded over the sides of the glass. This will help stabilize the bag. Spoon the choux pastry into the bag and pipe six tall kisses onto the circles on one of the sheet pans, about 2 in [5 cm] high, using half your batter. You'll pipe your second batch right before you bake it.

Dust the piped kisses with confectioners' sugar, then put the baking sheet in the oven and immediately lower the heat to 400°F [200°C]. Bake for 35 minutes, until the ptysie are puffed and a rich golden brown. Poke each puff with a toothpick to vent the steam from inside and let them dry out with the oven on and the door open for about 15 more minutes. Remove the puffs and gently transfer to a cooling rack.

Reheat the oven to 425°F [225°C], and pipe the second batch of kisses. Bake and cool the second batch as you did the first. Once the puffs have cooled to room temperature, cut each in half horizontally through the middle.

Shortly before you're ready to serve the ptysie, prepare the whipped cream. In the chilled bowl of your stand mixer fitted with the whisk attachment, add the whipping cream, confectioners' sugar, and vanilla. Beat on medium-high speed until the whipped cream is stiff and stable.

Generously spoon the whipped cream onto the base of each puff for a rustic look, or pipe with an open star-shaped tip, then cover with the top of each puff. Dust with confectioners' sugar. Serve immediately.

Ginger and Rhubarb Cream Puffs

Ptysie z Imbirem i Rabarbarem

This is a play on the plain ptysie that zips up the whipping cream with spicy ginger and balances it out with a sweet-sour rhubarb compote. While this dessert takes advantage of springtime rhubarb, you can substitute any number of fruits that pair well with ginger, like black currants, raspberries, strawberries, apricots, plums, and pears. Simply let your fruit rest with the sugar and spice until it has leaked out its juices, then cook into a quick fruit topping, just like with the rhubarb recipe here.

NOTE: These can be made half-sized for a more bite-sized dessert. If you prefer a sweeter rhubarb topping, add a couple extra tablespoons of sugar.

MAKES 12 large or 24 small ptysie

RHUBARB FILLING

19½ oz [550 g] rhubarb, washed and cut into eighths
5 Tbsp [60 g] granulated sugar
3 Tbsp [35 g] candied ginger, finely chopped
Juice of ½ lemon
1 tsp ground ginger
1½ tsp cornstarch

DOUGH

1 batch Choux Pastry (page 290)

WHIPPED CREAM

17½ oz [500 g] whipping cream
½ cup [60 g] confectioners' sugar
1 tsp ground ginger
1 tsp vanilla extract
1 Tbsp finely chopped candied ginger

TOPPING

Confectioners' sugar, for dusting

The night before you want to bake your ptysie, prepare the rhubarb filling. Combine the rhubarb, sugar, candied ginger, lemon juice, and ground ginger in a medium mixing bowl, cover, and refrigerate overnight. In the morning, the rhubarb will have softened and released its juices. Stir in the cornstarch until no lumps remain, then transfer the mixture to a medium saucepan. Bring to a simmer over medium-low heat and cook for a few minutes, until the rhubarb has softened and the juices have thickened. Set aside to cool, then refrigerate, covered airtight, until ready to use.

Prepare your choux pastry according to the recipe on page 290.

While the dough rests and before you pipe it, chill the bowl of your stand mixer and the whisk attachment in the fridge. Preheat the oven to 425°F [225°C] with the convection setting turned off. On two baking sheets lined with parchment paper, use a pencil to trace evenly spaced 2¾ in [7 cm] circles, six on each sheet. Flip the paper over. These circles will be your guides.

Prepare a large pastry bag with a large open star tip, then set it inside a tall glass or measuring cup with the sides of the pastry bag folded over the sides of the glass. This will help stabilize the bag. Spoon the choux pastry into the bag and pipe six tall kisses onto the circles on one of the sheet pans, about 2 in [5 cm] high, and using half your batter. You'll pipe your second batch right before you bake it.

Dust the piped kisses with confectioners' sugar, then put the baking sheet in the oven and immediately lower the heat to 400°F [200°C]. Bake for 35 minutes, until the ptysie are puffed and a rich

cont'd

golden brown. Poke each puff with a toothpick to vent the steam from inside and let them dry out with the oven on and the door open for about 15 more minutes. Remove the puffs and gently transfer to a cooling rack.

Reheat the oven to 425°F [225°C] and pipe the second batch of kisses. Bake and cool the second batch as you did the first. Once the puffs have cooled to room temperature, cut each in half horizontally through the middle.

Shortly before you're ready to serve the ptysie, prepare your whipped cream. In the chilled bowl of your stand mixer fitted with the whisk attachment, add the whipping cream, confectioners' sugar, ground ginger, and vanilla and whisk on medium-high speed until the whipped cream is stiff and stable. Fold in the candied ginger with a spatula.

Generously spoon the whipped cream onto the base of each puff for a rustic look, or pipe with an open star-shaped tip. Spoon a portion of rhubarb filling on each, then cover with the top of the puff and dust with confectioners' sugar. Serve immediately.

Little Nest Cruller Donuts

Gniazdka

My friend Paul says he likes to eat cruller donuts six at a time. To get his stats up, he says. Not cholesterol, just donut numbers—though it will certainly do both. It sorta makes sense, if eating donuts for the sake of quantity is your thing. Crullers are made from choux pastry, resulting in an unusually light and delicate donut. In Poland, land of donuts, crullers have one of three names depending on who you ask. Hiszpańskie pączki (Spanish donuts), Wiedeńskie pączki (Viennese donuts), or gniazdka—which, adorably, means *little nests*.

NOTE: Double the recipe if making donuts for a larger group. The glazes in the recipe are all good options, but no need to make them all at once! Make as few or as many flavors as your stomach desires.

MAKES 10 to 12 donuts

DOUGH

1 batch Choux Pastry (page 290), made with 4 eggs rather than 5

FOR FRYING

8½ cups [2 L] sunflower oil

VANILLA GLAZE

1 cup [120 g] confectioners' sugar
1½ Tbsp [20 g] whole milk
½ tsp vanilla extract
⅛ tsp vanilla seeds (optional)
Pinch of kosher salt

COFFEE GLAZE

1 cup [120 g] confectioners' sugar
1 Tbsp brewed strong coffee or espresso
½ Tbsp whole milk
Pinch of kosher salt

LEMON–POPPY SEED GLAZE

1 cup [120 g] confectioners' sugar
1 Tbsp whole milk
½ tsp vanilla extract
1½ tsp lemon juice
1 Tbsp poppy seeds
1 tsp grated lemon zest

Prepare the choux pastry according to the recipe on page 290, using only 4 rather than 5 eggs. This will make your dough a bit thicker and stand up well to the resting period and deep fry. Fill a large pastry bag fitted with a wide star tip with choux pastry.

Cut twelve 5 in [13 cm] squares of parchment paper. Hold a square of paper steady with one hand, then with the other hold the pastry bag a couple inches above the paper and pipe a 3 to 4 in [7.5 to 10 cm] donut onto each square of parchment paper. (If you need a guide, dip the mouth of a drinking glass into flour and press it gently onto the parchment before piping. This will leave a thin visible ring you can use as your guide.) Repeat with the remaining choux. Once all the donuts are piped onto their papers, let them air dry for at least 30 to 45 minutes before you heat your oil.

Shortly before your donuts finish resting, in a medium saucepan or home deep fryer, heat the sunflower oil until the temperature measures 350°F [180°C]. There should be at least 3 in [7.5 cm] of oil in the pan. Deep frying is an important time to use a thermometer—if the oil is too cool, the donuts will be slick and oily; too hot and they'll burn. If you don't have a kitchen thermometer, test the oil by dropping a little bit of dough into the oil. If the oil is ready, the dough should immediately bubble and turn golden fairly quickly.

cont'd

While your oil heats, line a baking sheet or cooling rack with a thick layer of paper towels. This is where your donuts will drain after frying.

Once the oil is hot, lower your donuts one at a time into the oil using a slotted metal spatula. They'll sink and then rise back to the surface and the paper will naturally separate from the donuts. Don't yank the paper off the donuts, as this could make holes. Once the donut is a deep golden brown, 2 to 3 minutes, use the spatula to flip it. (If you flip too early, your donut could collapse or split.) Fry the other side until equally golden brown.

Once your donut is fully fried, carefully remove it with the spatula and put it ridged-side up on the draining rack. Continue frying the rest of the donuts.

Once the donuts are all fried, mix up the glazes of your choice. In a small bowl, combine all the ingredients for the vanilla, coffee, or lemon-poppy seed glaze, whisking until smooth. If you like your glazes thicker or thinner, feel free to adjust the milk as needed. Dip either just the tops of the crullers or toss the whole thing in for an all-around glaze.

Serve fresh and warm.

Eclairs

Eklery

I know, I know. These are just eclairs spelled the Polish way. But as happens with foodways, things travel and become staples of faraway bakeries and, in their way, become of that place too. You'd be hard pressed to show me a cake shop in Poland without one of these rustic-style eclairs. Yes, in the high-end pastry shops, be it in Gdańsk, Poznań, Wrocław, or Warsaw, you can find as obsessively symmetric an eclair as in any French patisserie, tidy lines and sleek fondant glaçage. But there's something wonderfully homey about the casual eklery you can buy with a glass mug of tea at any old cukiernia that gush pudding with every bite.

NOTE: The individual components of these eclairs can be made up to 2 days in advance. Store the budyń in the fridge and the eclair shells in an airtight container.

MAKES 16 eklery

Double batch Pudding (Budyń, page 342), cooled
1 batch Choux Pastry (page 290)
¼ cup [30 g] confectioners' sugar
1 batch Chocolate Glaze (page 350)

Prepare the pudding according to the recipe on page 342, then allow to fully cool for an hour or two in the fridge.

Prepare the choux pastry according to the recipe on page 290.

While the choux rests, preheat the oven to 400°F [200°C] with the convection setting turned off. Line two baking sheets with parchment paper. Trace out two rows of four 4 in [10 cm] lines on each, then flip over the paper. These lines will be your guide.

Once the choux is ready to use, fit a large pastry bag with a large star tip, then set it inside a tall glass or measuring cup, the sides of the pastry bag folded over the sides. This will help stabilize the bag as you fill it. Spoon in your choux pastry, then pipe straight lines on one of the prepared sheets, letting the piping tip drag at an angle along the paper. It can be helpful to weigh down the paper or pin it to your pan to keep it still while piping.

Sprinkle the tops of the eclairs with confectioners' sugar, then put the first pan in the oven and immediately lower the heat to 350°F [180°C]. Bake for 35 minutes, until the eclairs are puffed and rich golden brown. Open the oven door partway with the heat still on and let the eclairs dry out for about 15 more minutes. Remove the pan from the oven, flip over the pastry shells, and use a toothpick to poke a couple holes in the underside to release steam. Bring the oven heat back to 400°F [200°C], then pipe your second tray of eclairs and repeat the process for the second batch.

Once the eclair shells and pudding are cooled, cut the eclair shells in half horizontally through the middle using a serrated knife. Use a whisk to whip the pudding until smooth. Prep a pastry bag with any wide round tip and fill with the pudding. Pipe pudding onto the bottom halves of each shell. You can also just spoon it on for a more rustic look. Either way, it's nice to be a little generous; you're gonna wanna see the cream leaking out the sides. When you think you've put on too much cream, put more. Bakers are sensual people. Let's do this.

Finally, make the chocolate glaze according to the recipe on page 350. Dip the top half of each eclair into the chocolate glaze or brush on the glaze with a pastry brush, then place it atop the filled bottom half. Let the glaze dry for about 30 minutes, then serve.

If you have leftovers, store them airtight in the fridge. They'll get softer there but will stay delicious for 2 to 3 days.

/6

EXTRAS: FILLINGS, CREAMS & TOPPINGS

The signature fillings and toppings of many Polish sweets—jammy plum butter; crumbly streusel; thick poppy seed paste; golden milk caramel; rich walnut filling; and more—make up the distinct and regional palate of Polish baking, typical of not just Poland but much of Central and Eastern Europe. Depending on where you're baking, some of these are easier to find in stores than others, but all can be made from scratch.

Candied Orange Peel

Kandyzowana Skórka Pomarańczowa

Candied orange peel is a widely used garnish for glazed yeast pastries or mixed in with nut and poppy seed pastes. Despite the northerly climate, citrus fruits have been available in Poland for longer even than tomatoes, imported from Central Asia as early as the fifteenth century. In the mid-seventeenth century, King Jan III had something of a passionate obsession with citrus fruits and cultivated everything from lemons to bitter oranges in his climate-controlled orangeries at the Wilanów Palace on the outskirts of Warsaw. Luxurious and rare at the outset, citrus eventually made its way into everyday pastries, particularly in the form of candied orange peel, studding the tops of donuts and yeast cakes. Making your own is a clever way to use up orange peels and achieve a livelier taste than you ever could with store-bought.

MAKES about 4 cups [600 g]

6 medium navel oranges, washed and scrubbed
5 cups [1 kg] granulated sugar
4½ cups [1 L] water
Caster sugar, for rolling (optional)

To prep the oranges, slice off about ½ in [1 cm] from the top and bottom of each orange with a paring knife. Score the length of each orange from top to bottom, through the pith and just to the fruit, dividing the peel into five even segments. Peel off each portion, keeping the pith attached to the skin. Cut the peels into long, thin strips.

Bring a medium to large saucepan of water to a boil on medium-high heat. Add the peels and boil for 10 minutes. Drain and rinse the peels with cold water. Bring a fresh pot of water to a boil, then repeat the boiling and draining process two more times. This will soften the peels and remove any bitterness.

After the third boil and drain, combine the granulated sugar and water in the same saucepan and bring to a low boil on medium heat until all the sugar has dissolved. Add the softened peels and keep at a simmer for about 1 hour, or until the white pith is transparent and the syrup is boiling with slow, marble-sized bubbles.

Use a slotted spoon or spatula to remove the peels from the syrup and arrange on a cooling rack set over paper towels to catch drips. (Save the extra orange syrup to use as a glaze on pastries or a flavored simple syrup for iced drinks.) Wait until the peels are cool enough to handle and roll in caster sugar, if desired. Leave the peels to dry for 3 days, covered with cheesecloth to keep off dust and insects. Once dry, store the candied peel in an airtight container in a cool, dry place for up to 4 months.

Plum and Apricot Fillings

Powidła and Apricot Lekvar

Powidła, or lekvar, is a thick, sweet paste made from small blue Italian or prune plums. It is one of the best fruit fillings for cookies and cakes because it doesn't spread the way jam tends to.

The traditional method made with fresh fruit requires three days of boils, reductions, bakes, and sugar additions. It's a lot of work, and I'm just gonna tell you: It's devastating to get to day two, look aside for just a moment and—*wham!*—your powidła is burned and ruined. But there's a great hack for getting around this: dried fruits. Your powidła will come together in half an hour.

Use this recipe for a classic prune powidła as well as apricot lekvar. For other thick fillings to be used in cookies, donuts, and turnovers, try dried cherries, cranberries, or any other plump dried fruit you get your hands on. For a bit of fun, I add a few pieces of candied ginger to the first simmering step.

MAKES about 2½ cups [650 to 700 g]

17½ oz [500 g] soft dried prunes or apricots
2 cups plus 2 Tbsp [500 g] water
1 cup [200 g] sugar
½ tsp ground cinnamon (optional)
1 Tbsp lemon juice

In a medium saucepan, combine the dried fruit, water, sugar, and cinnamon (if using), then cover and bring to a simmer over low heat. Cook, stirring occasionally, until the fruit is soft and bloated, about 30 minutes. Remove the saucepan from the heat and stir in the lemon juice. Use an immersion blender directly in the saucepan or pour the mixture into a blender or food processor and blend until smooth. Pour into a heatproof container and allow to cool to room temperature. Use right away or cover and refrigerate for up to 3 weeks or freeze for up to 6 months until ready to use.

Cherry Filling

Frużelina Wiśniowa

This cherry filling works as well with sweet cherries as sour cherries. Use as a topping for cheesecakes (pages 308 and 311) and Danishes (page 163) or as a filling for puff pastry turnovers (page 263).

MAKES about 3½ cups [400 to 450 g]

17½ oz [500 g] pitted sweet or sour cherries (fresh or thawed frozen works fine)
⅔ cup plus 1 Tbsp [160 g] demerara sugar
1 Tbsp lemon juice
Seeds from ¼ vanilla pod or 1 tsp vanilla extract
1 Tbsp cornstarch
Pinch of kosher salt (optional)

Toss the cherries, sugar, lemon juice, and vanilla seeds (if using) in a medium mixing bowl and set aside for 1 hour, stirring a couple times while it sits. After an hour, the juice will have leaked from the cherries, and they will be sitting in quite a bit of liquid. Stir in the cornstarch until no lumps remain, then transfer everything to a medium saucepan.

On low heat, bring the mixture to a simmer and allow it to bubble for a few minutes, until the juices have thickened and gotten a little gelatinous. If using salt or vanilla extract, stir them in now. Transfer to a heatproof bowl, remove the vanilla pod (if used), and allow everything to cool before using. Use immediately, store in the fridge in an airtight container for several days, or store frozen for up to several months.

Apple Filling

Frużelina Jabłkowa

This apple filling is used in the recipe for rożki (page 263), puff pastry fruit turnovers, but it can also be used as an alternative filling in kruche slab cakes (pages 199, 203, and 221), as filling for rogale (page 121), or a topping for various yeast Danishes. The incorporation of starch helps it hold up in any number of baked items without leaking.

MAKES about 2½ cups [400 to 450 g]

17½ oz [500 g] peeled, cored apples, cut into ½ in [1 cm] dice

3 Tbsp [40 g] demerara sugar

1 tsp ground cinnamon

1 Tbsp lemon juice

1 tsp cornstarch

In a medium mixing bowl, toss the apples, sugar, cinnamon, and lemon juice. Set aside for 1 hour, stirring a couple times while it sits. After an hour, the juice will have leaked from the apples and they will be sitting in a good amount of liquid. Stir in the cornstarch until no lumps remain, then transfer everything to a medium saucepan.

On low heat, bring the mixture to a simmer and allow it to bubble for a few minutes, until the juices have thickened and gotten a little gelatinous. Transfer to a heatproof bowl and allow to cool before using. Use immediately, store in the fridge in an airtight container for several days, or store frozen for up to several months.

Poppy Seed Paste

Masa Makowa

Poppy seed filling is like black gold in Polish and Ashkenazi baking. Poppies have been cultivated in Central and Eastern Europe for centuries and hold special cultural meaning, symbolizing prosperity, abundance, and luck. While preground poppy seed is sold in every Polish supermarket, if it isn't available in your region, you can simply grind whole poppy seeds in a coffee grinder until you have a rough powder. If you don't have a coffee grinder, add whole poppy seeds with all the ingredients and cook as instructed, then grind into a paste in a food processor after. White poppy seeds, used in St. Martin's Croissants (page 164), can often be found at South Asian grocery stores.

MAKES 3½ to 4 cups [700 g]

1½ cups [250 g] ground poppy seeds (blue or white)
½ cup plus 1½ Tbsp [120 g] granulated sugar
2 Tbsp [42 g] honey
7 Tbsp [100 g] orange juice
1 Tbsp grated orange zest
¾ cup plus 1 Tbsp [200 g] whole milk
¼ tsp ground cinnamon
Pinch of kosher salt (optional)
⅓ cup [75 g] unsalted butter, cubed
1 tsp vanilla extract

In a medium saucepan, stir together the ground poppy seeds, sugar, honey, orange juice, zest, milk, cinnamon, and salt (if using) until well-mixed. On low heat, bring the mixture to a low simmer, then mix in the butter and let it melt. Keep the mixture on a low simmer for about 10 minutes, stirring constantly to prevent burning or sticking. At this point, the mixture will have thickened to a pudding texture. Remove the poppy seed mixture from the heat and stir in the vanilla. Allow to cool, then either use immediately or transfer to an airtight container. This will keep for up to a week in the fridge or up to several months in the freezer.

J BRACI
152
3 zł kg.
Paulared
b. soczysty, miękki
3 50 gr
zł kg.

Walnut Paste

Masa Orzechowa

This is a versatile and thick nut paste filling that can be used anywhere that poppy seed filling or powidła is used for a very different flavor profile, whether in babkas (page 142), yeast rolls like makowiec (page 159), hamantaschen (page 281), or stuffed rogale (page 121).

NOTE: If you don't have a food processor, you can buy preground walnuts for this recipe. Give them a short toss in a dry pan on medium heat until they start to get fragrant, then pour into a medium heat-proof bowl and set aside to cool. The extra step of toasting the nuts brings out loads of flavor.

MAKES about 3½ cups [650 g]

10½ oz [300 g] walnuts

7 Tbsp [100 g] unsalted butter, cubed and at room temperature

¾ cup [150 g] sugar

1 tsp cornstarch

1 tsp ground cinnamon

Pinch of kosher salt (optional)

2 eggs

1 tsp vanilla extract

1 Tbsp walnut liqueur or rum (optional)

Preheat the oven to 350°F [180°C] and line a rimmed baking sheet with parchment paper. Spread the walnuts evenly on the sheet and toast for 10 to 15 minutes, until fragrant and just browning. Pay careful attention not to burn. Remove the sheet of walnuts from the oven and allow to cool, then blitz in your food processor until you have a sandy walnut flour.

In the bowl of your stand mixer fitted with the paddle attachment, cream the butter and sugar on medium-high speed until pale and fluffy. Reduce the speed to low and mix in the ground walnuts, cornstarch, cinnamon, and salt (if using), scraping down the sides of the bowl with a spatula as needed. Mix in the eggs one at a time, then add the vanilla and liqueur (if using) and mix on low speed until a thick paste forms. Use immediately, or store airtight in the fridge for up to a week or for up to several months in the freezer. From frozen, thaw in the fridge. Allow the chilled paste to come to room temperature before beating briefly in your stand mixer to make it spreadable.

Gingerbread Spice

Przyprawa Korzenna do Piernika

The food historian and chef Maciek Nowicki told me that the history of piernik (gingerbread) is not what one might expect. Centuries ago, when trade routes made their way through wealthy towns like Toruń, Polish cuisine was heavy on spice and flavor, and piernik was used to season meats and savory dishes. Polish gingerbread—in which the spices were combined with flour—was not so much the cake or cookie it is today, but rather a means of preserving spices for use in cooking.

While the practice of cooking with gingerbread spices mostly fell out of favor in the eighteenth century when the French influence on Polish cuisine did away with the heavy flavor in favor of trendier and, some would say, blander dishes, the use of gingerbread in savory cooking persisted in Jewish kitchens. As recently as 1929, in his controversial book *The Jews of Poland: Recollections and Recipes*, Edouard de Pomiane documented several Jewish fish and meat dishes seasoned with gingerbread spices. While few of its savory applications still exist, gingerbread as a sweet treat has evolved and earned an important place in Polish Christmas baking.

The gingerbread spice mix is heavy not just on cinnamon, but on allspice and coriander, two ingredients less emphasized in Western European gingerbread. The following recipe is perfect for one batch of Pierniczki (page 255). It can be doubled or tripled and stored in your pantry in an airtight spice jar. If you don't have the time or desire to make your own spice mix, use store-bought gingerbread spice interchangeably by weight or volume in all gingerbread recipes in this book.

MAKES about 4½ Tbsp [35 g]

5 tsp ground cinnamon
2 tsp ground allspice
1 tsp ground nutmeg
1 tsp ground coriander
1 tsp ground ginger
½ tsp ground fennel seed
½ tsp ground cardamom
½ tsp ground black pepper
¼ tsp ground anise seed
¼ tsp ground cloves

Mix all the ingredients until combined. Store in an airtight jar at room temperature for up to 4 months.

Pudding

Budyń

Budyń, vanilla pudding cream, is a multipurpose filling for many cream cakes and Danishes. Nowadays most people buy powdered pudding packets, but good bakeries and home bakers are trending back toward the from-scratch. Similar to a classic pastry cream, Polish budyńie tend to add egg yolks to make an extra-rich custard.

MAKES about 1½ cups [350 g] or 3 cups [700 g] for a double batch

SINGLE BATCH

1 egg
2 egg yolks
5 tsp [15 g] cornstarch
1 Tbsp all-purpose flour
¼ cup [50 g] sugar
1 cup [250 g] whole milk
½ vanilla pod or 1 tsp vanilla extract
1½ Tbsp [25 g] unsalted butter

DOUBLE BATCH

2 eggs
4 egg yolks
3 Tbsp [30 g] cornstarch
2 Tbsp [20 g] all-purpose flour
½ cup [100 g] sugar
2 cups [500 g] whole milk
1 vanilla pod or 2 tsp vanilla extract
3½ Tbsp [50 g] unsalted butter

In a large heatproof bowl, whisk together the eggs, egg yolks, cornstarch, flour, and half of the sugar. In a saucepan, combine the milk, the remaining sugar, and the vanilla pod (if using) on low to medium heat until the sugar is melted and the milk is steaming. Remove the vanilla pod, then pour the hot milk into the egg mixture in a thin stream, whisking constantly to temper the eggs. This process prevents the eggs from scrambling. Once all the milk has been incorporated into the egg mixture, return it to the saucepan on medium-low heat. Whisk constantly over the heat until the mixture starts to thicken and bubble into a pudding consistency. Don't look away! The change happens suddenly. Continuing to whisk vigorously, allow the pudding to bubble for 3 minutes before removing it from the heat. If using vanilla extract, add it now, along with the butter, and stir until smooth. Pour the pudding into a shallow bowl and cover directly with plastic wrap to prevent a skin from forming. Refrigerate for 2 hours or up to overnight until cool. Before using, whisk until smooth. To store, refrigerate airtight for up to a week or freeze for up to a few months. From frozen, thaw overnight in the refrigerator before using.

VARIATION: STIFF BUDYŃ WITH AGAR AGAR

When budyń is used in an unbaked filling, as for Karpatka (page 314) or Napoleonka (page 225), I like to add a little agar agar powder for extra stability without compromising the texture with more starch or flour, which can make a cream grainy. Meanwhile, agar agar can help your cream hold up if left at room temperature without adding undesirable texture. This is especially useful when you want to cut a neat slice through a cake without the cream gushing.

Note: I use agar agar in place of gelatin because it keeps your dish vegetarian, it sets faster, and it's a bit less finicky. To use gelatin instead of agar agar, the ratio is 1 Tbsp gelatin powder to 1 tsp agar agar. Follow packet instructions for blooming and setting gelatin, as it's different than the method used here for agar agar.

To make stiff budyń, follow the instructions for regular budyń, simply adding the agar agar powder (⅛ tsp for a single batch or ¼ tsp for a double batch) to the saucepan along with the milk, sugar, and vanilla before heating.

Sweet Cheese Filling

Sweetened twaróg filling has a rich cheesecake flavor and, like Budyń (page 342), adds a creamy filling to countless Polish yeast pastries.

MAKES about 1⅔ cups [515 g]

12½ oz [355 g] twaróg or ricotta cheese
¼ cup [50 g] sugar
2 egg yolks
3 Tbsp [45 g] cream cheese
1 Tbsp all-purpose flour
1 tsp vanilla extract
Grated zest of ½ lemon or orange (optional)

Strain the twaróg by wrapping it in a cheesecloth and twisting the ends tightly to squeeze out the excess water. Then, in a medium mixing bowl, whisk the strained twaróg together with the sugar, egg yolks, cream cheese, flour, vanilla, and zest (if using) until all the ingredients are incorporated and you have a smooth paste.

Use immediately or store airtight in the fridge for up to a week.

Rose Paste

Płatki Róży Ucierane z Cukrem

All along the northern Baltic coast of Poland grow *Rosa rugosa*, common beach roses with bright fuchsia petals that smell absurdly fragrant. The petals are edible, and when churned with sugar and a bit of lemon juice make a dark pink filling for cookies and donuts. You can find the paste in Polish specialty stores, but in its summer season it's worth a little forage to make your own. *Rosa rugosa* is native to Asia but grows all over the world in areas with sandy soil; it is especially common along the eastern seaboard of the United States.

There's a przesąd—an old wives' tale—that says you must churn the petals in a clockwise direction. Churning it the other way will result in a bitter paste. Better safe than sorry.

NOTE: This can be made either by hand in a large mortar and pestle or in a food processor. If using a food processor, be sure to pulse only enough to make a paste and no more, otherwise you risk losing some of the aromatics and making the flavor a bit bitter.

MAKES about 1⅓ cups [315 g]

7½ cups [100 g] edible rose petals from *Rosa rugosa*
1 cup [200 g] sugar
1 Tbsp lemon juice

By mortar and pestle: Mix one third of the rose petals with one third of the sugar and 1 tsp of the lemon juice, and grind until a paste has formed. Remove the mixture from the mortar. Repeat twice more with the remaining ingredients, then mix all three batches together.

By food processor: Pulse the rose petals, sugar, and lemon juice until a thick paste has formed.

Transfer the paste to a jar and close tightly. Due to the sugar and lemon juice, the rose paste will last for months when refrigerated. Store airtight in the fridge for up to several months until ready to use.

Streusel

Kruszonka

Kruszonka is the crumb topping used to sweeten and add crunchy crumble to everything from yeast baking to coffee cakes. Make this up to a week ahead of time and keep airtight in the fridge.

MAKES 1¾ cups [375 g]

1¼ cups [150 g] all-purpose flour
7 Tbsp [50 g] confectioners' sugar
¼ cup [50 g] granulated sugar
9 Tbsp [125 g] unsalted butter, at room temperature

In a medium mixing bowl, whisk together the flour, confectioners' sugar, and granulated sugar. Use your hands to rub the butter into the dry ingredients until you have a crumbly texture and no visible pockets of butter remain. Chill for at least 20 minutes in the fridge before using in your recipes, or store airtight in the fridge for up to a week.

VARIATION:
Add 1 tsp ground cinnamon or 1 tsp grated lemon zest, or replace the granulated sugar with light brown muscovado sugar.

Dulce de Leche

Kajmak

Kajmak, a thickened and fudgy milk caramel analogous to dulce de leche, came to Poland in the eighteenth century as a luxury sweet via King Stanisław II August (not to be confused with Stanisław I, the king responsible for the baba au rhum). But the two similarly named kings is not even where the confusion over kajmak ends: The name itself can be misleading. The moniker comes from the former Ottoman empire, where it still exists today, except that in the modern Balkans and Turkey, kaymak is a kind of fermented clotted cream or cream cheese—a completely different food altogether.

Today kajmak is layered in wafers for Andruty (page 277), drizzled over serniki as a glaze, spread over mazurki for Easter, and more. In return for the effort of homemade, you'll have a richer flavor and color and more control over the texture.

MAKES 14 to 42 oz [400 g to 1.2 kg]

One to three 14 oz [400 g] cans sweetened condensed milk, paper labels removed

In a medium pot, add the cans, unopened and upright, and 2 to 3 in [5 to 7.5 cm] of water. Cover the pot and bring to a boil on medium-high heat. Boil for 2½ hours for a looser, more drizzleable texture, or 3 hours for a thicker paste. Flip the cans midway through the cooking process and refill the water as needed to maintain a consistent level. Resist the temptation to boil extra long—this can result in a bitter caramel or crystalization. After boiling, remove the cans from the water, allow to cool, and then open and use. The kajmak can be left in the sealed cans for up to 3 months, or, once opened, stored in a sealed container in the refrigerator for up to 2 weeks.

Plain or Lemon Glaze

Lukier

Lukier is the simple icing used to top everything, including yeasted buns, cakes, cookies, and donuts. There are a few varieties, and they can all be thinned or thickened to your liking. I suggest adding a bit less liquid than each recipe calls for, adding it spoon by spoon and mixing to check for your desired opacity and texture.

MAKES about 1 cup [285 g]

LUKIER

2 cups [240 g] confectioners' sugar
2 to 3 Tbsp [30 to 45 g] hot water or whole milk

LEMON LUKIER

2 cups [240 g] confectioners' sugar
2 to 3 Tbsp [30 to 45 g] lemon juice

THIN LUKIER

2 cups [240 g] confectioners' sugar
4 to 5 Tbsp [60 to 75 g] hot water, whole milk, or lemon juice

Whisk together the confectioners' sugar and water, milk, or lemon juice in a small mixing bowl until smooth. This doesn't keep so make your glaze as needed for your recipes and use immediately.

Royal Icing

Lukier Królewski

Primarily a decoration icing, Lukier królewski starts fluid and turns hard and crunchy as it dries. Pipe through a very fine tip to adorn Decorated Christmas Gingerbread (page 255).

NOTE: This icing can easily be colored with a drop or two of food coloring.

MAKES 1⅓ cups [430 g]

2 egg whites
3 cups [360 g] confectioners' sugar
1 Tbsp whole milk
1 tsp vanilla extract

In the bowl of your stand mixer fitted with the whisk attachment, whisk the egg whites on medium-high speed until frothy, then add the confectioners' sugar bit by bit until it's all incorporated. Continue whisking for another minute or two until a smooth, shiny, white glaze is formed. Decrease the speed to low, add the milk and vanilla, and mix until smooth.

Decorate your cakes or cookies immediately while the icing is liquid. The decorations will dry hard in 30 minutes to an hour. This doesn't keep, so make your royal icing as needed for your recipes and use immediately.

Chocolate Glaze

Polewa Czekoladowa

This chocolate glaze is softened just enough with butter or coconut oil to be poured or brushed onto gingerbread loaves, hamantaschen, cookies, or whatever you feel needs a little extra chocolate.

NOTE: For a more fluid glaze that sets softer, add 1 to 2 teaspoons [5 to 10 g] more butter or coconut oil.

MAKES 1 cup [215 g]

7 oz [200 g] semisweet chocolate, finely chopped, or chocolate chips

1 Tbsp unsalted butter or refined coconut oil

Melt the chocolate and butter in a double boiler or in short bursts in the microwave and stir together until smooth. Allow to cool for 5 to 10 minutes, then pour over cakes or dip in cookies. Chill the glazed dessert in the fridge until the glaze is set.

If making ahead, store the glaze in the refrigerator for about a week and warm to liquid over a double boiler before using.

Zestaw
5 zł

C

D

ACKNOWLEDGMENTS

This book wouldn't be possible without so many friends, family members, and experts sharing their knowledge, stories, and kitchens.

Thank You: Małgosia Minta, Jessica Nadziejko, Adam Frydrych, Ulka Minorczyk, Maciek Nowicki, Weronika Noganska, Adrian Klonowski, Maciej Sondij, Joanna Ciborowska, Michael Anklewicz, Zach Leighton, Dorota Minta, Rose Ta My, Łukasz Szlapa, Monika Walecka, Michał Pajdosz, Ania Płeska, Zosia Barto, Paweł Pierzchała, Morgan Engling, Molly Schneider, Jessica Flore Angel and Ed Cooke, Lea Stansal, Demetri Siafakas, Daniel Cohen, Magda Maślak, Alessia Di Donato, Mark Forsyth, Adrian Hornsby, Anne Freier, Hanna Geller, Laurie French, Elena D'Alto, Anne Applebaum, Ruth Bartlett, Dżenneta Bogdanowicz, Zackary Leon Furst, Kevin Powers, Dominika Buck, Radek Drabik, Andrzej Popławski, Piotr Wójcik, Aishah Bennett, Roman Kratochvila, Sasha Lurje, Howard Waldman, Deborah Stoloff, Régine Nebel, Ronit Vered, Noa Gur-Arie, Tim Mazurek, Melissa Jalali, Tal Hever-Chybowski, Claire Gilhuly, Vanessa Dina, Rebecca Springer, Natalia Mętrak-Ruda, Christine Laskowski, Leigh Eisenman, Peter Gierszewski, Jeremy Katz, Daniel Margulies, Helen Fine, Bobbi Haney, Sasha Karchenko, Gosia Letowska, Albert Judycki, Rachel Wells, Martyna Płażewska, Paul Henry, Nikos Tsepetis, the entire Fine Bagels team, the Maison de la Culture Yiddish in Paris, and all the wonderful strangers across Poland who had a chat with me in cafés, on the street, and, of course, in bakeries.

LAUREL KRATOCHVILA is an American-born writer and baker based in Berlin and trained in France. She runs the iconic bakery Fine Bagels. Her first book, *New European Baking*, was a finalist for a James Beard award in 2023.

MAŁGOSIA MINTA is a celebrated food journalist and photographer, as well as the author of five of her own cookbooks. Based in Warsaw, she was also the photographer for *New European Baking*.

Chronicle Books publishes distinctive books and gifts. From award-winning children's titles, bestselling cookbooks, and eclectic pop culture to acclaimed works of art and design, stationery, and journals, we craft publishing that's instantly recognizable for its spirit and creativity. Enjoy our publishing and become part of our community at www.chroniclebooks.com.